ON YOUR HEART

A THREE-YEAR DEVOTIONAL FOR FAMILIES

ON YOUR HEART

A THREE-YEAR DEVOTIONAL FOR FAMILIES

A.J. GENCO

DEUT. 6:6-7

FREE GRACE PRESS

On Your Heart: A three-year devotional for families

Copyright © 2021 by Ruthanne Genco Brown

All rights reserved. No part of this publication may be reproduced, stored in a retrieval system, or transmitted in any form by any means, electronic, mechanical, photocopy, recording, or otherwise, without the prior permission of the publisher, except as provided for by USA copyright law.

Scripture quotations are from the ESV® Bible (The Holy Bible, English Standard Version®), copyright © 2001 by Crossway, a publishing ministry of Good News Publishers. Used by permission. All rights reserved.

Scripture marked (NASB) taken from the New American Standard Bible (NASB) Copyright ©1960, 1962, 1963, 1968, 1971, 1972, 1973, 1975, 1977, 1995 by The Lockman Foundation, La Habra, CA. All rights reserved. Used by Permission. www.lockman.org.

Cover design by Scott Schaller

Printed in the United States of America.

Free Grace Press
1076 Harkrider
Conway, AR 72032
freegracepress.com

On Your Heart: A three-year devotional for families/A. J. Genco

ISBN: 978-1-952599-34-7

*For Natalie, Jessica, Caleb, Hunter, Shelby,
Andrew, Calvin, and Knox*

Contents

Foreword ix
Introduction by A.J. Genco xi
Year 1 1
Year 2 107
Year 3 213
Appendix: Read through the Bible Chart 319
A. J. Genco's Testimony 323

Foreword

Dear Reader,

In the early hours of December 29, 2016, I drove my husband of almost twenty years to the local emergency room because he had been suffering for several days from what we assumed was a horrible chest cold. The doctors diagnosed A.J. with an aggressive strain of bacterial pneumonia and intubated him almost immediately. Three days later, I walked out of the hospital on the arm of a friend then sat in the backseat of my pastor's car as he drove me to my mother's home—where I would somehow comfort our children, who were waiting for news of their daddy. One moment I was stroking A.J.'s arm, kissing his forehead, and telling him I loved him, and the next, God was calling him home.

In 2003, A.J. set out to write a devotional for our family. I watched him year after year—ten years all total—labor over it, and while I was always proud of the work A.J. put into writing *On Your Heart,* it was not until he was gone from this earth that I realized the incredible gift he had left us.

My husband was radically saved at the age of nineteen during Air Force basic training. From the first moment God opened his heart, he had a hunger for the truth. His heart's cry was to see his children walking in the truth, and he took his role of disciplining them seriously. As long as I can remember, he led us in daily family devotions.

What you have in your hands was never intended for publication. My desire in publishing it now is to honor the legacy he left, and honestly, I feel it would be selfish to keep it to ourselves.

My prayer is that your family would be blessed by this resource and you would be inspired to leave a spiritual legacy for your own family.

Soli Deo gloria!

Ruthanne Genco Brown

Introduction

by A. J. Genco

Why Did I Write *On Your Heart*?

On January 16, 2003, the space shuttle *Columbia* blasted off for a sixteen-day voyage in orbit. The mission commander was USAF Colonel Rick Husband—a devoted follower of Christ and dedicated husband and father of two. Knowing that during the mission he would be unable to personally lead family worship, he videotaped himself leading devotions for his two children for each day he was to be in space. After watching their last video devotions on the morning of February 1, the Husband family drove to the Kennedy Space Center to watch their husband/daddy return. But in God's unsearchable providence, he didn't.

At 207,000 feet above Texas, *Columbia* disintegrated due to heat buildup in the left wing, which had been damaged during liftoff. Rick Husband went directly from the second heaven of space to the third—the dwelling place of God. Though Rick Husband will never be able to personally lead his family in devotions in this life, they have a legacy of his teaching on videotape to treasure for the rest of their lives and to pass down to future generations. Imagine just how precious those tapes are to his family! Yet Rick's legacy is not only important for his family but also for ours. Shortly after the *Columbia* tragedy, I heard this story about Rick's gift of recorded devotions, and God used it to challenge me: What spiritual legacy would I leave to my family?

Rick Husband's example reminds me of another father who recorded a copy of his teaching for his children. King Solomon wrote this to his children almost three thousand years ago:

> Hear, O sons, a father's instruction,
> and be attentive, that you may gain insight,
> for I give you good precepts;
> do not forsake my teaching.
> When I was a son with my father,
> tender, the only one in the sight of my mother,
> he taught me and said to me,
> "Let your heart hold fast my words;
> keep my commandments, and live."
> – Proverbs 4:1–4

Rick Husband shared with Solomon (and his father, David) a passion to teach his children the precious words of God. None of them intended their teaching to be a sentimental heirloom. They understood that the words of God are the words of life and are not just to be heard and heeded, but as another father before them commanded, they are to be "on your heart" (Deut. 6:6). That other father was Moses, and it is God's command through him to parents of all time that has provided the foundation and title for this written spiritual legacy I am passing down to you:

> And these words that I command you today shall be on your heart. You shall teach them diligently to your children, and shall talk of them when you sit in your house, and when you walk by the way, and when you lie down, and when you rise.
> – Deuteronomy 6:6–7

My children, it is in obedience to this command that I have written *On Your Heart*. It is only one of a multitude of ways to study God's Holy Word, but I want you to have this so you will always remember what I have striven to teach you and may use it to teach your children as well.

You see, God's command to diligently teach your children does not end with me but is also a command for each of you when—Lord willing—He blesses you with families. I will not consider my mission of discipling you complete until you successfully disciple your children—my grandchildren. In turn, your mission will not be complete until your children pass on the torch of faith to their children—your grandchildren—and so on, until our Lord returns. This is a serious responsibility and one that requires much more than regular family worship; it is a lifelong, 24/7 commitment. Yet this task is not a burden but a labor of love, for like the apostle John, "I have no greater joy than to hear that my children are walking in the truth" (3 John 1:4).

May God be pleased to use *On Your Heart* to help you—and multiple generations of our family walk in the truth.

What is *On Your Heart*?

We live in an age of instant foods and drive-through windows. We want patience, and we want it now! However, there's no instant formula or drive-through lane for discipleship. The title of Eugene Peterson's devotional commentary on the Psalms of Ascent captures what I believe is the essence of discipleship: *A Long Obedience in the Same Direction: Discipleship in an Instant Society*. This "long obedience" is not easy—our Lord Himself said, "The way is hard that leads to life, and those who find it are few" (Matt. 7:14). This lifelong journey of discipleship requires serious preparation and hard work. I have written *On Your Heart* as a spiritually muscular guide to help our family and, if it pleases the Lord, future generations of our family through this long road of obedience called discipleship.

To do this, *On Your Heart* contains daily devotional lessons covering the text of Scripture from Genesis to Revelation in a three-year cycle for the whole family. One cycle gives us enough time to cover the Scripture but leaves much depth unexplored. That's why we repeat the cycle, so that in subsequent cycles, as each member of the family is three years older, we can dig deeper and modify the applications to the changing needs of our family. The following is a specific breakdown of how it works.

Daily Lessons

Daily lessons consist of two main parts: a *Read through the Bible* section for parents and older children and a *Family Worship* lesson for the whole family. Read through the Bible is a reading schedule that covers the entire Bible in three years. The reading for each day is normally one, sometimes two, chapters of Scripture. On Monday through Saturday, the order is generally Genesis to Revelation but with the Gospels spread out so that at least one is read each year. On the Lord's Day, we do something special and read a psalm or a portion of a psalm. We call this our "Psalm for Sunday." I use the daily Read through the Bible reading as the basis for my personal devotions and as preparation to lead the Family Worship lesson later that day.

The Family Worship lesson for each day begins with a Scripture reading that is normally a subset of the Read through the Bible text. (I have made exceptions for chapters that contain "adult" content, such as the Song of Solomon.) After the reading, each lesson contains questions for fathers to use to help their family understand and apply the text. I've tried to include easier questions for younger children as well as challenging questions for older children and adults. Scripture references follow some questions and normally give clues to the answer. Those in **bold** are part of the Family Worship reading and should be read when you get to that part of the lesson. Those in *italics* are an optional part of the reading and are intended for reference and further study. Occasionally I refer to the Baptist Confession of Faith and the Nicene Creed, each of which can be found online. Finally, each lesson ends with a suggestion of how to respond to God in prayer.

To the Glory of God!

My beloved children, *On Your Heart* is an imperfect product of your very imperfect father, but I offer it up with the prayer that our triune God may use it to enable you to "grow in the grace and knowledge of our Lord and Savior Jesus Christ. To him be the glory both now and to the day of eternity. Amen" (2 Peter 3:18).

May any good that comes from this redound to the glory of God alone.

Soli Deo gloria!

Year 1

*"And these words that I command you today shall be **on your heart**."*
– Deuteronomy 6:6

Year 1   Week 1

Sunday

Read through the Bible: Psalm 1
Family Worship: Psalm 1:1–6

What doesn't a godly man do? What does he do? What does he delight in? How is he like a well-watered tree? Who is the perfect godly man? How are the wicked different? How are they like chaff? How can you be more like the godly man? Let's pray for hearts that delight in, meditate on, and walk in "the law of the Lord."

Monday

Read through the Bible: Genesis 1
Family Worship: Genesis 1:1–31

What did God create? What did He think of His work? By whom and for whom were all things created? *John 1:1–3; Col. 1:16*. Why did Christ create all things? **Ps. 19:1**; *Isa. 43:7*. How does creation declare God's glory? *Rom. 1:19-20*. How can we? *1 Cor. 10:31*. Let's praise God for the wonder of creation and pray for the grace to glorify and enjoy Him forever! *Hymn: "All Creatures of Our God and King."*

Tuesday

Read through the Bible: Genesis 2
Family Worship: Genesis 2:4–7, 18–24

How did God create Adam? Who is "the last Adam" who gives us spiritual life (1 Cor. 15:45)? What was "not good"? What did God do to complete His creation? How did He create the first woman? Why did He create her? How did the man respond to her? What has God given us so we would not be alone? *Ps. 68:6*. How can we show gratitude for our family? Let's begin by praising God for our family.

Wednesday

Read through the Bible: Genesis 3
Family Worship: Genesis 3:1–15

What did the serpent question? What should we do when someone questions the truth of God's Word? *2 Peter 1:19; Ps. 119:98*. To whom did Eve listen? How did sin change Adam and Eve's relationship with God? *Eph. 2:1–3*. Do sinners seek God apart from grace? *Rom. 3:11.* Who seeks sinners? *Luke 19:10.* Who is the woman's Offspring—bruised but victorious over Satan and sin on the cross? *Heb. 2:14.* What should we do when we sin? *Luke 15:18.* Let's pray for the grace to run to the One who seeks and saves us.

Thursday

Read through the Bible: Genesis 4
Family Worship: Genesis 4:1–12

Whose offering was acceptable to God? Why? **Heb. 11:4.** How did Cain respond? Why did he murder his brother? **1 John 3:12.** What attitude underlies his question, "Am I my brother's keeper?" Are we our brother's keeper? **1 John 3:11.** How can you be your brother's keeper today? Who is the ultimate brother's keeper? *Heb. 2:11.* Let's pray for hearts so filled with love that we rejoice to be our brother's keeper.

Friday

Read through the Bible: Genesis 5
Family Worship: Genesis 5:21–24; Hebrews 11:5

What did Enoch do with God? *Gen. 6:9; Mic. 6:8.* What kind of relationship is pictured by walking with God? *Gen. 3:8.* What did God do for Enoch? Where did He take him? *2 Kings 2:11; 1 Thess. 4:17.* How does Enoch's salvation from death magnify God's grace? Rom. 6:23. Who will take us to Himself? *John 14:3.* How can we walk with God? *1 John 1:7.* Let's pray for the grace to walk with God.

Saturday

Read through the Bible: Genesis 6
Family Worship: Genesis 6:5–22

What were Adam's descendants like? How was Noah different? Which came first: God's grace or Noah's righteousness? *Eph. 2:8–9.* Why did God plan to flood the earth? *Rom. 6:23.* What way of salvation did He provide? Who does the ark picture? How is the ark a picture of Christ? *1 Peter 3:20–21.* How can we escape the flood of God's just judgment for our sin? Let's pray for the grace to turn from our sin and flee for refuge into the ark of Christ.

Year 1   Week 2

Sunday

Read through the Bible: Psalm 2
Family Worship: Psalm 2:1–6

Whom do the rulers of the world rage against? How did they rage against King Jesus at His first advent? **Acts 4:23–31.** How does God respond to their raging? How did the disciples respond to their raging? How do people today rage against Christ and His Word? How should we respond? Let's praise God for our risen King and pray for the power of His Spirit to speak and obey His Word with all boldness.

Monday

Read through the Bible: Genesis 7
Family Worship: Genesis 7:1–5

Why did Noah build the ark? **Heb. 11:7.** Whom did he fear? Why? *Matt. 10:28.* How did he show reverent fear and faith? What is the connection between fearing God and faith? *Pss. 33:18; 147:11.* Between faith and obedience? *James 2:18.* How can you demonstrate reverent fear and faith? Let's pray for hearts filled with reverent fear and obedient faith.

Tuesday

Read through the Bible: Genesis 8
Family Worship: Genesis 8:14–22

What was the first thing Noah did when he got out of the ark? How did the Lord respond to Noah's worship? Did the flood change man's heart? *Gen. 6:5; Ps. 58:3.* How was God's grace magnified in His promise? Who is the ark of salvation? Who is the only sacrifice for sin? How should we respond to God for the gift of salvation in the ark of Christ through the cross of Christ? Let's worship Him!

Wednesday

Read through the Bible: Genesis 9
Family Worship: Genesis 9:8–17

What is a covenant? Who sets the terms of all covenants between God and man? What did God promise in this covenant? What is the sign of the covenant? What is the purpose of the rainbow? How does a reminder for God magnify His grace? *Heb. 6:17–18*. What will you think of the next time you see a rainbow? Let's pray that God would remind us of His grace at the sight of every rainbow.

Thursday

Read through the Bible: Genesis 10
Family Worship: Genesis 9:20–27

What did Noah do that was sinful? *Eph. 5:18*. How did Ham dishonor his father? *Mark 7:10; Prov. 17:9*. How did Shem and Japheth honor their father? What were the consequences for Ham? *His son would dishonor him by being the father of a cursed, sinful line (the Canaanites)*. Who is the perfect Son who always honors His Father? *John 8:29*. How can you honor your father and mother when they sin? Let's pray for hearts to honor God by honoring our father and mother.

Friday

Read through the Bible: Genesis 11
Family Worship: Genesis 11:1–9

Why did the people want to build such a high tower? How did this violate God's command? *Gen. 9:1*. Whose name were they trying to glorify? How did the Lord judge them? What was the result? Whose name should we glorify? *Ps. 115:1*. How can we work together to glorify God's name rather than our own? Let's pray for the grace to "magnify the Lord" and "exalt his name together" (Ps. 34:3).

Saturday

Read through the Bible: Genesis 12
Family Worship: Genesis 12:1–3

What did God promise to do for Abraham? What did God give him that those who built the tower of Babel sought for themselves? Why did God choose to bless Abraham? *Josh. 24:2–3; Rom. 9:15–16*. How are all the families of the earth blessed in him? **Gal. 3:7–9**; *Rev. 7:9–10*. In which offspring of Abraham is this fulfilled? *Gal. 3:16, 29*. How can our family be "blessed along with Abraham"? Let's praise God for the grace to be children of Abraham by faith.

Year 1 — Week 3

Sunday

Read through the Bible: Psalm 3
Family Worship: Psalm 3:1–6

What was troubling David? What did he do with his troubles? What happened when he began to pray? Who was his shield? Have you ever been so troubled about something that you couldn't sleep? How did David sleep? **Ps. 4:8.** Is there anything troubling you now? What should we do with our troubles? *1 Peter 5:6–7.* Let's cry out to the Lord with our troubles and trust Him to be our shield.

Monday

Read through the Bible: Genesis 13
Family Worship: Genesis 13:2–13

Who blessed Abraham with riches? *Prov. 10:22.* Why was there strife between Abraham's and Lot's herdsmen? Who had the right to choose first and have the best land? What did Abraham do instead? What did Lot choose? Why? What was spiritually dangerous about Lot's choice? *1 Cor. 15:33; 2 Tim. 2:22.* How can children be like Abraham when there is strife over a toy or game? Let's pray for the grace to be magnanimous like Abraham.

Tuesday

Read through the Bible: Genesis 14
Family Worship: Genesis 14:17–20

Who was Melchizedek? What did he do for Abraham? What did Abraham give him? Who else in Scripture is both king and priest? How does Melchizedek prefigure Christ? *Ps. 110:4;* **Heb. 5:5–6; 7:1–3.** How is Jesus greater? What should we give our greater King-Priest? *Rom. 12:1.* Let's give the tithe—and ourselves—to Him in worship.

Wednesday

Read through the Bible: Genesis 15
Family Worship: Genesis 15:1–6

Who was Abraham's shield? What was Abraham's concern? What did God promise him? How did he respond to God's promise? How was he made righteous (justified) before God? **Rom. 4:1–3.** How are we justified before God? **Rom. 4:22–25**; *3:28; Baptist Confession of Faith (BCF) 11:1.* How have you responded to God's promise of justification by faith? Let's pray for hearts to believe the Lord and for lives to show it, like Abraham.

Thursday

Read through the Bible: Genesis 16
Family Worship: Genesis 16:1–3*, 15–16

*Adult Content (AC) vv. 2, 4. What had God promised Abraham earlier? What was the apparent problem? What was Sarah's solution? Who designed marriage? What is God's design for marriage? *Gen. 2:24, cited Mark 10:7–8; Eph. 5:31.* Does God need our help to fulfill His promises? Reflect: Is there any problem you are trying to solve using worldly means rather than God's design? Let's ask God to show us and lead us to a greater trust in Him and obedience to His Word.

Friday

Read through the Bible: Genesis 17
Family Worship: Genesis 17:1–8, 15–21

With which of Abraham's sons did God establish His covenant? How did Abraham respond to the renewed promise? Who is the ultimate offspring of Abraham, in whom this covenant is fulfilled? **Gal. 3:16.** How do we become heirs of the Abrahamic covenant? **Gal. 3:29.** How should we respond to God for making us "fellow heirs with Christ" (Rom. 8:17)? Let's laud Him—and laugh with joy!

Saturday

Read through the Bible: Genesis 18
Family Worship: Genesis 18:1–15

Who appeared to Abraham? How did he respond to the Lord's appearance? *Gen. 3:8.* What would you do if God showed up at our front door? What did God promise? How did Sarah respond? Why? "Is anything too hard for the Lord?" **Jer. 32:17.** Is there anything "hard" we need the Lord—the Maker of heaven and earth—to do for us? What should we do? Let's run to the Lord in prayer and ask Him to do for us what only He can.

Year 1 Week 4

Sunday

Read through the Bible: Psalm 4
Family Worship: Psalm 4:4–5; Ephesians 4:26

Who was angry yet never sinned? *Mark 10:14.* What is the difference between anger that is and is not sinful? *Num. 20:10-12.* What should we do when we're angry? What is the difference between taking time to "ponder" and allowing anger to fester? How can anger hinder our ability to "offer right sacrifices" (worship)? *Matt. 5:22-24.* Let's pray for the grace to resolve our anger without sinning.

Monday

Read through the Bible: Genesis 19
Family Worship: Genesis 18:20–21; 19:12–17, 24–26, 29

Who destroyed Sodom? Why? Why did God save Lot? Why did Lot's wife look back? *1 John 2:15.* How does this account magnify God's justice? His grace? How will the return of our Lord be like this? **Luke 17:28-32.** How should we prepare? Let's pray that God would be merciful to our family and remove the love of the world from our hearts.

Tuesday

Read through the Bible: Genesis 20
Family Worship: Genesis 20:1–13

What did Abraham initially say about Sarah? Was this the truth? What's the difference between a half-truth and a lie? Why did he lie? What happened to Sarah? Who protected her? Who should have protected her? What does this show us about God's view of the marriage covenant? Reflect: Have you ever told a half-truth to get out of trouble? What should we do instead? *Eph. 4:15, 25.* Let's pray for the integrity to speak the truth, the whole truth, and nothing but the truth.

Wednesday

Read through the Bible: Genesis 21
Family Worship: Genesis 21:1–7

Who enabled Sarah to have a baby? How did she respond? How was her laughter here different from when she first heard God's promise? *Gen. 18:12.* How had her faith changed? **Heb. 11:11.** How did Abraham grow strong in his faith? **Rom. 4:18–21.** How can we grow strong in our faith? Let's give glory to God for what He did in Abraham's family and for what He's doing in ours—and laugh for joy.

Thursday

Read through the Bible: Genesis 22
Family Worship: Genesis 22:1–19

What promise had God made concerning Isaac? Why did He tell Abraham to sacrifice him? What do you think was going through Abraham's mind as he walked with his son? **Heb. 11:17–19.** How is Abraham a type of the Father? How are Isaac and the ram types of Christ? How are we like Isaac? Who "did not spare his own Son but gave him up for us" (Rom. 8:32)? How should we respond to our heavenly Father for providing a substitute for us? Let's praise Him!

Friday

Read through the Bible: Genesis 23
Family Worship: Genesis 23:1–4

Who promised to give Abraham the land he was in? Did he experience the fulfillment? **Heb. 11:8–10, 13–16.** What was he ultimately looking forward to? In what sense are we also "strangers and exiles on the earth"? **1 Peter 2:11;** *1:1, 17;* **Phil. 3:20.** How should we live as strangers and exiles? Let's pray for the grace to think of ourselves as strangers and exiles while we look forward to the heavenly city.

Saturday

Read through the Bible: Genesis 24
Family Worship: Genesis 24:1–28, 50–51, 57–67

What did Abraham tell his servant to do? Why didn't he want Isaac to have a Canaanite wife? *Gen. 9:25; 2 Cor. 6:14; 1 Cor. 7:39.* Who ultimately chose Rebekah? How did the Lord guide each family in this important decision? Though our customs are different today, how can families help their children make wise decisions about marriage? Let's pray that the Lord would give our family wisdom in preparation for marriage and would give our children godly spouses.

Year 1   Week 5

Sunday

Read through the Bible: Psalm 5
Family Worship: Psalm 5:1–8

Who is holy and hates sin? Was David without sin? How could he enter God's house? *Eph. 2:4*. How can we enter God's house? How can God allow sinners into His presence and remain holy? *Rom. 3:23-26*. How should we respond to God for His steadfast love to unworthy sinners like us? Let's praise Him and pray He would lead us in His righteousness.

Monday

Read through the Bible: Genesis 25
Family Worship: Genesis 25:19–26

Who enabled Rebekah to have children? What were the babies doing in her womb? Why? Who would inherit the covenant promises? Who chose Jacob over Esau? Why? **Rom. 9:10-12**. Why did God choose some sinners over others for salvation? *Rom. 9:15*. When did He choose them? *Eph. 1:4*. How does unconditional election exalt God and humble man? How should the unworthy chosen respond to God? Let's humbly worship Him. *Hymn: "Tis Not that I."*

Tuesday

Read through the Bible: Genesis 26
Family Worship: Genesis 25:27–34; 26:34–35

What was Esau like? *Heb. 12:16*. What was the covenantal importance of the birthright? What value did Esau place on spiritual things? Reflect: Based on your daily actions, how important are spiritual things to you? Who was passionate for God, even from childhood? *Luke 2:49*. How can we cultivate a greater passion for the things of God? Let's begin by praying for hearts passionate for the things of God.

Wednesday

Read through the Bible: Genesis 27
Family Worship: Genesis 27:1–45

Whom did Isaac want to bless? Why? *Gen. 26:27-28*. Whose providence overruled Isaac's will? *Gen. 25:23; BCF 5:4*. What did Rebekah and Jacob do? What should they have done? How did their deceit harm their family? Does the end justify the means? How does each family member show a lack of trust in God? How can we prevent deceit from dividing our family? Let's pray for a greater love for the truth, a greater trust in God, and a greater love for one another.

Thursday

Read through the Bible: Genesis 28
Family Worship: Genesis 28:10–22

What did Jacob see in his dream? Who is like a ladder that reaches from heaven to earth? **John 1:51;** *14:6; 1 Tim. 2:5.* What did God promise Jacob? How did he respond? How was his response to God's promise different from Abraham's? *Gen. 15:6.* How should we respond to God for the new covenant promises He freely gives through Christ? Let's praise God for Christ—the only stairway to heaven.

Friday

Read through the Bible: Genesis 29
Family Worship: Genesis 29:15–30*

*AC vv. 21, 23, 30. Whom did Jacob want to marry? What happened to the deceiver? *Gal. 6:7.* Who can never be deceived? What sin runs in this family? *Ex. 20:5.* Is there a certain sin which seems to be our family's weakness? What can we do about it? Let's ask the Lord to sanctify us in this area, and keep this sin from being further passed down.

Saturday

Read through the Bible: Genesis 30
Family Worship: Genesis 29:31–35

How did the Lord bless Leah? Why did He bless her? *Ps. 34:18.* In being despised and rejected, who was Leah a shadow of? *Isa. 53:3.* Which son of Jacob is the ancestor of Christ? *Matt. 1:2.* How does our Lord's genealogy magnify His grace? Does God choose to love people because they are beautiful or popular? *1 Cor. 1:26–29.* How did Leah respond to God for giving her Judah? How should we respond to God for giving us Judah's greater Son? Let's "praise the Lord" for His grace to the unloved and unlikely.

Year 1 Week 6

Sunday

Read through the Bible: Psalm 6
Family Worship: Psalm 6:1–3

Who "disciplines the one he loves" (Heb. 12:6)? What was troubling David? What did he do with his troubles? What did he ask the Lord not to do? What did he ask Him to do? Are you troubled by sickness, sadness, or sin? What should we do with our troubles? **Heb. 4:16.** So "let us then with confidence draw near to the throne of grace, that we may receive mercy and find grace to help in time of need."

Monday

Read through the Bible: Genesis 31
Family Worship: Genesis 31:1–9, 14–24, 41–42

What did God tell Jacob to do? How did he respond? Whom did he give credit to for his prosperity? How had Jacob matured spiritually since he had left Canaan? How was he still the same? Reflect: How have you matured spiritually? In what areas do you need further growth? Let's pray that the Lord would help us grow in spiritual maturity.

Tuesday

Read through the Bible: Genesis 32
Family Worship: Genesis 32:3–15, 22–32

What did Jacob fear? What did he do about it? How did God answer his prayer? Who wrestled with Jacob? How is this a picture of prayer? *Luke 18:1–8; 22:41–44.* What did Jacob want? How did God bless him? How did Jacob/Israel change physically because of striving with God? Spiritually? Has God called you to do something beyond your own strength? *Luke 9:23.* What should you do? Let's pray that God would increase our spiritual strength as we wrestle with Him in prayer.

Wednesday

Read through the Bible: Genesis 33
Family Worship: Genesis 33:1–11

How did God answer Jacob's prayer for reconciliation? How did Jacob treat Esau? How did Esau receive Jacob? What did Jacob do to make things right with Esau for the stolen blessing? *Gen. 32:13–15*. Who had graciously given Jacob everything? What do we need to do when we've wronged someone? Reflect: Do you need to make anything right with a sibling—or anyone else? Let's pray that God would show us anyone we've wronged and help us make it right.

Thursday

Read through the Bible: Genesis 34*
Family Worship: Genesis 35:1–4

*AC: ch. 34. Who spoke to Jacob? What did God tell Jacob to do? What did Jacob tell his family to do? What does this show us about the spiritual condition of Jacob's family? About the importance of a father's spiritual leadership in the home? What do we need to "put away" or "purify" as a family to get ready to meet with God? *Eph. 4:25–32; 1 Peter 1:22*. Let's put away our sin now as we come into God's presence.

Friday

Read through the Bible: Genesis 35
Family Worship: Genesis 35:9–15

Who blessed Jacob? How did God bless him? How did Jacob respond? How did Jacob's name change to Israel reflect the change God was making in his character? *Gen. 32:28; Matt. 16:17–18*. Which did Jacob act more like: the deceiver or one who strives with God? How has God changed you since coming to know Him? How can we live less like the old self and more like the new self? *Eph. 4:20–24*. Let's pray for the grace to become more like the new self in the likeness of Christ.

Saturday

Read through the Bible: Genesis 36
Family Worship: Genesis 37:1–11

What did Joseph dream? What did his dreams reveal about God's plans for him? What did Joseph's brothers think of him? What did their hatred reveal about their hearts? Can a person hate his brother and love God? *1 John 4:20*. In being beloved by his father and hated by his brothers, who was Joseph like? *John 7:3–7; Luke 19:14*. How can we prevent this kind of sibling rivalry in our family? Let's pray for hearts free from jealousy and a home filled with brotherly love.

Year 1 — Week 7

Sunday

Read through the Bible: Psalm 7
Family Worship: Psalm 7:1–2, 12–17

Who will judge the unrepentant? What is the wicked man like? Where does his wickedness come from? *Luke 6:45; James 1:14–15.* What are the consequences of his sin? *Gal. 6:7–8.* How are all of us like him? *Rom. 7:21–23.* What should we do before we give birth to evil? After? Let's prepare for worship by repenting of any known sin—and any sin within.

Monday

Read through the Bible: Genesis 37
Family Worship: Genesis 37:12–36

What did Joseph's brothers do to him? Why? How did God providentially protect Joseph? How did his brothers try to cover up their sin? In being sold by his brothers, who was Joseph like? *Matt. 26:14–16.* What can happen in a family when jealousy and hatred are unresolved? Are there any unresolved conflicts brewing in our family? Let's pray for the grace to resolve conflict quickly and redemptively.

Tuesday

Read through the Bible: Genesis 38*
Family Worship: Genesis 39:1–6a

AC: ch. 38. Who was with Joseph? What did the Lord do for him? For his master? *Gen. 12:3.* In his obedience as a servant, how did Joseph foreshadow Jesus? *Phil. 2:6–8.* What do you think it was like being a slave in a foreign land? How is Joseph an example of remaining steadfast under trial? **James 1:2–4, 12.** How can you be more like him? Let's pray for the grace to remain steadfast under trial.

Wednesday

Read through the Bible: Genesis 39
*Family Worship: Genesis 39:6b–23**

AC: vv. 7–18; paraphrase for young disciples. What did Joseph do when tempted? Why? What was the cost of obedience? What would have been the cost of disobedience? *Prov. 7:13–27; Ps. 51:4.* What did God do for Joseph in prison?

In remaining steadfast under temptation, who was Joseph like? *Matt. 4:1–11.* What should we do when tempted? *2 Tim. 2:22.* Let's pray for hearts to flee from sin and pursue Christ.

Thursday

Read through the Bible: Genesis 40
Family Worship: Genesis 40:1–23

What did Joseph do for Pharaoh's officers? How was he "rewarded"? What did Joseph dream when he was younger? *Gen. 37:5-10.* Why hadn't God fulfilled his dreams yet? **Ps. 105:17–19.** Does God always fulfill His promises? Does He always fulfill them when and how we think He should? In enduring suffering before receiving what was promised, who was Joseph like? *Heb. 12:2.* How can you be more like them? *Heb. 12:1; 10:36.* Let's pray for the grace to "run with endurance the race that is set before us" (Heb. 12:1).

Friday

Read through the Bible: Genesis 41
Family Worship: Genesis 41:1–16, 25–45

What did Pharaoh dream? What did the dreams mean? What did Egypt need? How had Joseph been a "discerning and wise" manager? In being exalted from suffering to sovereignty, who was Joseph like? *Phil. 2:8–11.* What will Jesus do for those who are faithful over what He's given them? **Matt. 25:21.** How can you be a "good and faithful servant" today? Let's pray for the grace to be good and faithful servants.

Saturday

Read through the Bible: Genesis 42
Family Worship: Genesis 42:1–28

How were Joseph's dreams fulfilled? In having his brothers bow the knee to him, who was Joseph like? *Gen. 41:43; Phil. 2:10.* What effect did Joseph's rough treatment have on his brothers? When bad things happen to us, is it always because of our sin? *Gen. 50:20.* Reflect: What does it normally take to bring you to repentance—the discipline of the Word or of the rod? *Prov. 23:13-14.* Let's pray for tender hearts that respond to the Word before the rod is necessary.

Year 1 — Week 8

Sunday

Read through the Bible: Psalm 8
Family Worship: Psalm 8:1–9

How much greater is God than man? What seemed to surprise David about God? What position in creation did God give to man? Who is the perfect Man who has dominion over all? **Heb. 2:5–9.** How should we respond to the majestic God-man? Is worship just for adults? **Matt. 21:15–16.** Let's worship the LORD, our Lord, praying for eyes to see His majesty and mouths prepared with praise.

Monday

Read through the Bible: Genesis 43
Family Worship: Genesis 43:1–15

What did Judah offer to be? Which greater Son of Judah is our pledge of safety? *John 6:39.* How had Judah changed? *Gen. 37:26.* How can you protect your younger siblings? What did Jacob tell his sons to bring to Joseph? If we're in a store and receive too much money back as change, what should we do? Let's praise God for Christ, our pledge of safety, and pray for the grace to reflect Him in showing selfless love.

Tuesday

Read through the Bible: Genesis 44
Family Worship: Genesis 44:1–18, 30–34

How did Joseph test his brothers? Why do you think he did it? What effect did it have on Judah? What did he offer to do? In offering to give himself for his brother and bear his blame, who was Judah like? *Eph. 5:25.* How can you practice sacrificial love in our family? Let's praise God for Christ our substitute and pray for the grace to reflect Him in showing sacrificial love.

Wednesday

Read through the Bible: Genesis 45
Family Worship: Genesis 45:1–15

Who sent Joseph to Egypt? What was God's purpose? What might have happened to the covenant family had Joseph not gone to Egypt? Has anything bad happened to you that later turned out for good? How can understanding God's good purpose in His providence help us face future trials? *Rom. 8:28.* Let's praise God for His providence and pray for the grace to trust Him even before His specific purpose is clear.

Thursday

Read through the Bible: Genesis 46
Family Worship: Genesis 46:1–7, 26–27

What is the first thing Jacob did on his journey to Egypt? Who spoke to Jacob? What did God promise him? How had God blessed Jacob's family? *Gen. 47:27; Ps. 127:3–5.* How many were in his family? How has God blessed our family? How should we respond to God for blessing us with children? Let's praise Him! *Dad: thank God specifically for each child.*

Friday

Read through the Bible: Genesis 47
Family Worship: Genesis 47:7–12

What did the spiritually mighty patriarch do for the temporally mighty Pharaoh? How was Jacob's family blessed by Pharaoh? How was Pharaoh blessed by Jacob's family? How is this a fulfillment of God's promise to Abraham? *Gen. 12:3.* How have we been blessed by Jacob's family? *Eph. 2:11–22.* Which greater Son of Israel has blessed us by making us part of Israel? How should we respond to Him? Let's praise Him!

Saturday

Read through the Bible: Genesis 48
Family Worship: Genesis 48:1–16

Who was Jacob's Shepherd? *John 10:11.* How did the Good Shepherd bless Jacob? How did Jacob bless Joseph? How were the grace and sovereignty of God magnified in choosing to bless the younger children of Jacob and Joseph? How has God our Father chosen to bless us? *Eph. 1:3–6.* How should we respond to our heavenly Father for His blessing? Let's praise Him! *Dad: pray a blessing over each child.*

Year 1 — Week 9

Sunday

Read through the Bible: Psalm 9
Family Worship: Psalm 9:1–2

Who does "wonderful deeds"? What are some of the wonderful deeds of God recorded in the Bible? What are some of the wonderful deeds God has done in your life? How did David respond to God for His wonderful deeds? How should we? Let's "give thanks to the LORD with [our] whole heart" for His many "wonderful deeds."

Monday

Read through the Bible: Genesis 49
Family Worship: Genesis 49:1, 8–10

What will happen to Judah "in days to come"? Who is "the Lion of the tribe of Judah" (Rev. 5:5)? How is our Lord like a lion? How is Genesis 49:10 being fulfilled in Christ? *Matt. 28:18–20.* How should we respond to the divine Lion King? Let's praise Him and pray He would continue to expand His kingdom of grace to "the obedience of the peoples."

Tuesday

Read through the Bible: Genesis 50
Family Worship: Genesis 50:15–21

What was the brothers' purpose in selling Joseph into slavery? What was God's purpose? Who promises to work all things together for good? **Rom. 8:28–29.** What is the ultimate "good" He promises? How was Joseph conformed to the image of Christ? Reflect: Has the struggle with evil left you bitter or better? Let's pray that God would make us better by conforming us to the image of His Son.

Wednesday

Read through the Bible: John 1
Family Worship: John 1:1–5, 14

Who is "the Word"? Is He God or man? *BCF 8:2.* What would it be like to become an ant? How is this like what God did? How is the Incarnate Word like the inspired Word? *John 14:6; 17:17.* How is He like God's spoken word in Genesis 1? How can we know God? **John 1:18.** How should we respond to the incomprehensible God who made Himself known by becoming one of us? Let's worship Him and pray we would come to know Him more fully as we see His glory revealed in His Word.

Thursday

Read through the Bible: John 2
Family Worship: John 2:1–11

What was the problem at this wedding? What would have happened to the celebration without more wine? Who "richly provides us with everything to enjoy" (1 Tim. 6:17)? How does the abundant wine of this feast picture the joy of salvation? *Isa. 25:6-9.* How does it foreshadow Jesus's own wedding supper? *Rev. 19:7-9.* How can we celebrate the joy of salvation in our home? Let's praise God for the joy of family and the joy of salvation.

Friday

Read through the Bible: John 3
Family Worship: John 3:1–8

To see the kingdom of God, what must happen? Who causes us to be "born again"? What kind of birth did Nicodemus think Jesus was talking about? What kind of birth did Jesus really mean? How is spiritual birth like physical birth? *2 Cor. 5:17; Eph. 2:5.* How is the work of the Holy Spirit like the wind? How can our lives show the evidence of the Spirit's work? *Gal. 5:22-23.* Let's pray for the wind of God's Spirit to blow in our family and give us life/revival.

Saturday

Read through the Bible: John 4
Family Worship: John 4:5–15

Why did the woman come to the well? Who is the well of salvation? *Isa. 12:3.* What water did Jesus offer? *John 7:37-39; Isa. 44:3.* What do we need water for? How is the Holy Spirit's work in salvation like water? *Ezek. 36:25-27; Titus 3:5.* What did the woman need to do to receive this "gift of God"? What do you need to do to experience the reviving, cleansing power of living water? Let's come to the well of salvation and ask for an outpouring of living water on our family.

Year 1 — Week 10

Sunday

Read through the Bible: Psalm 10
Family Worship: Psalm 10:1, 12–18

Who promises to always be with us? *Matt. 28:20.* What troubled the psalmist? Does God really hide Himself in times of trouble? Why did he feel that way? Has it ever felt like that to you? What happened to the psalmist's faith as he brought his complaint to God? What should we do when we feel like God is hiding from us during a time of trouble? Let's pray for the faith to take our feelings straight to God.

Monday

Read through the Bible: John 5
Family Worship: John 5:24–29

Who has life in Himself? What will happen to all the physically dead at Jesus's command? *1 Thess. 4:16.* What happens now to the spiritually dead who hear His voice? *Eph. 2:1–5.* How do we hear Jesus's voice? **John 5:39–40.** What does He give those who hear His Word and believe? When does eternal life begin? How can we live as those who have eternal life now? Let's pray for ears to hear our Savior's voice and lives that reflect His resurrection power.

Tuesday

Read through the Bible: John 6
Family Worship: John 6:26–35, 48–51

Who is "the bread of life"? What kind of bread did the people think Jesus was talking about? What did He really mean? How is "living bread" like physical bread? How is it different? How does eating bread picture faith? If "you are what you eat," then what are you spiritually—fluff or buff? How can we grow stronger in our faith? Let's ask our Father to "give us this day our daily [living] bread" (Matt. 6:11).

Wednesday

Read through the Bible: John 7
Family Worship: John 7:37–39

What did Jesus invite the thirsty to do? How does drinking picture faith? What did He promise those who come and drink? Who is this "living water"? What needed to happen before the full new covenant outpouring of the Holy Spirit? *Acts 1:8–9*. What should a person be like who has rivers of living water flowing from his heart? *Gal. 5:22–23; cf. Mark 7:21–22*. Reflect: What do your actions and attitudes say about what is flowing from your heart? Let's pray for hearts overflowing with the living water of the Holy Spirit.

Thursday

Read through the Bible: John 8
Family Worship: John 8:12; 3:19–21

When you turn over a rock, what do the insects underneath do? Why? How are sinners like this? Why do sinners love darkness? Why do they hate the light? Who is "the light of the world"? How is Jesus like light? What do His followers have? *1 John 1:7*. What should we do when the light of God's Word exposes our sin? Let's pray for hearts that love the light of truth and hate the darkness of our sin.

Friday

Read through the Bible: John 9
Family Worship: John 9:1–7, 13–17, 24–41

Who is "the light of the world"? What two types of blindness did the man have? What happened the first time the man born blind met the Light of the World? The second time? What type of blindness did the Pharisees have? What happened when they encountered the Light? *John 3:19–20; 12:40*. How can we see the Light today? *Ps. 119:18, 105, 130*. How are you responding to the light of His Word? Let's ask the Light of the World to open the eyes of our hearts.

Saturday

Read through the Bible: John 10
Family Worship: John 10:1–15

Who is "the good shepherd"? *Ps. 23:1*. What does a shepherd do? How is Jesus like a shepherd? What did the Good Shepherd give for His sheep? How do His sheep respond to His voice? How do they respond to strangers? How can we discern our Shepherd's voice? He is calling us now through His Word—how shall we respond? Let's pray for hearts tuned to hear and follow only the Good Shepherd.

Year 1   Week 11

Sunday

Read through the Bible: Psalm 11
Family Worship: Psalm 11:1–7

What problem was David facing? To where were people telling him to flee? What did he do instead? What is a refuge? Who is our refuge? What are some "mountains" (temporal sources of security) people take refuge in? According to verses 4–7, how is the Lord a greater refuge? *Ps. 46:1–3.* Where will you flee for refuge the next time trouble comes? Let's pray for hearts to flee to Christ alone for eternal refuge.

Monday

Read through the Bible: John 11
Family Worship: John 11:1–4, 17–27, 38–44

Who is "the resurrection and the life"? What was wrong with Lazarus? What did Jesus do for him? Why? How is Lazarus's resurrection a picture of salvation? *Eph. 2:1–6.* After being raised, what did Lazarus need to take off? How does this picture sanctification? *Eph. 4:22.* Reflect: What "grave clothes" do you need to put off? Let's pray that Christ would be "the resurrection and the life" to our family.

Tuesday

Read through the Bible: John 12
Family Worship: John 11:45–53; 12:9–11

Who is "the resurrection and the life"? How did people respond to Lazarus's resurrection? How did the Pharisees respond? Do miracles guarantee belief? *John 12:37–40; Luke 16:31; BCF 5:6.* What does God use to build our faith? *John 20:31; Rom. 10:17.* How should we respond to this and the other miracles in Scripture? *Heb. 2:1–4.* Let's praise God and pray He would use His Word to strengthen our faith.

Wednesday

Read through the Bible: John 13
Family Worship: John 13:1–17

Who "came not to be served but to serve, and to give his life as a ransom for many" (Mark 10:45)? *Phil. 2:7–8.* What did Jesus do for the disciples? Why?

In addition to dirty feet, in what sense was one disciple unclean? *Titus 3:3–5*. Washing feet was a servant's task—why didn't one of the disciples do it? How can we follow our Lord's example in serving one another? Let's pray for servants' hearts—then roll up our sleeves and serve.

Thursday

Read through the Bible: John 14
Family Worship: John 14:1–6

How would you respond to someone who said, "All roads lead to heaven"? Who is the Way, the Truth, and the Life? How is Jesus "the way"? *John 10:9; Acts 4:12*. The truth? *John 1:17*. The life? *John 11:25*. What is Jesus preparing for us? What did He promise to do when He returns? How can these promises comfort troubled hearts? Increase our joy? Inflame our love and devotion? How can we prepare for our Savior to take us to His glorious home? Let's believe, rejoice in, love, and worship the only Way, Truth, and Life.

Friday

Read through the Bible: John 15
Family Worship: John 15:1–8

Who is "the true vine"? How is Jesus like a vine? How are we like branches? What do we do with dead branches on a tree? How is this like Judas? What do living branches produce? What kind of fruit can you bear to glorify God? *Gal. 5:22–23*. Can we bear fruit by ourselves? What do we need to do to bear much fruit? Let's pray for the grace to abide in the Vine and bear fruit to the glory of God.

Saturday

Read through the Bible: John 16
Family Worship: John 16:4b–15

Where was Jesus going? Why was this advantageous? Who is the "Helper"? What would He do for the world? For the disciples? For Jesus? How did the Holy Spirit "guide [the disciples] into all the truth"? *2 Peter 1:21*. How does He guide us into all the truth? *1 Cor. 2:12*. What is something the Holy Spirit has helped you understand through our study of John? Let's praise God for the Helper and pray He would guide us to understand and obey the truth of the Word.

Year 1 — Week 12

Sunday

Read through the Bible: Psalm 12
Family Worship: Psalm 12:1–8

Whose words are pure and perfect? What was David's concern? What are the words of the wicked like? Which of these is the greatest temptation for you: lying, flattery, or boasting? How are God's words different? *John 17:17; 14:6.* How can we better reflect Christ with our words? *1 Peter 2:22; Eph. 4:25.* Let's praise God for His pure and trustworthy words and pray for lips to speak words more like His.

Monday

Read through the Bible: John 17
Family Worship: John 17:1–5

What did Jesus pray for? How did He glorify the Father? *Phil. 2:5-8.* How did the Father answer His prayer? *Phil. 2:9-11.* Who gives eternal life? To whom does He give eternal life? What is eternal life? What is the difference between knowing about God and knowing God? How can we know God? *John 1:18; 3:16; 14:7.* How can we get to know Him better? *John 17:17; Ps. 119; 1 John 1:3-6.* Let's pray for the grace to know God more intimately every day.

Tuesday

Read through the Bible: John 18
Family Worship: John 18:33–38a

Who is the "King of kings" (Rev. 19:16)? Is Jesus's kingdom of this world? How is His kingdom different? Who listens to His voice? What is truth? *John 14:6; 17:17.* Whose voice did Pilate listen to? **John 19:12-16.** Which king did the people listen to? Where do we hear King Jesus's voice? How can we tell if we're really listening? *John 14:15.* How can you better listen to our King? Let's worship King Jesus—praying for ears to hear His commands and hearts to quickly obey.

Wednesday

Read through the Bible: John 19
Family Worship: John 19:16b–22, 28–30

Who is the King of glory? *Ps. 24:7-10.* What did Jesus say just before He died? The phrase "It is finished" was a business term meaning a debt was paid in full.

What "debt" did Jesus pay on the cross? **Col. 2:13–14;** *BCF 8:5*. How is our sin like a debt? Can we pay it? How should we respond to the King of glory for paying our sin debt with His life? Let's worship and thank Him. *Hymn: "Man of Sorrows."*

Thursday

Read through the Bible: John 20
Family Worship: John 20:24–31

Why didn't Thomas believe at first? What changed his mind (and heart)? What did he call Jesus? Who is our Lord and God? Do you have to see to believe? *Heb. 11:1*. Instead of seeing Jesus physically, what has God given us so we might believe? *Rom. 10:17*. What have you learned about our Lord in John's Gospel? How should we respond? **1 Peter 1:8–9.** Let's believe, rejoice, and worship our risen Lord and God. *Hymn: "Christ the Lord Is Risen Today."*

Friday

Read through the Bible: John 21
Family Worship: John 21:1–14

Who is Lord of creation? How did Jesus show His power over creation? His involvement in the ordinary things of life? His desire to fellowship with His people? How did Peter respond to Him? How does Jesus invite us to dine with Him? *Rev. 3:20; 1 Cor. 10:16*. How can we fellowship with Him in the ordinary? *1 Cor. 10:31*. Let's pray for hearts that dive in to opportunities to be with Jesus.

Saturday

Read through the Bible: Exodus 1
Family Worship: Exodus 1:1–22

Who promised to make Jacob's family into a great nation in Egypt? *Gen. 46:3*. What happened to Jacob's family there? How did the Egyptians respond? *Gen. 15:13*. What did Pharaoh command the midwives to do? Why? Did they do it? Why not? How did God reward them? What should we do if someone tells us to do something against God's law? *Acts 5:29*. Let's praise God for our family and pray for hearts to fear and obey Him rather than men.

Year 1   Week 13

Sunday

Read through the Bible: Psalm 13
Family Worship: Psalm 13:1–6

Who "will never leave you nor forsake you" (Heb. 13:5)? What was David's concern? Does the Lord ever really hide His face from us or forget about us? How might it feel like that sometimes? What did David do when he felt like that? What should we do? How can worship help us through those times? Let's pray for hearts to trust in, rejoice in, and sing to the Lord no matter the circumstances.

Monday

Read through the Bible: Exodus 2
Family Worship: Exodus 2:1–10

Why did Moses's mother have to hide him? In being saved as an infant from the wrath of the king, who was Moses like? *Matt. 2:13–18.* How did God providentially protect Moses? Who moved the heart of the princess to adopt him? *Prov. 21:1.* How was Moses's older sister a bold helper? How can you be a helper with your younger siblings? Let's pray for hearts eager to help, protect, and serve one another.

Tuesday

Read through the Bible: Exodus 3
Family Worship: Exodus 3:1–15

Was Moses seeking God? Who was seeking Moses? How did God reveal Himself to Moses? Why did Moses have to take his shoes off? Why did he hide his face? By what name did God reveal Himself? Who is the great "I Am"? **John 8:58.** What does this name reveal about God's nature? How should we approach our holy, self-existent Lord? "Let us offer to God acceptable worship, with reverence and awe, for our God is a consuming fire" (Heb. 12:28–29).

Wednesday

Read through the Bible: Exodus 4
Family Worship: Exodus 4:1–17

Did Moses want to be the one to deliver Israel? Why not? What did God promise to do for him? "Who has made man's mouth?" Can God call us to do things we don't want to do? Does He call us to do things we can't do in our own strength? Why? *2 Cor. 12:9-10*. What is God calling you to do right now? How are you responding? Let's pray for the faith to trust and obey no matter what God calls us to do.

Thursday

Read through the Bible: Exodus 5
Family Worship: Exodus 5:1–9, 22–23

Who always keeps His promises? What did God promise to do through Moses? How did Pharaoh respond? How did Moses respond to God? Is it easy to obey God? What are the potential "costs" of obeying God? What are the costs of disobedience? When something God has promised doesn't immediately happen, what should we do? Let's pray for the faith and patience to obey God no matter the cost.

Friday

Read through the Bible: Exodus 6
Family Worship: Exodus 6:1–9

Who always keeps His promises? What covenant did God make with Abraham, Isaac, and Jacob? What did He promise to do for Israel? How did they respond to God's promises? Why? What kind of slavery has Jesus redeemed us from? *John 8:34, 36*. To what greater "promised land" is He bringing us? *Rev. 21*. How should we respond to God for these greater promises to the church? Let's thank and praise Him!

Saturday

Read through the Bible: Exodus 7
Family Worship: Exodus 7:1–13

What miracle did Moses and Aaron perform? What effect did it have on Pharaoh? Who ultimately hardened his heart? Why did God harden Pharaoh but show mercy to Moses, a murderer (*Ex. 2:12*)? *Ex. 9:16; Rom. 9:14-18*. Did Pharaoh deserve God's mercy? What do all sinners deserve? How should we respond to God for choosing to be merciful to us? *Rom. 11:33-36*. Let's praise God for His sovereign mercy!

Year 1   Week 14

Sunday

Read through the Bible: Psalm 14
Family Worship: Psalm 14:1a

Who created the world? What does the fool say in his heart? Why is this foolishness? How has God made plain the truth of His existence? **Rom. 1:18–23.** What do fools do with the truth? What awaits those who suppress the truth about God? What would we be apart from the grace of God? How can we be the opposite of fools? *Ps. 19:1–2, 7; 2 Tim. 3:14–15.* Let's praise God for revealing Himself to us in His Word and in His world so we can know and worship Him.

Monday

Read through the Bible: Exodus 8
Family Worship: Exodus 8:20–32

Who is "the LORD in the midst of the earth"? How did God judge Egypt? How did God put a division between His people and Pharaoh's people? *Rev. 9:4.* How has God set the church apart from the world? *John 17:9; Eph. 1:3–4.* How did Pharaoh respond to the fly judgment? How did Moses respond to his proposed compromise? What should we do when others ask us to compromise God's Word? Let's pray for the grace to stand firm against compromise.

Tuesday

Read through the Bible: Exodus 9
Family Worship: Exodus 9:13–35

Whom does the earth belong to? What could the Lord have done to quickly deliver His people? Why did He instead use a series of judgments? *Rom. 9:17.* How did God judge Egypt this time? What merciful warning did He give them? How did Pharaoh's servants respond to God's word? Why? Did Pharaoh fear the word of the Lord? How can you tell? How can you show reverence for God's Word? Let's pray for hearts to fear, pay attention to, and obey God's Word.

Wednesday

Read through the Bible: Exodus 10
Family Worship: Exodus 10:1–20

Who hardened Pharaoh's heart? Why? Who was Moses to tell about God's mighty acts? *Deut. 6:7.* Whom did Pharaoh agree to let go? Who did Moses say needed to go? How old do children have to be to worship? *Matt. 21:15–16.* Who said: "Let the little children come to me" (Matt. 19:14)? How can we worship the Lord as a family? Let's worship Him now, praying for the grace to be faithful in family worship.

Thursday

Read through the Bible: Exodus 11–12:20
Family Worship: Exodus 12:1–13

How was the Lord going to judge Egypt? How could Israel be saved from judgment? What is the significance of the term *Passover*? Who is our Passover Lamb? **1 Cor. 5:7.** How is Christ the fulfillment of the Passover lamb? **1 Peter 1:18–19.** What judgment do all deserve? *Rom. 6:23.* How can we be saved from judgment? Let's pray that God would look at the blood of Christ and pass over our sins.

Friday

Read through the Bible: Exodus 12:21–51
Family Worship: Exodus 12:21–36

How did the Lord judge Egypt? How did Pharaoh respond? How did the Egyptians respond? How were future generations to remember this deliverance? **Ex. 13:3–9.** Who is our Passover Lamb? What ritual meal has Jesus given us to remember our deliverance from sin? *1 Cor. 11:23–26.* How can better understanding Passover help you better prepare for the Lord's Supper? Let's praise God for passing over our sin and pray for hearts prepared to dine with Him.

Saturday

Read through the Bible: Exodus 13
Family Worship: Exodus 13:17–22

Where did God lead the people? How did God lead them? Who was in the pillars of cloud and fire? *1 Cor. 10:1–4.* What has God given us today to lead us that the Israelites of this time didn't have? *1 Cor. 10:11; Ps. 119:105.* Where is God leading us? *2 Peter 3:13.* How can we follow the pillars of cloud and fire today? Let's pray for eyes focused on Christ through His Word as He leads us to the true promised land.

Year 1   Week 15

Sunday

Read through the Bible: Psalm 15
Family Worship: Psalm 15:1–5

Who shall dwell with God? Who has ever lived perfectly as described here? Does this psalm describe the way of salvation or the way of life for God's people? How should God's people speak? Who should be our heroes? What should we do when we promise something? Which of these is the hardest for you? Let's pray for the grace to "walk blamelessly" in Christ (and repent quickly when we don't).

Monday

Read through the Bible: Exodus 14
Family Worship: Exodus 14:5–31

What did Pharaoh do after he let Israel go? Who hardened his heart? Why? How did the Lord save Israel and gain glory over Pharaoh? What did Israel have to do to be saved? How did the people respond to God and Moses before their salvation? After? Does God help those who help themselves, or does He help the helpless? What do we need to do to be saved? *Rom. 10:9-10.* Let's confess our helplessness and praise God for His glorious grace.

Tuesday

Read through the Bible: Exodus 15
Family Worship: Exodus 15:1–18

Who triumphed gloriously over Pharaoh and his army? How did Moses and the people respond to God for their salvation? What do the people exalt about God? How did Jesus triumph gloriously over rulers and authorities? *Col. 2:15.* How should we respond to God for so great a salvation? *Rev. 15:3-4.* Let's worship God for His glorious triumph at the Red Sea, at the cross, and at the empty tomb.

Wednesday

Read through the Bible: Exodus 16
Family Worship: Exodus 16:1–15, 31

What problem did the people face? What did they do about it? Whom were the people ultimately grumbling against? Do you ever complain? What should you do instead? What did God provide for the people? Who is the ultimate bread from heaven? *John 6:31-35.* How is Jesus like manna? How is He greater? *John*

6:48–51, 58. How should we respond to God for giving us the Bread of Life? Let's praise and thank Him.

Thursday

Read through the Bible: Exodus 17
Family Worship: Exodus 17:1–7

What problem did the people face? What did they do about it? What should they have done? What did they learn from the manna? What did Moses do? Who was the Rock who provided water for them? **1 Cor. 10:1–4.** When stricken on the cross, what kind of water did Jesus provide for us? *John 4:13–14; 7:37–39; 19:34.* What can we learn from the example of the Israelites? **1 Cor. 10:6, 11.** Let's pray for hearts washed from quarreling and overflowing with living water.

Friday

Read through the Bible: Exodus 18
Family Worship: Exodus 18:13–27

Who is the perfect leader? What was wrong with the way Moses was leading the people? What was Jethro's solution? What would Moses be directly responsible for? What was he to delegate? How is this principle of delegation of authority reflected in our government? In the church? *Acts 6:1–6.* What can you do to help manage the workload in our home? Let's pray for the grace to be able servant-leaders.

Saturday

Read through the Bible: Exodus 19
Family Worship: Exodus 19:1–6

Who bore Israel on eagles' wings? What did God call Israel out of the darkness of Egypt to be? What did the people need to do to be God's "treasured possession"? What did God call the church out of the darkness of sin to be? **1 Peter 2:9–10.** What did the church have to do to become God's "own possession"? How should we respond to God for calling us His people by grace alone? Let's "proclaim the excellencies of him who called [us]."

Year 1   Week 16

Sunday

Read through the Bible: Psalm 16

Family Worship: Psalm 16:8–11

In whom did David trust? What was his confidence concerning death? Where did he find "fullness of joy"? Whom was he ultimately talking about? **Acts 2:25–32.** How did Jesus fulfill this prophecy? What confidence can this give us concerning death? Where do you find fullness of joy? Let's praise God for the resurrection of Christ and pray for hearts that experience fullness of joy in His presence.

Monday

Read through the Bible: Exodus 20

Family Worship: Exodus 20:1–17

Who gave us His law? Is the law a way *to* life or a way *of* life? *Rom. 3:20.* What do the Ten Commandments tell us about loving God? *Matt. 22:36–40; John 14:15.* What do they tell us about loving our neighbor? Have you perfectly obeyed the Ten Commandments? Who has? How can you be more like Christ this week? Let's ask the Lord to forgive us and empower us to love Him by obeying His law.

Tuesday

Read through the Bible: Exodus 21

Family Worship: Exodus 20:12

How should children treat their parents? Who always honors His Father? *John 8:29.* What does God promise children who honor their parents? *Eph. 6:1–3.* How does your relationship with your parents reflect your relationship with God? *Matt. 15:1–9 (Ex. 21:17); 1 Tim. 1:9 (Ex. 21:15); Rom. 1:28–32; 2 Tim. 3:1–5.* How can you honor your parents? Let's pray for hearts to honor our heavenly Father by honoring our earthly father and mother.

Wednesday

Read through the Bible: Exodus 22

Family Worship: Exodus 22:1, 4–6

What was the penalty if a man caused his neighbor's crops to be ruined by accident? What was the penalty for stealing an animal? What if the thief sold the animal? Let's say you accidentally broke one of your sibling's toys; what should you do? How would it be different if you broke it on purpose? Who made full restitution for our sins? Let's pray for hearts to quickly make things right whenever we wrong someone.

Thursday

Read through the Bible: Exodus 23
Family Worship: Exodus 23:2

Who is always right? Is the majority always right? What was an Israelite supposed to do when "the many" wanted to commit an injustice? When you're away from us and a group of so-called friends tries to get you to do something wrong by saying, "Everyone's doing it," what should you do? **Prov. 1:10.** Let's pray for the spiritual backbone to stand up for what is right even when "the many" are doing wrong.

Friday

Read through the Bible: Exodus 24
Family Worship: Exodus 24:3–11

What did Moses read to the people? How did they respond? How did Moses ratify the covenant with the people? **Heb. 9:15–22.** What did the blood symbolize? With whose blood are we brought into covenant with God? *1 Peter 1:2.* What privilege did the elders of Israel have as a result of being in covenant with God? How can we eat and drink with God? *Matt. 26:26–28.* How should we respond to God for the greater revelation, blood, and privileges of the new covenant? Let's worship Him! *Hymn: "Nothing but the Blood."*

Saturday

Read through the Bible: Exodus 25
Family Worship: Exodus 25:8–9, 40

What did God instruct Moses to make? What was the purpose of the tabernacle? *Ex. 25:22.* How was he to make it? Why was it so important to make it exactly as God had shown him? **Heb. 8:5; 9:23–24.** Who decides how man should worship God? *BCF 22:1.* How should we worship God today? *John 4:23–24.* Are we worshiping God according to His pattern or ours? Let's pray that God would show us and lead us to worship Him "in spirit and truth" (John 4:24).

Year 1   Week 17

Sunday

Read through the Bible: Psalm 17

Family Worship: Psalm 17:13–15

How are "men of the world" blessed? What happens to all their abundance when they die? How are the people of God blessed? *Eph. 1:3–14.* Whose face shall believers behold in heaven? *Ps. 11:7; Rev. 22:4.* How can knowing we will see God face to face help us persevere through trials? Let's pray for the grace to experience God through both blessing and trial while we live with the end in sight.

Monday

Read through the Bible: Exodus 26

Family Worship: Exodus 26:1

What was the purpose of the tabernacle? *Ex. 25:8.* Who is our tabernacle? How is Christ the fulfillment of the tabernacle? **John 1:14** (Note: *dwelt* is literally *tabernacled*.); *2:19–21; 14:6; 1 John 1:1–3.* How would you respond if the president called and said he wanted to visit with us? How should we respond when Almighty God comes to live with us? Let's praise God for dwelling (tabernacling) with us in Christ.

Tuesday

Read through the Bible: Exodus 27

Family Worship: Exodus 26:31–33; Hebrews 9:1–10

What were the two divisions of the tabernacle? What divided them? Who could go into the Most Holy Place? How often? Who is our High Priest? *Heb. 9:11–12.* What happened to the veil when Jesus died? **Matt. 27:50–51.** What did this symbolize? *Heb. 10:19–20.* Now that Christ has opened the way to God, what should we do? *Heb. 10:22.* Let's draw near and worship God in the Most Holy Place.

Wednesday

Read through the Bible: Exodus 28

Family Worship: Exodus 28:1

Who was Moses to appoint as high priest? Who is our High Priest? What does a high priest do? **Heb. 5:1–6.** How is Christ like Aaron? How is He greater? *Gen. 14; Heb. 7:25.* Since we have an infinitely greater High Priest, what can we do when we sin against God? *Heb. 4:14–16.* "Let us then with confidence draw near to the throne of grace, that we may receive mercy and find grace to help in time of need" (Heb. 4:16).

Thursday

Read through the Bible: Exodus 29
Family Worship: Exodus 29:1, 19–21

How were Aaron and his sons consecrated as priests? Why was blood necessary? *Heb. 9:22.* Who is our High Priest? **Heb. 7:26–28.** Did Christ need to be consecrated with ram's blood? Why not? What did our perfect High Priest do for us that Aaron couldn't? *2 Cor. 5:21.* How should we respond to our perfect High Priest who "offered up himself" for sinners like us? Let's worship Him! *Hymn: "Man of Sorrows."*

Friday

Read through the Bible: Exodus 30
Family Worship: Exodus 30:11–13

What did Israelites have to pay as a ransom for their lives under the law? Who fulfilled this ransom/tax? **Matt. 17:24–27.** Did Jesus and Peter really have to pay the ransom/tax? Why not? What do children owe their parents? What do they pay? What do all people owe God? What do His children pay? Who paid our ransom? At what price? **Matt. 20:28.** How should we respond to the One who gave "his life as a ransom for many"? Let's thank and praise Him!

Saturday

Read through the Bible: Exodus 31
Family Worship: Exodus 31:1–11

Who gives "able men" their ability? What did God give to Bezalel? How did he serve God? Do you have to be a pastor or missionary to serve God? How can each of you serve God? *Col. 3:17, 23.* How can we hone the abilities God has given us for greater service? Let's pray for the grace to glorify God with the abilities He's given us.

Year 1   Week 18

Sunday

Read through the Bible: Psalm 18
Family Worship: Psalm 18:1–3

Who was David's strength and rock? How was God his strength and rock? His fortress and stronghold? His shield and deliverer? How has God been these for you? How did David respond to God for being all these for him? How should we? Let's "call upon the LORD, who is worthy to be praised." *Hymn: "A Mighty Fortress Is Our God."*

Monday

Read through the Bible: Exodus 32
Family Worship: Exodus 31:18–32:8, 15–24

Who wrote the Ten Commandments? What were the people doing while God was writing the law? What did the breaking of the tablets symbolize? What kind of leadership did Aaron provide? What excuse did he make? What should you do when you break God's law? *1 John 1:9.* Reflect: Do you repent quickly, or make lame excuses and blame others? Let's pray for hearts quick to take responsibility and repent.

Tuesday

Read through the Bible: Exodus 33
Family Worship: Exodus 33:12–23

Who is so glorious that no man shall see His face and live? *1 Tim. 6:16.* What did Moses pray for? How did God respond? How would He show Moses His glory? How is God glorified through sovereign grace? *Rom. 9:15–16.* How can we cultivate a passion like Moses for God's glory? Let's pray for hearts passionate to know God, His ways, and His glory. *Hymn: "Immortal, Invisible, God Only Wise."*

Wednesday

Read through the Bible: Exodus 34
Family Worship: Exodus 34:1–10

How did the Lord answer Moses's earlier prayer to see His glory? What did God reveal about Himself? How did Moses respond? In the new covenant, in whom did God reveal Himself, His glory, His grace, and His Word? *John 1:14, 17–18.*

How should we respond to this revelation of our awesome God? Let's worship the Lord and thank Him for being to us "a God merciful and gracious, slow to anger, and abounding in steadfast love and faithfulness."

Thursday

Read through the Bible: Exodus 35
Family Worship: Exodus 34:29–35

With whom had Moses been speaking? How was Moses changed as a result? How did the people respond? Why? Who is our covenant Mediator? *1 Tim. 2:5.* How is He more glorious than Moses? *John 1:14; Heb. 1:3.* How is the new covenant He mediates more glorious than the old? **2 Cor. 3:7-11.** How should we respond to God for giving us an infinitely more glorious Mediator and covenant? Let's worship Him "with reverence and awe" (Heb. 12:28).

Friday

Read through the Bible: Exodus 36
Family Worship: Exodus 35:20–29; 36:2–7

Who gives craftsmen their skill? *Ex. 35:30–35.* What did the people do to help build the tabernacle? With what attitude did they do it? *2 Cor. 9:7.* What was the result? What can we do to help the work of our church? What can you do to help our family? With what attitude should we do these things? Let's pray that God would move each of our hearts to be cheerful givers and workers at home and in church.

Saturday

Read through the Bible: Exodus 37
Family Worship: Exodus 37:1–9

Who promised to meet with His people by the ark of the covenant? **Ex. 25:22.** What precious metal covered the ark? What would you do with that much gold? What is the value of gold compared to the value of knowing and worshiping God? *Phil. 3:8.* How can we prepare for the privilege of meeting with God tomorrow in corporate worship? Let's pray for hearts passionate for the "surpassing worth of knowing Christ Jesus [our] Lord" (Phil. 3:8).

Year 1 — Week 19

Sunday

Read through the Bible: Psalm 19
Family Worship: Psalm 19:7–11

Whose Word is perfect? *John 17:17.* What words did David use to describe God's Word? What effect does God's Word have on God's people? What effect has it had on you? How valuable is God's Word? Why is it to be desired more than gold? How can we ensure God's Word has its full effect in us? *James 1:22.* Let's praise God for His perfect Word and pray He would use it to do as He has spoken in each of us.

Monday

Read through the Bible: Exodus 38
Family Worship: Exodus 38:24–25

How much gold and silver did the people give for the construction of the tabernacle? *2,193 lbs. of gold and 7,544 lbs. of silver.*[1] What book has God given us that is more valuable than all that? **Pss. 119:72,** *127; 19:10.* How can you honor God's Word as more precious than gold and silver? *Deut. 6:6-9; Matt. 6:21.* Let's praise God for His Word and pray for hearts to treasure it far above gold and silver.

Tuesday

Read through the Bible: Exodus 39
Family Worship: Exodus 39:1, 5, 7, 32, 42–43

Who commanded Moses to build the tabernacle? Would God have been pleased if the people had done only part of what He commanded? Or substituted their own plans? When God commands you to do something, how should you do it? Do you? When your parents tell you to do something, how should you do it? Do you? Let's pray for hearts faithful to do according to all God has commanded.

Wednesday

Read through the Bible: Exodus 40
Family Worship: Exodus 40:1–2, 16, 34–38

What did God do when the people completed the tabernacle? In whom is God's

---

[1] *The Reformation Study Bible*, note for Exodus 38:25.(Sanford, FL: Reformation Trust, 2015), 151.

glory now revealed? *John 1:14.* How should seeing God's glory in Christ transform God's people? **2 Cor. 3:18.** Into whose image are we being transformed? *Rom. 8:29.* How can we better reflect the image and glory of Christ? Let's pray for lives transformed by the Spirit to reflect the image and glory of Christ.

Thursday

Read through the Bible: Leviticus 1–2
Family Worship: Leviticus 1:1–5.

What is the penalty for sin? *Rom. 6:23.* How was this penalty paid in Old Testament sacrifices? What did the worshiper do before he killed his sacrifice? Why? How does this picture the imputation of guilt? Who bore the sin of all His people? *Isa. 53:5–6.* How did these Old Testament sacrifices prefigure Christ? *1 Peter 1:18–19; 3:18; 2 Cor. 5:21.* How should we respond to our sinless Savior for taking our sin and giving us His righteousness? Let's worship Him! *Hymn:* "Man of Sorrows."

Friday

Read through the Bible: Leviticus 3–4
Family Worship: Leviticus 4:27–31

What is a pleasing aroma to you? Why is it pleasing? In the Old Testament, what was a pleasing aroma to God? How does this picture the satisfaction of God's just wrath against sin? *Rom. 3:25–26.* Whose is now the only sacrifice with a pleasing aroma to God? **Eph. 5:2.** In the Old Testament, how did a sinner make things right with God and become pleasing to Him? How can we? *1 John 1:9; 2 Cor. 2:14–15.* Let's confess our sins and seek forgiveness in the God-pleasing sacrifice of Christ.

Saturday

Read through the Bible: Leviticus 5–6
Family Worship: Leviticus 6:1–7

Who commanded us to love our neighbor as ourselves? *Lev. 19:18.* What did God command a person to do who took something and lied about it? What was he to do first—make restitution or give a guilt offering? **Matt. 5:23–24.** Let's say a child finds some money, takes it, lies about it, then realizes his guilt—what should he or she do? Is there anything you need to make right before we go to church tomorrow? Let's pray for the grace to realize our guilt—and make it right.

Year 1   Week 20

Sunday

Read through the Bible: Psalm 20
Family Worship: Psalm 20:6–9

What did some kings trust in for military might? In what did David trust instead? What are some "chariots" people trust in today to make them powerful? To save them from sin and death? Whose is the only name "by which we must be saved" (Acts 4:12)? How can we trust the Lord's name rather than chariots in daily spiritual combat? Let's pray for the grace to "trust in the name of the LORD our God."

Monday

Read through the Bible: Leviticus 7
Family Worship: Leviticus 7:11–12

What kind of offering would an Israelite use to give thanks to God? What kind of "sacrifice" can we use to give thanks? **Heb. 13:15 (KJV)**; *Ps. 116:17.* How often? Through whom do we offer it? What are some things you would like to thank and praise God for? Let's "offer the sacrifice of praise to God . . . the fruit of our lips giving thanks to his name."

Tuesday

Read through the Bible: Leviticus 8
Family Worship: Leviticus 8:1–3, 30

Who were set apart from the congregation to serve as priests? Who is the church's High Priest? *Heb. 9:11–12.* Under Him, who are priests in the church? **1 Peter 2:5.** What kind of "sacrifices" do we offer? **Heb. 13:15–16.** What are some good things you could do as a pleasing sacrifice? What could you share? Let's pray that God would make us a family of priests quick to do good and share.

Wednesday

Read through the Bible: Leviticus 9–10
Family Worship: Leviticus 9:7, 16, 22–10:3

Did the Lord accept Aaron's offering? How do we know? Why did He accept it? Did He accept Nadab and Abihu's offering? Why not? Who decides how we should worship God? *BCF 22:1.* How are we to worship God today? *John*

4:23–24; Heb. 12:28b-29; BCF 22:2–6. Are we worshiping God "according to the rule"? Let's pray for wisdom from the Word to "offer to God acceptable worship, with reverence and awe, for our God is a consuming fire" (Heb. 12:28–29).

Thursday

Read through the Bible: Leviticus 11–12
Family Worship: Leviticus 11:44–47

Who is perfectly holy? *Heb. 7:26.* What are God's people to be? **1 Peter 1:14–16.** Why are we to be holy? What does it mean to be holy? *Eph. 4:22–32; 5:1–2ff.* How were the Old Testament laws about food a picture of holiness? Are there any unclean foods today? **Mark 7:19.** What are some sinful attitudes and actions you need to be separate from? What should you do instead? Let's pray for the grace to be more like Christ—holy as He is holy.

Friday

Read through the Bible: Leviticus 13
Family Worship: Leviticus 13:45–46; Mark 1:40–45

According to the law, what did a leper have to do? Why? What did Jesus do when a leper came close to Him? Why? What happened to him? How is sin like leprosy? Reflect: Is there any sin-leprosy in your life? Who is able to heal us from the leprosy of sin? Let's pray that God would show us the ugliness and seriousness of our sin—and heal us from it.

Saturday

Read through the Bible: Leviticus 14
Family Worship: Leviticus 14:1–2; Luke 17:11–19

After being healed, what did lepers need to do? What happened to the ten lepers that cried out to Jesus? What did they do? Why do you think only one of them came back to thank Him? How should you respond when a person does something nice for you? Who is able to heal us from the leprosy of sin? How should we respond when the Great Physician heals our spiritual leprosy? Let's praise and thank God for healing us from the leprosy of sin.

Year 1   Week 21

Sunday

Read through the Bible: Psalm 21
Family Worship: Psalm 21:1–7

What had David asked of God? What did God give him? What "rich blessings" has God given us? In whom has God given us "every spiritual blessing in the heavenly places" (Eph. 1:3)? How can we experience "the joy of [God's] presence"? Let's rejoice in God and ask Him to "make [us] glad with the joy of [his] presence.

Monday

Read through the Bible: Leviticus 15
Family Worship: Mark 5:24b–34

Who is the Great Physician? Why did the woman need the Great Physician? What had she said about Jesus? What did she do? Why did He sense her touch? Why do you think she was afraid to be publicly identified? *Lev. 15:25.* What disease do we need to be healed of? *Jer. 17:9.* What should we do about it? Let's reach out to the Great Physician in prayer, asking Him to heal the disease of our sin.

Tuesday

Read through the Bible: Leviticus 16
Family Worship: Leviticus 16:34

How often did the high priest make atonement for Israel? **Heb. 9:7.** What did the yearly sacrifices do? **Heb. 10:1–4.** What couldn't they do? Who is our High Priest? How often did Christ make atonement? **Heb. 10:11–14.** What did His sacrifice accomplish? How should we respond to our great High Priest for making full and final atonement for us? Let's praise Him and pray that by His offering He would indeed perfect and sanctify us. *Hymn:* "Nothing but the Blood."

Wednesday

Read through the Bible: Leviticus 17–18
Family Worship: Leviticus 18:1–5

What did God tell His people to do? What did He tell them not to do? Why? Is the law a way of salvation or a way of life for God's people? **Gal. 3:10–12.** Have you perfectly obeyed God's law? Who has? If not by the law, how are we saved? *Eph. 2:8–9*. After being saved, how should God's people live? *Eph. 2:10; John 14:15*. Let's pray for the grace to live as God's obedient people.

Thursday

Read through the Bible: Leviticus 19
Family Worship: Leviticus 19:17–18

How does God command us to treat others? Why love "as yourself"? *Eph. 5:29*. Who loved us this way? Which is the second greatest commandment in the law? **Matt. 22:36–40**. How does love fulfill the law? **Rom. 13:8–10**. What are some practical ways you can "love your neighbor as yourself" in our family? Outside our family? Let's pray for the grace to love others as we love ourselves.

Friday

Read through the Bible: Leviticus 20
Family Worship: Leviticus 20:22–26

To whom did Israel belong? How were they to live? What did the separation of clean and unclean animals picture about their relationship to the nations? To whom do we belong? How are we to live? What are we to be separate from? *Compare Acts 10:9–15, 28; 2 Cor. 6:14–18; 1 Peter 1:14–16*. How can we be separate from the world and still love our neighbor as ourselves? Let's pray for the discretion to love fellow sinners without becoming "yoked" to them or their sin.

Saturday

Read through the Bible: Leviticus 21
Family Worship: Leviticus 19:1–3

What does God command His people to be? Why? *Eph. 4:24; 5:1*. What is one important way children practice holiness? *Eph. 6:1–3*. What does it mean to *revere*? *"To show devoted deferential honor to."*[2] What are some ways you can express reverence for your parents? Who perfectly reveres His Father? What is the connection between reverence for parents and reverence for God? Let's pray for hearts to show reverence for God by revering our parents.

---

2 *Merriam-Webster Online*, s.v. "revere," accessed October 2, 2019, https://www.merriam-webster.com.

Year 1   Week 22

Sunday

Read through the Bible: Psalm 22
Family Worship: Psalm 22:1, 7–8, 14–18

To whom did David turn when going through a severe trial? About whom was he ultimately talking? **Matt. 27:27-50.** How is this psalm fulfilled in Christ? Why did Jesus feel like He was being forsaken by God? *Isa. 53:3-6, 10; Rom. 3:25-26; 1 Peter 3:18.* How should we respond to the One who was forsaken so that we could be forgiven? Let's worship our crucified and risen Savior. *Hymn: "Man of Sorrows."*

Monday

Read through the Bible: Leviticus 22
Family Worship: Leviticus 22:17–22

What did sacrificial animals need to be in order to be acceptable? Who is the true "lamb without blemish or spot"? (1 Peter 1:19). How would a blemished animal fail to foreshadow Christ? What kind of attitude would the offering of a blemished animal reflect? **Mal. 1:8, 14.** What kind of sacrifices do we offer today? *Heb. 13:15-16.* How can we ensure our offerings are "without blemish"? *BCF 16:6.* Let's pray for unblemished hearts to give our best to the Lord.

Tuesday

Read through the Bible: Leviticus 23
Family Worship: Leviticus 23:39–43

What is a booth (or tabernacle)? Why did God tell His people to dwell in booths for seven days? How were they to celebrate? Who came to "tabernacle" among us? *John 1:14.* In what sense do we dwell in tents? *2 Cor. 5:1; Heb. 11:13-16.* How can we celebrate our exodus from sin and our pilgrimage to the promised land of the new earth? Let's rejoice and worship our risen Lord while we live with the end in sight.

Wednesday

Read through the Bible: Leviticus 24
Family Worship: Leviticus 24:17–21

What was the penalty for murder? For taking an animal's life? How does the phrase "eye for eye" picture the judicial principle of proportionality? Did this law permit personal revenge or limit penalties in civil justice? Who corrected the abuse of this law? **Matt. 5:38–41.** What did Jesus do when He was slapped? *Matt. 26:67–68; 1 Peter 2:23.* What should you do when someone insults you? *1 Peter 3:9; 1 Thess. 5:15.* What if you are physically attacked? *1 Sam. 19:10; John 8:59.* Let's pray for the grace to return good for evil.

Thursday

Read through the Bible: Leviticus 25
Family Worship: Leviticus 25:8–10

What did God command Israel to do every fifty years? Who fulfilled the Jubilee by proclaiming "liberty to the captives"? **Luke 4:18–19.** In what sense does Jesus give us liberty? *John 8:34–36.* How should we live after being set free from captivity to sin? *Rom. 6:17–18; Gal. 5:1.* Let's praise God for setting us free from sin—and pray for the grace to live like it!

Friday

Read through the Bible: Leviticus 26
Family Worship: Leviticus 26:3–12

What did God promise to do for Israel if they obeyed Him? How fully did Israel experience this? Who came by grace to dwell with His church? **2 Cor. 6:16.** How would you act if the president came over for dinner? How should we act knowing that God lives in us? *2 Cor. 6:17–7:1.* Let's pray that God would give us a greater awareness of His presence—and help us act accordingly.

Saturday

Read through the Bible: Leviticus 27
Family Worship: Leviticus 27:30; Malachi 3:8–10

What did God command His people to give Him? How is not giving the tithe "robbing" God? Who "gives to all mankind life and breath and everything" (Acts 17:25)? Who gave 100 percent of Himself for us? *2 Cor. 8:9.* What does God promise for those who tithe? How can we make sure we are giving "the full tithe"? With what attitude should we give it? *2 Cor. 8:5; 9:7.* Let's pray for hearts to cheerfully give ourselves and our tithes to the Lord.

Year 1   Week 23

Sunday

Read through the Bible: Psalm 23
Family Worship: Psalm 23:1–6

Who is "the good shepherd" (John 10:11)? What does a shepherd do for his sheep? What does the Good Shepherd do for His sheep? Where does He lead us? What does He feed us? *John 6:51.* What security does He give us? How do sheep respond to their shepherd? *John 10:4.* How should we respond to the Good Shepherd? Let's praise Him and pray for hearts to follow Him and rest in Him "forever."

Monday

Read through the Bible: Numbers 1
Family Worship: Numbers 1:1–3, 45–46

How many descendants had God promised to give Abraham? *Gen. 15:5.* What does the census tell us about the progress of God's promise? In whom are people now counted as children of Abraham? *Gal. 3:29.* How many children will he have in heaven? *Rev. 7:9.* Who always fulfills His promises? How can knowing this strengthen our faith when we don't see the immediate fulfillment of God's promises? Let's praise God for always keeping His promises.

Tuesday

Read through the Bible: Numbers 2
Family Worship: Numbers 2:1–9

What would Israel's camp have been like if everyone camped and marched wherever they wanted? What did God do to prevent chaos in the camp? What would our family be like if everyone did what he or she felt like? Where can we find our family's "marching orders?" *Col. 3:18–21.* What can you do to prevent chaos in our home? Let's pray for the grace to do everything "decently and in order" (1 Cor. 14:40).

Wednesday

Read through the Bible: Numbers 3
Family Worship: Numbers 3:11–13; 18:15; Exodus 13:1–2

Why did God consecrate the firstborn? Whom did He use in place of the firstborn for tabernacle service? Who fulfilled the imagery of the firstborn? **Luke**

2:22–32; *Col. 1:15, 18; Rom. 8:29; Heb. 1:6.* What did God's firstborn Son do for us that the Levites never could? How did Simeon respond to God's firstborn? How should we? Let's praise God for setting apart His firstborn and only Son for our salvation.

Thursday

Read through the Bible: Numbers 4
Family Worship: Numbers 4:21–28

What role did God assign the Gershonites? Whom did He put in charge? What would have happened if either didn't do their jobs? Who assigned different roles in the church? **Rom. 12:3–8.** How is the church like a body? What would happen if a part of your body didn't do its "job"? How can we serve the body of Christ? How can you serve our family? Let's pray for the grace to serve as "God has assigned."

Friday

Read through the Bible: Numbers 5
Family Worship: Numbers 5:5–7

Who commanded us to love our neighbor as ourselves? *Matt. 22:39.* What did God command a person to do if he sinned against his neighbor and later realized his guilt? *Lev. 6:1–7.* Why was it not enough to confess his sin? *Matt. 5:23–24; 1 John 4:20.* Why was it not enough to give an equal replacement? *Ex. 22:1–4.* Is there anything you need to make right with a neighbor or sibling before we worship? Let's pray for the grace to realize our guilt—and make it right.

Saturday

Read through the Bible: Numbers 6
Family Worship: Numbers 6:22–27

What kind of a face do I make when I'm pleased with you? How is it different when I'm not pleased? What is pictured by the Lord's face shining upon us? *Pss. 31:16; 67:1; 80:3.* Who is our High Priest who prays for us? *John 17:9; Heb. 7:25.* In what ways does God make His face shine upon us in Christ? *Eph. 1:3–14.* How should we respond? Let's praise and thank God for making His face shine upon us in Christ! *Fathers: Close by pronouncing this blessing on your family.*

Year 1   Week 24

Sunday

Read through the Bible: Psalm 24
Family Worship: Psalm 24:1–10

"Who is this King of glory?" *Rev. 19:16.* "Who shall ascend [His] hill . . . and stand in his holy place?" *Matt. 5:8.* Who "has clean hands and a pure heart"? Reflect: What sinful actions need to be washed from your hands? What sinful attitudes from your heart? How can we wash ourselves from sin? *Isa. 1:16; 1 John 1:9.* Let's cleanse our hands and hearts in repentance and worship the risen King of glory.

Monday

Read through the Bible: Numbers 7
Family Worship: Numbers 7:1–9

What did the chiefs of Israel give as an offering? What would they be used for? *Num. 4:24-26, 31-33.* Why didn't the Kohathites get any? Who told Moses to accept these very practical gifts? Are there any practical needs our church or missionaries have that we can help meet? What are some practical ways you can help around the house? Let's pray for eyes to see practical ways we can help others.

Tuesday

Read through the Bible: Numbers 8
Family Worship: Numbers 7:89–8:3

How did God speak to Moses? What did He say? What practical purpose did the lamps serve? Who is "the light of the world" (John 8:12)? How does God speak to us? **2 Peter 1:19.** How is God's Word like a lamp? **Ps. 119:105; Prov. 6:23.** What truth has God illumined for you recently? What do we need to do with the lamp of God's Word? Let's pray for hearts to "pay attention" to the lamp of God's Word.

Wednesday

Read through the Bible: Numbers 9
Family Worship: Numbers 9:15–23

Who was in the pillars of cloud and fire? *1 Cor. 10:1-4.* What did the Lord do when He wanted the people to move out? How can we see when God is "moving" today? *John 3:8; 5:19–20*. What are some things only God can do in us? *John 14:26; 16:8, 13*. How can we join the Spirit's work when we see Him moving? *1 Cor. 3:5–9; Acts 8:26–39*. Let's pray for eyes to see when God is moving and hearts quick to join Him.

Thursday

Read through the Bible: Numbers 10
Family Worship: Numbers 10:33–36

What was the Lord seeking for Israel? Who is our resting place? What rest is Christ leading us to? *Heb. 4:9–10; Rev. 14:13; 21:1–27*. What enemies is He scattering? *1 Cor. 15:24–26; Rom. 5:10*. Reflect: What sin-enemies need to be scattered from your life? How can we participate in our Savior's rest and victory? *Heb. 4:3, 11*. Let's pray as Moses did: "Arise, O LORD, and let your enemies be scattered." *Ps. 68:1*.

Friday

Read through the Bible: Numbers 11
Family Worship: Numbers 11:1–6, 10, 18–23, 31–34

Who delivered Israel out of slavery and provided them with food? How did the people respond to God's provision? How was their complaining a rejection of the Lord? *Ps. 78:17–32*. What were the consequences? What has God provided for us? Have you ever complained about His provision? What should we do instead? **Phil. 2:14-15.** Let's each thank God for something we've complained about in the past.

Saturday

Read through the Bible: Numbers 12
Family Worship: Numbers 12:1–15

What complaints did Miriam and Aaron have against Moses? What do you think was the root of this sibling rivalry? What causes sibling rivalry in our home? Is there anything you need to make right with a sibling? How did God respond? How was Moses unique? How should he have been treated? Who is the head of the church? How is Christ greater than Moses? *Phil. 2:5–11; Heb. 3:1–6*. What spiritual leaders has He given us? How should we treat them? *Heb. 13:17*. Let's praise God for Christ and the leaders He's placed over us.

Year 1 — Week 25

Sunday

Read through the Bible: Psalm 25
Family Worship: Psalm 25:12–14

Who can have friendship with God? What does God do for His friends? Who was called "a friend of God" (James 2:23)? *2 Chron. 20:7; Isa. 41:8.* Who laid down His life for His enemies to make them His friends? **John 15:13–15;** *Rom. 5:8, 10.* How should we live as friends of God? **Ps. 25:4–5;** *John 14:15.* Let's pray for the grace to live as friends of God.

Monday

Read through the Bible: Numbers 13
Family Worship: Numbers 13:1–3, 25–33

What did the spies find in the promised land? What did Caleb say they should do? What did the other spies say? What made the difference between the two reports? **1 John 5:4.** Who is leading us through the wilderness of the world to the promised land of heaven? What difficulties do we need to overcome en route? How do we overcome the world? Let's pray for overcoming faith like Caleb's.

Tuesday

Read through the Bible: Numbers 14
Family Worship: Numbers 14:1–10, 26–35

How did Israel respond to the report of the spies? How did Moses, Aaron, Caleb, and Joshua respond to the people? How did God respond? Why was this congregation not able to enter the promised land? **Heb. 3:7–19.** Who is leading us to the promised land of heaven? How can we encourage one another to remain faithful en route? Let's pray for the grace to encourage one another and endure in faith.

Wednesday

Read through the Bible: Numbers 15
Family Worship: Numbers 15:27–31

What is an unintentional sin? How was it forgiven? How does sinning "with a high hand" picture defiance? How could this be forgiven? How is this like one who professes Christ then deliberately rejects Him? **Heb. 10:26–31.** Whose is the only "sacrifice for sins"? How can you be forgiven if you reject it? Reflect:

Have you been defiant with your parents? Spouse? Boss? The government? God? If so, what should you do? Let's confess our sins, cling to the cross, and raise our hands—unclenched—in praise to Christ.

Thursday

Read through the Bible: Numbers 16:1–40
Family Worship: Numbers 16:1–5, 11, 19–35

What was Korah's complaint? Against whom was he ultimately rebelling? How was this an example of sinning "with a high hand" (Num. 15:30)? What were the consequences? *Num. 26:11.* How are false teachers in the church like Korah? **Jude 8, 11.** How can we stand clear of "Korah's rebellion"? Let's pray for hearts to humbly submit to biblical authority.

Friday

Read through the Bible: Numbers 16:41–17:13
Family Worship: Numbers 16:41–50

How did the people respond to the judgment of Korah? How should they have? What were the consequences? What did Moses do? Who "stood between the dead and the living" to atone for our sin? *1 Tim. 2:5–6.* How should we respond to God's just judgment of sinners? *Rom. 11:20b; 2 Cor. 5:10–11.* Let's pray for hearts to fear God and for grace to "persuade others" (2 Cor. 5:11).

Saturday

Read through the Bible: Numbers 18
Family Worship: Numbers 17:1–18:1, 5

Whom did God choose to be Israel's high priest? How did He signify this? How would Aaron protect the people from God's wrath? Who is our High Priest? How did God publicly and powerfully signify this? *Rom. 1:4; Acts 17:31.* How did Jesus protect us from God's just wrath for our sins? *1 John 2:2; 4:10.* How should we respond to our divine High Priest? Let's praise and thank Him in reverent fear.

Year 1 — Week 26

Sunday

Read through the Bible: Psalm 26
Family Worship: Psalm 26:1–12

Where is some place you love to be? Where do you hate to be? Where did David hate to be? Where did he love to be? Why the difference? Who is now "the place where [God's] glory dwells"? *John 1:14; Heb. 1:3.* In which assembly do we meet with Him? *Matt. 18:20; Heb. 12:22-24.* How can we cultivate a greater love for the body of Christ? Let's pray for hearts that "hate the assembly of evildoers" and "love the habitation of [God's] house."

Monday

Read through the Bible: Numbers 19
Family Worship: Numbers 19:1–7

Where was the red heifer sacrificed? How did the place of sacrifice symbolize the removal of sin from God's people? Who "suffered outside the gate in order to sanctify the people"? **Heb. 13:11-14.** In what sense must believers go "outside the camp"? *Num. 11:24-26.* Are you willing to bear the reproach Jesus endured? Let's go to Him now, praying for the grace to endure reproach as we seek the heavenly city.

Tuesday

Read through the Bible: Numbers 20
Family Worship: Numbers 20:2–13

What did the Lord tell Moses to do? What did he do instead? How closely do you follow instructions? What were the consequences? How did Moses's role as mediator make this sin more serious? *Luke 12:48; James 3:1.* Who is our sinless Mediator? Who is the Rock, struck to supply living water? *1 Cor. 10:4; John 7:37-39.* Have you ever lost your temper? What is a better way to deal with anger? *Ps. 4:4; Eph. 4:26.* Let's pray for the grace to control our temper.

Wednesday

Read through the Bible: Numbers 21
Family Worship: Numbers 21:4–9

How did the people sin? How did the Lord judge them? How did they respond? What means of grace did God provide? Who did the bronze serpent picture?

John 3:14–15. How was it a type of Christ? How are we like Israel? Have your words been more like poison or medicine? *James 3:8.* What must we do to be healed from the poison of sin? Let's confess our sin and look to Christ alone for the only remedy.

Thursday

Read through the Bible: Numbers 22
Family Worship: Numbers 22:1–35

What did Balak want Balaam to do? What did Balaam say he would do? Do you think his spiritual-sounding words were genuine? How did God expose the greed in his heart? **2 Peter 2:15–16; Jude 11**; *BCF 5:4, 6.* Who can make even a donkey speak? Should we believe everyone who sounds "spiritual"? *Matt. 7:15–23.* Reflect: Have you ever tried to sound spiritual to hide the truth? Let's pray for the discernment not to be fooled by feigned spirituality in others or ourselves.

Friday

Read through the Bible: Numbers 23
Family Worship: Numbers 23:13–20

What did Balak hope Balaam would do? Did God change His mind about blessing Israel? Why not? Who can never lie or change His mind? *Heb. 6:18; Titus 1:2; Mal. 3:6; James 1:17.* Who is truth? *John 14:6.* How can this truth about God build our faith? *Rom. 11:29.* If God is this way, what should His people be like? *Ex. 20:16; Eph. 4:25.* Let's praise God for His unchangeable character and irrevocable promises.

Saturday

Read through the Bible: Numbers 24
Family Worship: Numbers 24:15–19

What did Balaam say would rise from Israel? What would this star/scepter do? How do these symbols picture kingship? *Matt. 2:1–2; Gen. 49:10.* Who is the "bright morning star" (Rev. 22:16)? Who rules the nations "with a rod [scepter] of iron" (Rev. 19:15)? How should we respond to this risen Star/King? Like the wise men, let's rejoice "exceedingly with great joy" (Matt. 2:10) and worship Him.

Year 1 — Week 27

Sunday

Read through the Bible: Psalm 27
Family Worship: Psalm 27:4–6

Whose house did David desire to dwell in? Why? What are some aspects of God's nature that reveal his beauty? *BCF 2:1.* How is "the beauty of the Lord" reflected in His creation? How can we reflect His beauty in our behavior? *1 Peter 3:4.* In worship? *John 4:23; 1 Cor. 14:40.* In the arts? *Ex. 35:30–35.* Let's pray for hearts to recognize, "gaze upon," and reflect "the beauty of the Lord."

Monday

Read through the Bible: Numbers 25
Family Worship: Numbers 25:1–5*

*Adult Content What did the daughters of Moab do? Whose idea was this? **Num. 31:16; Rev. 2:14.*** What does this tell us about Balaam's true nature? Whom should we be "yoked" to? *Matt. 11:29.* What are some "stumbling blocks" that could seduce us away from following Christ? *2 Cor. 6:14.* How can we guard ourselves from these? *Ps. 27:4.* Let's pray as our Lord taught us: "Lead us not into temptation, but deliver us from evil" (Matt. 6:13).

Tuesday

Read through the Bible: Numbers 26
Family Worship: Numbers 26:1–4, 51, 63–65

How many fighting men were counted? Is this more or less than forty years earlier? *1,820 less (Num. 1:46).* Did the earlier generation fail to enter the land because of the size of their army or the size of their faith? *Heb. 3:19.* Should we trust in the size of our church to accomplish God's work? *Zech. 4:6.* Whom should we trust? Let's pray for the faith to trust not in the size of our army but in the size of our God.

Wednesday

Read through the Bible: Numbers 27
Family Worship: Numbers 27:12–23

What was Moses's concern for the congregation? *Mark 6:34.* What are sheep like without a shepherd? How did God answer his prayer? How was Joshua equipped for leadership? Who is "the good shepherd" (John 10:11)? Who was given to us by the Lord to keep us from being like sheep without a shepherd? *Eph. 4:11-16.* How are you being equipped for service? Let's praise God for—and pray for—the leaders He's given us.

Thursday

Read through the Bible: Numbers 28
Family Worship: Numbers 28:7

What was offered with each lamb? Whose blood was poured out for us? **Matt. 26:27-28.** In what sense was Paul poured out like a drink offering? **Phil. 2:17; 2 Tim. 4:6; 2 Cor. 12:15.** How can you be poured out for the Lord? *Rom. 12:1.* Let's praise God for the blood of Christ poured out for us and pray for the grace to give ourselves completely in His service.

Friday

Read through the Bible: Numbers 29
Family Worship: Numbers 29:40

What did Moses tell the people? Did he skip anything or summarize? Why not? *Deut. 4:2; Jer. 26:2.* Where do we find everything the Lord has commanded us? Have you ever read through the whole Bible? If we don't, how will we know everything the Lord has commanded us? Let's pray for hearts hungry for "every word that comes from the mouth of God" (Matt. 4:4, cited from Deut. 8:3).

Saturday

Read through the Bible: Numbers 30
Family Worship: Numbers 30:3-8; 1 Corinthians 11:3

Who is the head of Christ? Who is the head of a man? Who is the head of a wife? Is headship based on superiority of personhood or on divinely given roles? *Gen. 1:27; John 10:30.* Who is ultimately responsible for a woman's vow? How can this protect women? How can we practice Christlike headship in our home? *Col. 3:18-21.* Let's pray for greater Christlikeness in the roles He's given us.

Year 1   Week 28

Sunday

Read through the Bible: Psalm 28

Family Worship: Psalm 28:6–9

Who was David's strength and shield? What else was the Lord for David? How is the Lord our strength? Our shield? Our saving refuge? Our shepherd? How did David respond to God? How should we? With our prayer and our song, let's "give thanks to him."

Monday

Read through the Bible: Numbers 31

Family Worship: Numbers 31:8

What finally happened to Balaam? Why? *Num. 31:16*; **Josh. 13:22**. What is divination? *Using magic to try to discover the future or God's secret will.* What does God's Word warn us about divination? **Deut. 18:9–14**. Instead of trying to discover God's secret will, what should we focus on instead? **Deut. 29:29**. Where do we find God's revealed will? Let's pray for hearts focused on obeying God's revealed will in His Word.

Tuesday

Read through the Bible: Numbers 32

Family Worship: Numbers 32:1–6, 16–27

What did the people of Reuben and Gad ask Moses? What was Moses's concern? What was the tribes' solution? What kind of war is the church fighting? *2 Cor. 10:3–5; Eph. 6:10–20; 1 Peter 2:11; Rev. 12:11, 17; 13:7*. How can we help our brothers around the world engaged in spiritual warfare? Who will finally crush all the church's enemies? *Rom. 16:20; Rev. 17:14*. Let's pray that God would enable us and our brothers and sisters to be "good soldier[s] of Christ Jesus" (2 Tim. 2:3).

Wednesday

Read through the Bible: Numbers 33

Family Worship: Numbers 33:50–56

Who commanded Israel to drive out the Canaanites? What would happen if they disobeyed? How would the Canaanites be "barbs" and "thorns"? **Ps. 106:34–38**; *Deut. 12:29–31*. What could be a snare leading us to sin? What did Jesus command us to do with things that cause us to sin? **Matt. 18:7–9.** Does He want us to literally cut off body parts or ruthlessly remove snares to sin? Are there any snares to sin you need to cut off? Let's pray for the grace to cut off anything that causes us to sin.

Thursday

Read through the Bible: Numbers 34
Family Worship: Numbers 34:1–2

What land did God promise to Abraham and his offspring? **Gen. 15:18.** How was He beginning to fulfill this promise? Who is the ultimate Offspring of Abraham? *Gal. 3:16.* How has God expanded this promise for Abraham's offspring in Christ? **Rom. 4:13**; *Matt. 5:5; 2 Peter 3:13.* How should we respond to God for His grace to expand His promises and faithfulness to fulfill them? Let's worship Him!

Friday

Read through the Bible: Numbers 35
Family Worship: Numbers 35:1–3

What did God command Israel to give to the Levites? Instead of land, who was the Levites' inheritance? **Num. 18:20; Deut. 10:8–9.** In addition to their duties in the tabernacle, what were the Levites to do for the people? **Deut. 33:10.** What are we to share with those who teach us? **Gal. 6:6.** What is something special we can do for our pastor? Let's pray that God would show us and use us to bless our pastor.

Saturday

Read through the Bible: Numbers 36
Family Worship: Numbers 35:9–12

What did the Lord provide to protect a manslayer from judgment? What did the manslayer need to do to be protected? Who was provided by God for sinners to be protected from judgment? **Rom. 8:1**; *Ps. 18:2; 46:1.* What do we need to do to be protected? **Heb. 6:18**; *Ps. 31:1–2.* How is fleeing for refuge a picture of faith? Let's confess our guilt and flee by faith to Christ, our city of refuge.

Year 1 — Week 29

Sunday

Read through the Bible: Psalm 29
Family Worship: Psalm 29:1–11

Who is supreme over the angels? How should the angels respond to God? Who is supreme over creation? What is a thunderstorm like? What can we learn about God from a thunderstorm? *Ps. 19:1; Rom. 1:20.* How is the voice of the Lord like a storm? *Jer. 23:29.* How should we respond to Him whose voice is "powerful" and "full of majesty"? Let's "ascribe to the LORD the glory due his name."

Monday

Read through the Bible: Deuteronomy 1
Family Worship: Deuteronomy 1:3–5

Who gave His law to Moses? After forty years of wandering, what did Moses do for the people? Why was it important to explain the law to this new generation? Who will explain God's Word to the next generation of our family? How can you be prepared to explain God's Word to your children? *Deut. 6:6–7.* Let's pray that God would enable each generation of our family to faithfully explain His Word to the next.

Tuesday

Read through the Bible: Deuteronomy 2
Family Worship: Deuteronomy 2:1–8a

Who provided Mount Seir to Esau? How had God provided for His people? How are both examples of God's common grace? *Matt. 5:45; Acts 14:17.* In addition to His common grace for all, how does God especially care for His people? *1 Tim. 4:10; 2 Peter 1:3–11; BCF 5:7.* How has God been gracious to us? Let's praise God for providing us with all we need for life and godliness.

Wednesday

Read through the Bible: Deuteronomy 3:1–4:8
Family Worship: Deuteronomy 4:1–2

What "is the only sufficient, certain, and infallible rule of all saving knowledge, faith, and obedience" (BCF 1:1.1)? What did Moses warn Israel about? What are the consequences for intentionally corrupting God's Word? **Rev. 22:18–19.** What are some ways we could inadvertently add to or take from God's Word?

Matt. 15:3-9. Is there any confusion in our home between family rules and God's rules? Let's pray for the wisdom to apply God's Word without adding to or taking from it.

Thursday

Read through the Bible: Deuteronomy 4:9–49
Family Worship: Deuteronomy 4:32–40

What are we to know in our hearts? How many Gods are there? How did the one and only God show His power and love to Israel? How did He show His power and love to the church? What should we do in response to this knowledge of God? What has God promised those who know and obey Him? Let's pray for hearts filled with—and lives changed by—the knowledge of God. *Optional: Pray Eph. 1:16-23.*

Friday

Read through the Bible: Deuteronomy 5
Family Worship: Deuteronomy 5:1, 22–29

Who wrote the Ten Commandments? How did the people respond to the revealed glory and greatness of God? What did God think of their response? What does God desire beyond confession of fear? *Jer. 32:39-40.* How should we respond to the glory and greatness of God revealed in His Word? *Heb. 12:28-29.* How can we show a proper fear of God in worship? In all of life? Let's pray for hearts and minds to fear God and obey Him forever.

Saturday

Read through the Bible: Deuteronomy 6
Family Worship: Deuteronomy 6:4–7

How many Gods are there? Which commandment is the greatest? **Mark 12:28-30.** How do we show our love for God? What is the difference between having God's words merely in your head and having them "on your heart"? How are parents to show their love for God? When and where should we discuss God's words? Let's pray that our home would be saturated with God's words, His words would be on our hearts, and our hearts would be devoted to God.

Year 1 — Week 30

Sunday

Read through the Bible: Psalm 30
Family Worship: Psalm 30:1–5

What did God do for David? In what sense was his weeping at night turned to joy in the morning? Whom did God literally raise up from death and restore to life? How was the disciples' sorrow turned to joy? **John 16:20–22.** Describe a time when God has turned your sorrow to joy. When will He turn all our sorrows into joy? *Rev. 21:4.* How should we respond to the One who turns our sorrow into joy? Let's "give thanks to his holy name."

Monday

Read through the Bible: Deuteronomy 7
Family Worship: Deuteronomy 7:6–8

What is a treasured possession of yours? What is God's "treasured possession"? *1 Peter 2:9.* Why did God set His love on Israel? Why did He set His love on us? *Eph. 1:4–6.* Who chose a people for Himself out of mere free grace and love? *BCF 3:5.* How should we respond to Him who chose us to be His treasured possession? *Deut. 6:5; 1 John 4:19; Matt. 13:44.* Let's praise Him and pray for hearts that treasure Him in return.

Tuesday

Read through the Bible: Deuteronomy 8
Family Worship: Deuteronomy 8:1–3

Why did the Lord let Israel hunger? How is God's Word like bread? Which of God's words are important? Who is the Bread of Life? How did Jesus's experience parallel Israel's? **Matt. 4:1–4.** How was He proven greater? What was His source of strength? What is our source of spiritual strength? Let's pray for hearts hungry for the bread of God's Word.

Wednesday

Read through the Bible: Deuteronomy 9
Family Worship: Deuteronomy 9:1–8

Who would go before Israel "as a consuming fire"? Why did God give Israel the promised land? Were they better than the Canaanites? Is God bringing the church to the heavenly promised land because of our righteousness?

1 Cor. 1:26–29. Are we better than those not chosen? Can anyone boast about being called by God? Why not? How should we respond to God for calling stubborn sinners like us? Let's humbly praise and thank Him.

Thursday

Read through the Bible: Deuteronomy 10
Family Worship: Deuteronomy 10:12–15

To whom belong heaven and earth? Whom did the Lord choose to "set his heart in love on"? Who are these offspring today? *Gal. 3:7, 16, 29.* What does God require of those He has set His special love on? How can you show wholehearted fear of God? Wholehearted love for Him? Let's praise God for setting His heart in love on us and pray for hearts devoted to fear, love, obey, and walk with Him.

Friday

Read through the Bible: Deuteronomy 11
Family Worship: Deuteronomy 11:18–21

Whose words are these in the Bible? What are we to do with God's words? What is pictured by binding God's words on our hands? *James 1:22.* Making them as frontlets on our foreheads? *2 Cor. 10:5; Phil. 4:8.* Writing them on our doorposts? *Deut. 6:7; Col. 3:16–21.* What do you need to do to make God's Word the rule of your actions? Your thoughts? Our home? Let's pray for the grace to saturate and sanctify every part of our lives with God's Word.

Saturday

Read through the Bible: Deuteronomy 12
Family Worship: Deuteronomy 12:1–7, 12, 28–32

What did God command Israel to do to the Canaanite idols and places of worship? Why? Who decides how God is to be worshiped? *John 4:24; BCF 22:1.* How did God command Israel to worship Him? Should we look at the world or other religions to get ideas on how to worship God? Where should we look? How are we to worship God? *1 Cor. 11:23–34; Col. 3:16; 1 Tim. 4:13; 2 Tim. 4:1–2.* Let's pray for hearts overflowing with joyful, biblical worship.

Year 1 — Week 31

Sunday

Read through the Bible: Psalm 31
Family Worship: Psalm 31:1–5

What did David ask God to be for him? What did he commit to the Lord? How did this show his trust in God? Who quoted these words on the cross? **Luke 23:44–46.** How did Jesus literally fulfill David's words? How can we commit our spirits to God? *Rom. 12:1.* Reflect: Is there any part of your life you have not totally committed to the Lord? Let's recommit ourselves totally into God's hands.

Monday

Read through the Bible: Deuteronomy 13
Family Worship: Deuteronomy 13:1–5

Should we believe everyone who does miracles? Why not? *2 Thess. 2:9–12.* What was Israel to do if a "prophet" performed a sign and then told them to worship other gods? What should the church do with false prophets? **1 Cor. 5:13;** *Matt. 18:15–20.* Who is fully God and man? What should we do if someone comes to our home teaching a different "Jesus"? **2 John 7–11.** Let's pray for such love for God and His truth that we would immediately recognize and reject deceivers.

Tuesday

Read through the Bible: Deuteronomy 14
Family Worship: Deuteronomy 14:22–27

Who gives us the power to make wealth? *Deut. 8:18.* What did God command His people to offer Him each year? What did He tell families to do with a portion of the tithe? *Deut. 12:5–7.* How can we practice joyful, family worship in our giving? *2 Cor. 9:7.* In the Lord's Supper? Let's pray for hearts to be a family of cheerful givers and joyful worshipers.

Wednesday

Read through the Bible: Deuteronomy 15
Family Worship: Deuteronomy 15:1–2, 7–11

What did God command Israel to do every seven years? Who released us from our debt of sin? *Col. 2:14.* How would some people be tempted to treat their poor brothers close to the year of release? Why? What did our Lord say about this kind of ungracious attitude? **Luke 6:34–36.** How can we imitate our Father's mercy to the needy? How can we practice generosity in our family? Let's ask God to give us hearts more like His—merciful, loving, and generous.

Thursday

Read through the Bible: Deuteronomy 16
Family Worship: Deuteronomy 16:9–12

What did God tell Israel to do seven weeks after Passover? *Note: This was a celebration of the firstfruits of the wheat harvest (Ex. 34:22), also called "Pentecost" because it occurred fifty days after the last feast (Lev. 23:15–16).* What blessing (whom) did God pour out on the church at Pentecost? *Acts 2:1-4.* In what sense was the outpouring of the Spirit the firstfruits of even greater blessings? **Rom. 8:23**; *Eph. 1:13-14.* What are some "firstfruit" blessings we can praise God for today? *Rom. 8:16, 26.* Let's praise God for the firstfruits of the Spirit.

Friday

Read through the Bible: Deuteronomy 17
Family Worship: Deuteronomy 17:14–20

What did the Lord say Israel's king must *not* do? What did He command him to do? Did Israel's kings obey these commands? Who is the King of Kings? How did King Jesus fulfill these commands? *John 1:14.* How can we apply these commands to be good subjects of King Jesus? *Josh. 1:8; Ps. 1:2; Col. 3:16.* Let's pray for hearts passionate to read and obey God's Word every day.

Saturday

Read through the Bible: Deuteronomy 18
Family Worship: Deuteronomy 18:15–19

Whom did God promise to raise up for the people? What does a prophet do? Who is this Prophet? **Acts 3:18-24.** Whom do all the words of the prophets point to? *Luke 24:25-27; Rev. 19:10.* Where do we find God's words given by the prophets? What do you need to do in response to these words? Reflect: How well have you been listening? Let's pray for hearts passionate to listen to God's Word and to obey.

Year 1   Week 32

Sunday

Read through the Bible: Psalm 32
Family Worship: Psalm 32:1–5

Who is able to forgive sin? Who is blessed? What did David feel like when he tried to cover up his sin? What did he do to be forgiven? Did God forgive David because of his good works? *Rom. 4:6-8.* Have you ever felt the weight of guilt like David? What do you need to do about it? Let's confess our sin and praise God for the blessedness of forgiveness.

Monday

Read through the Bible: Deuteronomy 19
Family Worship: Deuteronomy 19:15–21

Who is both the perfect Judge and true Witness? *John 8:16-18.* How many witnesses were required to establish a charge? *Matt. 18:16; 1 Tim. 5:19.* Why? What were the consequences for a malicious witness? What effect would swift justice have on the nation? How could our nation apply these principles? How could our family? What should we do with false witnesses? Let's pray for hearts to be true witnesses and for wisdom to be just in discipline.

Tuesday

Read through the Bible: Deuteronomy 20
Family Worship: Deuteronomy 19:15; Matt. 18:15–17

Who is the head of the church? What did Jesus say to do if a brother sins against you? What if he refuses to repent? What if he refuses to listen to the church? What is the goal of church discipline? *James 5:19-20.* What should you do if your sibling "sins" against you? What if you can't work it out? What if they won't listen to your parents? *We'll discuss that tomorrow.* Let's pray for the wisdom to deal biblically with conflict at home and at church.

Wednesday

Read through the Bible: Deuteronomy 21
Family Worship: Deuteronomy 21:18–21

What did God command Israel to do with an incorrigibly rebellious son? Though the Old Testament penalty no longer applies, what does it teach us about God's view of dishonoring parents? *Deut. 27:16; Rom. 1:30.* When would it be appropriate today for parents to turn their children over to the discipline of the church? Of the state? Who always honors His Father? How can you be more like Christ? *Eph. 6:1–3.* Let's pray for hearts to honor God by honoring our parents.

Thursday

Read through the Bible: Deuteronomy 22
Family Worship: Deuteronomy 22:1–4

Who told us to love our neighbor as ourselves? What was an Israelite supposed to do if he found a neighbor's animal? What if he saw an injured animal? What should you do if you find one of your sibling's toys left outside? What if you find someone's wallet or purse full of money? Let's pray for hearts filled with love for others and respect for their things.

Friday

Read through the Bible: Deuteronomy 23
Family Worship: Deuteronomy 23:24–25

What was an Israelite allowed to do when walking through a neighbor's field? What could he not do? How did Jesus's disciples make use of this merciful provision for travelers? **Mark 2:23–24.** Was it sinful? **Mark 2:27–28.** If someone tells us we're doing something sinful, what should we do? What is the supreme standard for right and wrong? *Mark 2:25; BCF 1:10; 21:2.* Let's pray for the discretion to walk according to God's Word and not be enslaved by the traditions of men.

Saturday

Read through the Bible: Deuteronomy 24
Family Worship: Deuteronomy 24:19–22

Who gives the power to make wealth? What did God command farmers to do? Why? How did Ruth benefit from this merciful provision? *Ruth 2.* Today the state gives money from our taxes to the poor—how might this undermine the incentive to work? How could our state system be made more biblical? *2 Thess. 3:10.* How can we help the poor while remaining good stewards? Let's pray for the wisdom to be merciful to the needy and good stewards of God's provision.

Year 1   Week 33

Sunday

Read through the Bible: Psalm 33
Family Worship: Psalm 33:1–9

Who created the heavens and the earth? By what did God create everything? *Heb. 11:3; 2 Peter 3:5.* Through whom did He create everything? *John 1:1–3; Heb. 1:2.* How does creation display God's power? *Ps. 19:1–6; Rom. 1:19–20.* How does it display His steadfast love? *Acts 14:17.* How should we respond to our awesome Creator? Let's shout and sing for joy, give thanks, play skillfully—and stand in awe of Him.

Monday

Read through the Bible: Deuteronomy 25
Family Worship: Deuteronomy 25:4

What law did God give concerning oxen? What would muzzling an ox do to its incentive to work? Was this law written ultimately for oxen? **1 Cor. 9:8–11; 1 Tim. 5:17–18.** Who said, "The laborer deserves his wages" (Luke 10:7)? How are Jesus's words pictured in this law? How can you earn your wages? *2 Thess. 3:10.* How does our pastor earn his wages? How can we show him double honor? Let's pray for hearts to honor our pastor with our respect and our riches.

Tuesday

Read through the Bible: Deuteronomy 26
Family Worship: Deuteronomy 26:1–11

Who answered Israel's cries and delivered them out of slavery and into the promised land? What did the Lord command them to do when they brought in their first harvest? What has God delivered us from? What have you prayed for recently? How has God answered? How should we respond to the Lord our God for all the good He has given us? *Heb. 13:15.* Let's worship Him and rejoice!

Wednesday

Read through the Bible: Deuteronomy 27
Family Worship: Deuteronomy 27:9–10, 26; Galatians 3:10

Who is under God's curse? Have you perfectly obeyed the law? Who has? Who redeemed us from the curse of the law? **Gal. 3:13–14;** *Deut. 21:22–23.*

How have we been blessed as a result? How should we then live? *John 14:15; Gal. 5:22-23*. How should we respond to the One who was cursed, that we might be blessed? Let's worship our Savior and pray for the Spirit's power to obey Him.

Thursday

Read through the Bible: Deuteronomy 28
Family Worship: Deuteronomy 28:1–6, 15–19

What did God promise Israel if they obeyed His Word? What would be the consequences if they disobeyed? Who gave us the full meaning of the law? *Matt. 5–7*. What did Jesus promise those who obey His word? **Matt. 7:24–27.** How does building a house on rock vs. sand picture the outcome of obedience vs. disobedience? Does obedience guarantee an easy life? *Matt. 5:2-12*. How can we build our lives on the rock? Let's pray for hearts to build our lives on the rock of obedience to God's Word.

Friday

Read through the Bible: Deuteronomy 29
Family Worship: Deuteronomy 29:29

How has God revealed Himself to us? *2 Tim. 3:16-17; Rom. 1:19-20; Ps. 19*. Whose words are these? Has God revealed everything there is to know? What are some "secret things" God has not revealed? *Matt. 24:36; Acts 1:7*. What should we focus on? What should we do with what God has revealed? Let's praise God for His Word and pray for hearts to "do all the words of this law."

Saturday

Read through the Bible: Deuteronomy 30
Family Worship: Deuteronomy 30:15–20

Who is our life? What choice did God set before His people? How could they "choose life"? How could they, in effect, choose death? What choice has God given us? **John 3:36.** How can we choose life? How can we show by our lives that we have chosen Christ? *James 2:17-18; BCF 11:2; 16:2*. What does God want us to choose? Let's pray for hearts to choose life in Christ and lives that show it.

Year 1 — Week 34

Sunday

Read through the Bible: Psalm 34
Family Worship: Psalm 34:1–8

Whom should we bless "at all times"? Why was David praising the Lord? In what way did he "taste" God's goodness? Have you tasted (experienced) God's goodness? How? How did you respond to Him? Are there others you know who need to taste God's goodness? Let's praise God for delivering and saving us and pray He would enable others to also "taste and see that [He] is good!"

Monday

Read through the Bible: Deuteronomy 31
Family Worship: Deuteronomy 31:9–13

Whose word did Moses write down? What did he command Israel to do with God's Word? *1 Tim. 4:13*. Who needed to hear the Word? Why were they to do this? When do you read or hear God's Word? What effect has it had on your life? Let's pray for hearts that "learn to fear the Lord [our] God" as we study through His Word every three years.

Tuesday

Read through the Bible: Deuteronomy 32
Family Worship: Deuteronomy 31:30–32:4

What is God like? What is His work like? What are His ways like? What is justice? *The principle or ideal of just dealing or right action.*[3] How are God's ways "justice"? Whose ways are the standard of right and wrong? What does our society use as a standard of right and wrong? How can we keep from being corrupted by society's false standards? Let's pray for the wisdom to compare all standards to the One whose work is perfect and ways are just.

Wednesday

Read through the Bible: Deuteronomy 33
Family Worship: Deuteronomy 33:26–29

Who "rides through the heavens to [our] help"? Who is like God? What is God like for His people? How is He our dwelling place? What does the word picture of "everlasting arms" tell us about how God relates to us? How is God

---

[3] *Merriam-Webster Online*, s.v. "justice," accessed October 4, 2019, https://www.merriam-webster.com.

our shield? Our sword? What are we as a result? How should "a people saved by the Lord" respond to Him? Let's praise Him and pray He would draw us close in His everlasting arms.

Thursday

Read through the Bible: Deuteronomy 34
Family Worship: Deuteronomy 34:1–12

How was Moses's prophetic ministry unique? Since this was written, who arose as an even greater prophet than Moses? **John 1:16–18.** How is Jesus like Moses? How is He greater? *Heb. 1:1–3; 3:1–6.* How should we respond to the One who not only speaks face to face with God for us but is Himself God? Let's praise God for revealing Himself to us through Moses and, preeminently, through His Son.

Friday

Read through the Bible: Joshua 1
Family Worship: Joshua 1:1–9

Who promised, "I will never leave you nor forsake you" (Heb. 13:5)? What did God tell Joshua to be? What did He say should never depart from his mouth? What did He command Joshua to do with His Word? What did He promise if Joshua obeyed? How can we meditate on God's Word day and night? *Deut. 6:7.* Let's pray for hearts passionate to meditate on and obey God's Word day and night.

Saturday

Read through the Bible: Joshua 2
Family Worship: Joshua 2:1–14*

*AC v. 1. Who is "God in the heavens above and on the earth beneath"? What had Rahab heard about the Lord? How did this affect the Canaanites? How did it affect Rahab? How has it affected you? How did Rahab express her faith? How did she show it? *Heb. 11:31; James 2:25.* How can we? How does Rahab's story demonstrate sovereign grace? *Matt. 1:5.* Let's praise God for His amazing grace in calling unworthy sinners like Rahab—and us—to Christ.

Year 1   Week 35

Sunday

Read through the Bible: Psalm 35
Family Worship: Psalm 35:19–24

What cause did David's foes have to hate him? What did he do about it? Who else was hated "without cause"? **John 15:18–21, 25.** What did Jesus say would happen to His disciples? How should we deal with those who hate us and hate our Lord without cause? Let's begin like David did by taking the situation—and our feelings—straight to God in prayer.

Monday

Read through the Bible: Joshua 3
Family Worship: Joshua 3:7–17

Who is "the Lord of all the earth" (Josh. 3:13)? What did God promise to do for Joshua? How did God show He was with Joshua? How did this strengthen Israel's faith for the coming war? **Josh. 4:14;** *Ex. 14:31.* How did God show He was with the apostles? *Heb. 2:3–4.* What did God give us through them to strengthen our faith? *Rom. 10:17.* Are you ready for the coming battle? Let's pray for faith fortified by God's Word.

Tuesday

Read through the Bible: Joshua 4
Family Worship: Joshua 4:1–7, 19–24

What did God command Joshua to do? What was the purpose for the memorial of stones? Who instituted two memorial signs in the church? *BCF 28:1.* What are they? What do baptism and the Lord's Supper remind us of? *Rom. 6:3–4; 1 Cor. 11:23–26; BCF 29:1; 30:1, cf. Josh. 5:1–10.* How should they affect our devotion? Let's pray that the sacraments would prompt teachable moments in our family—that we may fear the Lord forever.

Wednesday

Read through the Bible: Joshua 5
Family Worship: Joshua 5:13–15

Who appeared to Joshua? *Josh. 6:1–2.* How can you tell this was no mere man? Who is the only One who is both God and man? How was Joshua's experience similar to Moses's at the burning bush? How is Jesus like Joshua?

How is He greater? *Rev. 19:11-16*. How should we respond to our Commander—the greater Joshua—who is leading us to the greater promised land? Let's worship Him!

Thursday

Read through the Bible: Joshua 6
Family Worship: Joshua 6:1–5, 15–25*

*AC 6:17, 22, 25. Who made the wall of Jericho fall down? Who were the only people saved out of Jericho? How were both the grace and justice of God magnified in this? How will the return of Christ be similar? *2 Thess. 1:6-10*. How can we, like Rahab's family, be delivered from the coming judgment? **1 Thess. 1:9-10**. Let's praise God for our greater Joshua: "Jesus who delivers us from the wrath to come."

Friday

Read through the Bible: Joshua 7
Family Worship: Joshua 7:1–15, 20–26

Whose "ways are justice" (Deut. 32:4)? Why was God angry with Israel? What was Achan's sin? What were the consequences for Israel? For his family? *Deut. 5:9; Col. 3:5b*. How does this contrast with the effect of Rahab's faith? How is sin like a contagious disease? How might the sin of one member affect our family? Our church? Is there any unconfessed sin in your life? Let's pray for hearts to confess and deal redemptively with any sin in our family.

Saturday

Read through the Bible: Joshua 8
Family Worship: Joshua 8:1–22

Who gave Joshua the strategy to capture Ai? Who had given him the previous failed strategy? *Josh. 7:2-3*. How was the new strategy different? How was it different from that used to capture Jericho? How does this illustrate different means God uses to accomplish His purposes? *BCF 5:3*. Whose strategy should we follow in spiritual battle? Where do we find it? Let's pray for hearts to obey our heavenly Commander's strategy in His Word.

Year 1 — Week 36

Sunday

Read through the Bible: Psalm 36
Family Worship: Psalm 36:5–9

What is God's steadfast love like? Who is "the light of the world" (John 8:12)? Why do we need light? Why do we need His light? Who is "the fountain of life"? *John 4:14.* How is knowing Jesus like drinking from a river of delights? *Ps. 16:11; Isa. 25:6.* How would a starving man respond to a feast? How should we respond to the feast of God's steadfast love? Let's glorify God by enjoying Him and His feast forever.

Monday

Read through the Bible: Joshua 9
Family Worship: Joshua 9:3–21

What did the Gibeonites do? Why? What did Joshua do? What should he have done to keep from being deceived? *James 1:5.* What has God given the church to guard against our being deceived by "human cunning"? **Eph. 4:11–16.** Where do we find their teaching? How can you keep from being deceived? Who is the standard of spiritual maturity? Let's pray for greater maturity in Christ through the teaching of His Word.

Tuesday

Read through the Bible: Joshua 10
Family Worship: Joshua 10:1–15

Who is almighty over all creation? How did God fight for Israel? Did God's sovereignty mean Israel didn't have to fight? How much effort did Israel put into the fight? How much effort should we put into spiritual battle? **Col. 1:28–29.** How much effort did Paul put into his ministry? What did God do through him? Which spiritual discipline needs more effort in your life? Let's pray for hearts to be spiritual warriors, "struggling with all his energy."

Wednesday

Read through the Bible: Joshua 11
Family Worship: Joshua 11:16–20

Who is almighty over all people? What did God do to the Canaanites? Why? Who deserves God's mercy? *Rom. 3:23; 6:23.* Why does God show mercy to some and harden others? **Rom. 9:18–24.** Do we have any right to question God for this? Why not? How should we respond instead? *Rom. 11:33–36.* Let's praise God for choosing to show mercy to unworthy sinners like us. *Hymn: "Amazing Grace."*

Thursday

Read through the Bible: Joshua 12
Family Worship: Joshua 12:7

How does the conquest of Canaan picture the Christian life? **Eph. 6:10–20.** Who is our Commander? Who is our enemy? How can we stand firm against the forces of evil? What is "the sword of the Spirit"? How did Jesus use the Word in battle with the devil? *Matt. 4:1–11.* How does the armor correspond to the normal disciplines of the Christian life? How can we train to be more effective warriors? Let's pray for the Spirit's power to take up our armor and stand firm.

Friday

Read through the Bible: Joshua 13
Family Worship: Joshua 13:1

Why couldn't Joshua lead Israel to complete victory? Who is our ageless Joshua who will defeat all His enemies? How is the partially conquered promised land similar to the ongoing war for sanctification? **1 Peter 2:11;** *BCF 13:2–3.* Who is the enemy in this war? What are we to do with remaining sin? *Rom. 8:13.* Reflect: Are there any parts of the old self you have made peace with instead of putting to death? Let's pray for the grace to conquer remaining sin.

Saturday

Read through the Bible: Joshua 14
Family Worship: Joshua 14:6–14

What did the Lord promise Caleb? Why? How did Caleb respond to God's promise? Whom did Caleb credit for his enduring strength? How does Caleb model strong faith? How does he model enduring faith? **Heb. 10:36.** How can you live out active, enduring faith like Caleb? Let's pray for strong, enduring faith—like Caleb's.

Year 1   Week 37

Sunday

Read through the Bible: Psalm 37
Family Worship: Psalm 37:1–11

What did David tell us not to fret about? How are evildoers like grass? What should we do instead of fretting? How can you "delight yourself in the LORD"? Will the proud and powerful inherit the earth? Who will? **Matt. 5:5.** Who perfectly modeled the humble strength of meekness? *Matt. 11:29.* How can you practice meekness? Let's pray for the meekness of Christ to "delight [ourselves] in the LORD."

Monday

Read through the Bible: Joshua 15
Family Worship: Joshua 15:13–19

Who "gave us a spirit not of fear but of power and love and self-control" (2 Tim. 1:7)? What was Caleb's family like? How were they examples of bold, overcoming faith? *Judg. 3:9–10; 1 John 5:4.* How were they like Timothy's family? **2 Tim. 1:5–7.** How can we "fan into flame" the gift of bold, overcoming faith in our family? How can we pass it on? Let's pray that God would enable us to be a family of bold, overcoming faith.

Tuesday

Read through the Bible: Joshua 16
Family Worship: Joshua 16:4

What is an inheritance? What do you do to earn it? What inheritance did the people of Israel receive? What inheritance are we destined to receive? **1 Peter 1:3–5.** What did we do to earn it? How is our inheritance greater than Israel's? Who gained and continues to guard our inheritance? How should we respond to our Father for the imperishable inheritance of eternal life? Let's praise Him!

Wednesday

Read through the Bible: Joshua 17
Family Worship: Joshua 17:14–18

What inheritance did the people of Joseph receive? What did they have to do to possess it? How does their faith compare with Caleb's? *Josh. 14:12.* What do we have to do to possess our inheritance? **1 Peter 1:3-7**. What happens to our faith when we overcome trials? Who is praised as a result? What trials are grieving you? How can your faith be tested genuine? Let's pray for the faith to persevere through trials—to the praise, glory, and honor of Christ.

Thursday

Read through the Bible: Joshua 18
Family Worship: Joshua 18:1–3

Who promised Israel their land as an inheritance? Had all the tribes taken possession of it? How were the seven remaining tribes different from Caleb's family? *Josh. 15:14-19*. Which families heard God's promise? Which acted on that promise? How can we "take possession" of God's promises? *Heb. 4:11; 10:36*. Let's pray for hearts to "be doers of the word, and not hearers only" (James 1:22).

Friday

Read through the Bible: Joshua 19
Family Worship: Joshua 19:51

From whom did Israel inherit their land? From whom do children normally receive their inheritance? Are all people the children of God? *John 1:12-13*. What did God do so that we could be His heirs? **Rom. 8:14-17**. With whom are we "fellow heirs"? What can God's children call Him? *Mark 14:36*. How is God like a daddy? How should we respond to our "Abba, Father" for adopting us and making us joint heirs with Christ? Let's worship Him!

Saturday

Read through the Bible: Joshua 20
Family Worship: Joshua 20:1–2

Who commanded Israel to appoint cities of refuge? Through whom did God speak to them? Whose words are these in the Bible? **2 Peter 1:19-21;** *2 Tim. 3:16*. Who wrote them down for us? Who carried them along as they wrote? *Acts 4:25*. Since these are the very words of God, how should we treat them? Let's pray that God would give us a greater reverence for and obedience to His Word.

Year 1 — Week 38

Sunday

Read through the Bible: Psalm 38
Family Worship: Psalm 38:1–11, 15, 18, 21–22

What was wrong with David? Why was he sick? Is sickness always caused by sin? *Job; John 9:3.* Whom did he turn to in sickness? What should we do when we're sick? *James 5:13-15.* How did David's friends and family treat him? How should we treat those who are sick? *Matt. 25:36, 40.* Let's pray for hearts of compassion to minister to the sick as unto Jesus.

Monday

Read through the Bible: Joshua 21
Family Worship: Joshua 21:43–45

Who gave Israel rest from their enemies? In what sense was God's promise of rest complete? In what sense was it yet incomplete? **Heb. 4:8-11.** What is the final fulfillment of God's rest? *Rev. 14:13.* How is salvation-rest both a gift of grace and something we must strive for? *Eph. 2:8-10; Heb. 10:35-39.* How can we experience God's rest? *Matt. 11:28-30.* Let's pray for hearts that strive by faith to enter God's rest.

Tuesday

Read through the Bible: Joshua 22
Family Worship: Joshua 22:1–6

What did Joshua command the eastern tribes? Whom are we to cling to? What does it mean to cling to something? How do we cling to God? What is the relationship between loving God and obeying Him? **John 14:15, 21, 23.** What did Jesus promise those who love and obey Him? How can you show that you love Jesus today? Let's pray for hearts that cling to God in love—and show that love by obedience.

Wednesday

Read through the Bible: Joshua 23
Family Worship: Joshua 23:6–13

Whom was Israel to cling to? Whom were they not to cling to? What would happen if they did? How would it be dangerous for us to cling to unbelievers? **1 Cor. 15:33**; *2 Cor. 6:14.* Reflect: Is there anyone or anything you're clinging to that could be a snare to sin? How can we minister to unbelievers without clinging to them? Let's pray for hearts that "cling to the LORD" in love—and are free from snares to sin.

Thursday

Read through the Bible: Joshua 24
Family Worship: Joshua 24:14–15

Was all Israel serving the Lord? What choice did Joshua give them? What had he chosen for himself and his family? What are some false gods or false ideas of God that people serve today? Whom will you serve this day? How can we show that we've chosen as a family to serve the Lord "in sincerity"? *John 13:35.* Let's pray for the grace to say with our lips and our love: "as for me and my house, we will serve the LORD."

Friday

Read through the Bible: Judges 1
Family Worship: Judges 1:27–28

Who commanded Israel to completely drive out the Canaanites? Did Manasseh completely obey God? Is partial obedience acceptable to God? **Rev. 3:2–3.** What was wrong with the church at Sardis? What did Jesus command them to do? Reflect: Are you completely obeying God? Children: Are you completely obeying your parents? Let's pray that God would expose any partial obedience in our lives and gently lead us to repentance and full obedience.

Saturday

Read through the Bible: Judges 2
Family Worship: Judges 2:6–12

What was Israel's relationship with God like during Joshua's lifetime? What happened to the next generation? Who commanded parents to make His works known to their children? **Deut. 4:9.** Did the earlier generation obey this? What can we do to keep what happened to Israel from happening to our family? Who will make Christ known to your children? To their children? Let's pray for the grace to make Christ known to multiple generations of our family.

Year 1 — Week 39

Sunday

Read through the Bible: Psalm 39
Family Worship: Psalm 39:1

What is a muzzle? What is it used for? In what sense did David say he would muzzle himself? Why? *James 3:5–10.* Why do we especially need to control our speech near unbelievers? *Rom. 2:24.* Reflect: Have you said something recently you wish you hadn't? Who never sinned with His words? *1 Peter 2:22–23.* How can we honor God with our words? *Eph. 4:29.* Let's pray for the grace to muzzle our mouths.

Monday

Read through the Bible: Judges 3
Family Worship: Judges 3:7–12

What did Israel do after Joshua died? Who disciplined His people to draw them back to Himself? How did God discipline them? How did Israel respond? How did God deliver them? What happened after Othniel died? How could this cycle of apostasy occur today in people, families, and churches? How can we keep this from happening to us? Let's pray that God would bind our wandering hearts to Him with cords of grace. *Hymn: "Come Thou Fount."*

Tuesday

Read through the Bible: Judges 4
Family Worship: Judges 4:1–10, 12–16, 23

How does this chapter reflect the cycle of apostasy discussed yesterday? In the book of Judges, there is also a downward spiral in spiritual leadership—how did Barak show himself to be a weaker leader than Othniel? What does it say about Israel's men that a woman was judging Israel? What does it say about God's grace? *2 Cor. 12:9.* Who is the perfect role model of manly leadership? Sons: How can you prepare for leadership in the family? Let's pray that God would help us train our boys to "act like men" (1 Cor. 16:13).

Wednesday

Read through the Bible: Judges 5
Family Worship: Judges 5:1, 6–9

What does a mother do for her children? *1 Thess. 2:7.* Who comforts us as a mother comforts her children? *Isa. 66:13*. How was Deborah like a mother to Israel? *Judg. 4:4–9, 14*. What dangers did she see? What did she do about it? How can we exalt motherhood in our home? Daughters: How can you prepare to nurture your children? Let's pray for the grace to exalt—and prepare our girls for—the gift of motherhood.

Thursday

Read through the Bible: Judges 6
Family Worship: Judges 6:1, 7–17

Who appeared to Gideon? What did Gideon ask the Lord? How had He already answered? How is Gideon a weaker leader than his predecessors? If we're struggling in our faith, should we seek a sign? *Matt. 12:38–39*. What has God already given us to strengthen our faith? *Rom. 10:17*. Let's pray that God would use His Word to build our faith.

Friday

Read through the Bible: Judges 7
Family Worship: Judges 7:1–23

Why did God tell Gideon he had too many in his army? How many did Gideon end up with? How big was the Midianite army? *Judg. 8:10*. What did Gideon do to defeat the Midianites? What did God do? How were God's power and grace magnified in Gideon's weakness? *2 Cor. 12:9*. How are they magnified in ours? *Eph. 2:4–9*. Who should get the glory for any good works we do? Let's pray that God's power and grace would indeed be magnified in our weakness.

Saturday

Read through the Bible: Judges 8
Family Worship: Judges 8:22–28*

*AC 8:27 (*whored* = *committed spiritual adultery*). Whom did Israel want to rule over them? Who did Gideon say would rule them? How were his actions different from his pious words? *Judg. 8:30–31*. What is a snare? How was the golden ephod a snare? What are some things that could become snares to us, luring us away from God? How can we keep this from happening? Let's pray that God would help us identify and remove any potential snares from our lives.

Year 1   Week 40

Sunday

Read through the Bible: Psalm 40
Family Worship: Psalm 40:6–8

What does God delight in more than sacrifices and offerings? *1 Sam. 15:22.* What did David delight in? Who did David (and the Old Testament sacrifices) foreshadow? **Heb. 10:5–10.** How did Jesus fulfill David's words? What does the once-for-all sacrifice of Christ do for believers? How can we be more like David and his greater Son? Let's pray for open ears and hearts that delight to do God's will.

Monday

Read through the Bible: Judges 9
Family Worship: Judges 8:29–9:6*

*AC 8:33. Who created marriage to be between one man and one woman? *Mark 10:6–8.* How did Gideon depart from God's design? What do you think Gideon was trying to do by having so many sons? What kind of legacy did Gideon end up leaving? How can we leave a better legacy? Let's pray that God would make ours a family of multi-generational faithfulness to Him, His Word, and each other.

Tuesday

Read through the Bible: Judges 10
Family Worship: Judges 10:6–16

Who is the only living and true God? What steps of the cycle of apostasy do you see? What's different? Why didn't God deliver the people as soon as they cried out to Him? How did they respond to God's discipline? How did God respond to their repentance? Are you in a cycle of repeating and repenting of the same sin? Will more discipline be required to break the cycle? Let's pray for the grace to break the cycle of sin—before more discipline is required.

Wednesday

Read through the Bible: Judges 11
Family Worship: Judges 11:29–40

What did Jephthah do that showed great faith? **Heb. 11:32–34.** What did he do that was a wicked corruption of faith adopted from paganism? Who hates child sacrifice? *Deut. 12:31*. Should he have carried out his rash vow? *Lev. 5:4–6; 1 Sam. 25:34; BCF 23:5*. Have you ever done or said anything without thinking through the potential consequences? What should we do instead? Let's pray for the wisdom to think before we speak (and quickly repent if we don't).

Thursday

Read through the Bible: Judges 12
Family Worship: Judges 12:1–7

What were the Ephraimites angry about? What kind of leadership did Jephthah display in this explosive situation? How could he have handled this better? **Prov. 15:1**; *8:1–3*. Who is "slow to anger, and abounding in steadfast love" (Ex. 34:6)? If one of your siblings angrily accuses you, how should you respond? Let's pray for the discretion to defuse conflict redemptively with humility, wisdom, and love.

Friday

Read through the Bible: Judges 13
Family Worship: Judges 13:1–25

Who appeared to Manoah's wife? *Isa. 9:6*. What did He tell her? How did Manoah and his wife practice spiritual headship? How did they show their faith? Their fear of God? How were they different from the surrounding culture? How can we be more like them? Let's praise God for this refreshing picture of a godly home amid an ungodly culture and pray He would make ours so as well.

Saturday

Read through the Bible: Judges 14
Family Worship: Judges 14:1–20

Who made Samson strong? How did Samson show great physical strength? How did he show great spiritual weakness? How did God show His sovereignty? Which motivated Samson more: what was right is his eyes or God's? Reflect: Which motivates you more? How can we grow in spiritual strength? *Eph. 3:14–19*. Let's pray for the spiritual strength to be motivated by what is right in God's eyes rather than ours.

Year 1 — Week 41

Sunday

Read through the Bible: Psalm 41
Family Worship: Psalm 41:9

What happened to David? Who quoted this verse when He was betrayed by a friend? **John 13:18-30.** How was this Scripture fulfilled in Christ? Did Judas's betrayal take Jesus by surprise? Have you ever had anyone close to you betray you? How can we be better friends than Judas? *John 15:12-15.* Let's praise God for making us His friends and pray He would make us faithful friends to Him—and to each other.

Monday

Read through the Bible: Judges 15
Family Worship: Judges 15:1-16

How did the men of Judah show great weakness? How did Samson show great strength? Who gave Samson his strength? Whom did Samson give glory to? How could he have grown stronger in faith? *Rom. 4:20.* Reflect: Who receives the glory for what God has given you? What are some things you can give glory to God for? Let's pray for the grace to grow strong in faith as we give glory to God.

Tuesday

Read through the Bible: Judges 16
Family Worship: Judges 16:4-22

What kind of woman was Delilah? *Prov. 5:3-6.* How did Samson show a lack of discretion? What were the consequences? Who left Samson in order to discipline him? How can we protect ourselves from deceitful Delilahs? *Prov. 4:20-23; Ps. 119:9.* Let's pray for the discretion to guard our hearts and our ways in God's Word.

Wednesday

Read through the Bible: Judges 17
Family Worship: Judges 17:1-6

What happened between Micah and his mother? How did *they* decide to worship God? In whose eyes was this right? Was it right in God's eyes? *Deut. 12:8, 32.* Who decides how we are to worship? How can we ensure our worship is right in God's eyes? *John 4:24; BCF 22.* Let's pray for hearts to "worship in spirit and [the] truth [of God's Word]" (John 4:24).

Thursday

Read through the Bible: Judges 18
Family Worship: Judges 17:6–13

What kind of worship did Micah institute in his household? In whose eyes was this right? Who decides how we are to worship? What did Micah seek to gain from this arrangement? Who (or what) was Micah's god? *Judg. 17:2; Col. 3:5.* How might people today attempt to exploit Christianity for personal gain? *1 Tim. 6:3–6; Titus 1:11; 2 Peter 2:3.* Why do you worship God? Let's pray for hearts to worship God His way for His glory—not for gain.

Friday

Read through the Bible: Judges 19*
Family Worship: Judges 18:1–6, 14–26, 31

*AC ch. 19. What kind of god did the tribe of Dan serve? How did they get it? How does this dispute over an idol show the folly of idolatry? *Isa. 44:9–20.* Who is the only living and true God? How is He different from this idol? *Pss. 96:5; 115:2–8.* How might trusting in false views of God be like idolatry? What kind of God do you serve? Let's pray that God would reveal any false views we have of Him so that we might worship Him "in spirit and truth" (John 4:24).

Saturday

Read through the Bible: Judges 20
Family Worship: Judges 20:12–14, 21, 25, 46–48

Give an age-appropriate overview of chapter 19. What should the Benjaminites have done with the murderers? *Gen. 9:6.* What resulted from this travesty of justice? How does this show the need for swift and fair justice? *Prov. 21:15.* How does it show Israel's need for a godly king? *Judg. 21:25; Prov. 29:4.* Which King gives perfect justice? *Prov. 29:26.* How can we work for justice in our nation? Let's begin by praying that God would give our leaders the wisdom to govern with justice.

Year 1   Week 42

Sunday

Read through the Bible: Psalm 42
Family Worship: Psalm 42:1–6a

What is a thirsty animal like? How was the psalmist like that? For whom was he thirsty? How is God like a flowing stream? Where had the psalmist previously gone to satisfy his longing for God? Evidently something was keeping him from corporate worship—how did it affect him? How can we cultivate a thirst for God in corporate worship? Let's pray for hearts thirsty for God in private and public worship.

Monday

Read through the Bible: Judges 21
Family Worship: Judges 21:16–25

What problem did the Israelites face? Whose counsel did they seek? Whom did they fail to seek? What was their solution? In whose eyes was this right? Where has God told us what is right in His eyes? *John 17:17.* How can we make better decisions than Israel? *Isa. 8:20; James 1:5.* Let's pray for the wisdom to make decisions that are right in God's eyes.

Tuesday

Read through the Bible: Ruth 1
Family Worship: Ruth 1:1–18

Where was Naomi from? Where was Ruth from? What tragedy happened to them? What did Naomi tell Ruth to do? Why didn't she go? Who displayed His glorious grace in Ruth? How? How did Ruth express her faith? How was her vow different from Jephthah's? *Judg. 11:30–31.* How did she show her faith? How can we? *1 Tim. 5:8.* Let's pray for the grace to emulate Ruth's devotion to God and her family.

Wednesday

Read through the Bible: Ruth 2
Family Worship: Ruth 2:1–16

Who providentially arranged for Ruth to glean in Boaz's field? How did Ruth demonstrate her faith? How did Boaz demonstrate his? How does a mother bird provide refuge for her young? How is this a picture of what God does for us? *Pss. 36:7; 91:4.* How do we take refuge under His wings? How can you demonstrate your faith in your works? *James 2:18; 1 Thess. 4:11–12; 2 Thess. 3:10, 12.* Let's praise God for Christ our refuge and pray for the grace to show our faith by our works.

Thursday

Read through the Bible: Ruth 3
Family Worship: Ruth 3:1–13

Who created marriage? What was Ruth asking Boaz to do for her? How is Ruth's request in verse 9 similar to Boaz's blessing in 2:12? How does a bird covering its chicks picture what a husband should do for his wife? Boys: How can you prepare for this role? Girls: What qualities should you seek in a future husband? Let's pray that God would cause our sons and future sons-in-law to be Christlike protectors and providers.

Friday

Read through the Bible: Ruth 4
Family Worship: Ruth 4:1–6, 9–17*

*AC v. 13. What does it mean to redeem something? In what sense did Boaz redeem Ruth and Naomi? *Deut. 25:5–6.* Who is our Kinsman-Redeemer? How does Boaz picture Christ? Who was Ruth's great-grandson? How does this magnify God's grace? *Matt. 1:5; note also Boaz's mother.* How has God magnified His grace in us? *Eph. 2:11–22.* How should we respond? Let's worship our Redeemer, who bought us with His blood and brought us into His family.

Saturday

Read through the Bible: 1 Samuel 1
Family Worship: 1 Samuel 1:1–20

Why was Hannah sad? Who closed her womb? Why do you think God did that? What did Hannah do about the fact that she had no children? What are you praying passionately for? Who was Eli? What did he think of Hannah? Was he right? How did God bless Hannah? What does this story tell us about the power of prayer? The preciousness of children? Let's praise God for giving our family the precious gift of children and pray for greater passion in prayer.

Year 1   Week 43

Sunday

Read through the Bible: Psalm 43

Family Worship: Psalm 43:1–5

What problem was the psalmist facing? What did he ask for? Where do we find the light and the truth? *Ps. 119:105; John 8:12; 14:6; 17:17.* What (who) was the psalmist's "exceeding joy"? What should we do when we don't understand what God is (or isn't) doing? Let's pray that God would send His light and His truth to guide us and mold our hearts to find in Him our exceeding joy.

Monday

Read through the Bible: 1 Samuel 2

Family Worship: 1 Samuel 2:12–17, 23–25*

AC v. 22.* What were Eli's sons like? Whom did they ultimately treat with contempt? What did Eli do about it? What should he have done? *Deut. 21:18–21.* What did God think about Eli's failure to discipline? **1 Sam. 2:29; *3:13.* How can we keep our family from dishonoring God like this? *Heb. 12:7–11, 28–29.* Let's pray that God would help us practice loving, biblical discipline and joyful, reverent worship.

Tuesday

Read through the Bible: 1 Samuel 3

Family Worship: 1 Samuel 3:1–21

Who was calling Samuel? What did God tell him? How did he respond? How did God reveal Himself to Samuel? How does He reveal Himself to us? *Rom. 10:17; 1 Peter 1:23–25.* Can children hear God's voice in His Word? *Matt. 19:13–15; Eph. 6:1–3.* What is He telling you? How will you respond? Let's pray that God would reveal Himself to us through His Word and give us ears to hear and hearts to obey.

Wednesday

Read through the Bible: 1 Samuel 4

Family Worship: 1 Samuel 4:1–18

What did Israel try to do with the ark? Did it work? Why not? What should they have done? Who cannot be treated like a magic charm? How did God fulfill His word to Samuel in chapter 3? Will God automatically bless us because we go to church or carry Bibles? When we have a problem, where should we turn for guidance? *Isa. 66:2.* Let's pray for hearts to tremble at and obey God's Word.

Thursday

Read through the Bible: 1 Samuel 5
Family Worship: 1 Samuel 5:1–5

What did the Philistines worship? Was Dagon a real god? Who is the only "living and true God" (1 Thess. 1:9)? How did the Lord show that Dagon was a false god? What are some false gods that people serve today? How can we make sure there are no "Dagons" in our hearts? Let's pray that God would exalt Himself throughout the earth by causing all the Dagons of the world (and in our hearts) to fall before Him.

Friday

Read through the Bible: 1 Samuel 6
Family Worship: 1 Samuel 5:11–6:2, 7–16, 19–21

Why did the Philistines want to send the ark back? Why did the men of Beth-shemesh want to get rid of it? Did they treat the ark with reverence? *Num. 4:20.* Who is "able to stand before the LORD, this holy God?" *Heb. 9:24.* How must we worship God? **Heb. 12:28–29.** How can you be more reverent in worship? "Let us offer to God acceptable worship, with reverence and awe."

Saturday

Read through the Bible: 1 Samuel 7
Family Worship: 1 Samuel 7:3–12

What did Samuel tell the people to do? Did they? How can you tell? How did they handle the Philistine threat? How was this different from chapter 4? Who saved them? How was the Lord their "Ebenezer" (stone of help)? How has He been ours? How can we show that we've directed our hearts fully to the Lord alone? Let's "cry out to the LORD our God," praying that He would bind our wandering hearts to Him. *Hymn: "Come, Thou Fount."*

Year 1 — Week 44

Sunday

Read through the Bible: Psalm 44
Family Worship: Psalm 44:1–8

What had God done for His people in the past? Who told the psalmist about God's deeds? What did God do for him? Who was Israel's ultimate King? Who is yours? Who told you about God's mighty acts? Who will tell your children? What has God done for our family? How should we respond? Let's give thanks to our heavenly King!

Monday

Read through the Bible: 1 Samuel 8
Family Worship: 1 Samuel 8:1–10, 19–22

What did the people ask for? Why? Was the request for a king wrong in and of itself? *Deut. 17:14-20.* What was wrong with it? How was their demand a rejection of God's kingship? *1 Sam. 10:19; 12:12; Ps. 47:6-8.* What are some ways we might be tempted to be like the world? Who should we try to be like instead? Let's ask God to replace our desire to be like the world with the passion to be like Christ our King.

Tuesday

Read through the Bible: 1 Samuel 9
Family Worship: 1 Samuel 9:1–2, 15–17

What was noteworthy about Saul and his family? Was there anything noteworthy about him spiritually? How was he just the kind of king Israel asked for? *1 Sam. 8:20.* Who is the "King of kings" (Rev. 19:16)? How was King Jesus different from Saul? **Isa. 53:2–3.** Which kind of person does the world esteem? Which kind of person does God esteem? *Isa. 66:2; 1 Peter 3:4.* Whom do you esteem? Let's ask our King for hearts with the character He esteems.

Wednesday

Read through the Bible: 1 Samuel 10
Family Worship: 1 Samuel 10:17–24

What was Saul doing? *Gen. 3:8.* Can anyone hide from God? Why not? *Ps. 139:7-12.* Have you ever tried to hide from responsibility? Who had delivered Israel from all their oppressors? Whom did they now want to deliver them? In what sense was Israel trying to hide from God? What are some ways people try to hide from God today? What should we do instead? Let's draw near to God and pray as David did: "Search me, O God, and know my heart" (Ps. 139:23).

Thursday

Read through the Bible: 1 Samuel 11
Family Worship: 1 Samuel 11:1–11

Who chose Saul to be king? What had God called Saul to do as king? *1 Sam. 10:1.* How did He empower Saul to do this? What was the result? In the Old Testament, God gave special people the gift of the Spirit to empower them for service. To whom does He now give the Spirit? **1 Cor. 12:4–7.** For what purpose? What is God calling you to do? How is He empowering and equipping you? Let's pray that God would empower us to serve each other and our church "for the common good."

Friday

Read through the Bible: 1 Samuel 12
Family Worship: 1 Samuel 12:1, 16–25

Who was Israel's true King? **1 Sam. 12:12.** How had Israel forsaken God? Why would God never forsake His people? Why did He choose them? What did Samuel promise to do for them? What did he tell them to do? How is Samuel an example for parents? What are some great things God has done for us? How should we respond? Let's pray for the grace to "fear the LORD and serve him faithfully with all [our] heart[s]."

Saturday

Read through the Bible: 1 Samuel 13
Family Worship: 1 Samuel 13:5–15a

Why did Saul offer the sacrifice? Was it pleasing to God? Why not? *1 Sam. 15:22; Heb. 10:5–7.* Who only is both King and Priest? *BCF 8:9.* What were the consequences for Saul's disobedience? What kind of man did God seek to be king? How is Saul an example of religion without relationship? How can we instead be a people "after his own heart"? *Ps. 51:16–17.* Let's pray for hearts after God's own heart—broken over our sin and passionate for obedience.

Year 1   Week 45

Sunday

Read through the Bible: Psalm 45
Family Worship: Psalm 45:6–7

Which king is the psalmist talking about? **Heb. 1:8–9.** How is King Jesus greater than King Saul? How is His kingdom greater? What did God do for Jesus? *Acts 10:38; BCF 8:3.13.* How can we prepare to worship our King? *John 7:37–39.* Let's ask God to anoint us with the oil of gladness—the joy of His Spirit—as we worship our glorious King.

Monday

Read through the Bible: 1 Samuel 14
Family Worship: 1 Samuel 14:6–15, 20–23

Who can save "by many or by few"? Who was Jonathan? What did he do? What did the Lord do through him? How was he different from his father? How is he a role model for us in the battle against sin? What is something hard you can take the initiative to do? Let's pray for hearts of bold faith to take the initiative and do hard things.

Tuesday

Read through the Bible: 1 Samuel 15
Family Worship: 1 Samuel 15:1–23

What did God command Saul to do? *Deut. 25:17–19.* What did Saul do instead? Was God pleased? Why not? Which pleases God more: being "religious" or obeying Him? Was God's regret a change of mind or genuine grief over Saul's disobedience? Who is not a man that He should change His mind? **1 Sam. 15:29**; *Num. 23:19; Eph. 1:11.* Is there anything God has commanded you to do that you have not completely obeyed? Let's pray that God would show us those areas and lead us to complete obedience.

Wednesday

Read through the Bible: 1 Samuel 16
Family Worship: 1 Samuel 16:1–13

What characteristics do people typically focus on in others? Who "looks on the heart"? Reflect: Which do you spend more time on: outward appearance or matters of the heart? How was David different from Saul? *1 Sam. 9:2.* What kind of heart does God value? *1 Sam. 13:14; Matt. 5:8; 1 Peter 3:3-4.* How can we cultivate such hearts? *2 Peter 1:5-8.* Let's pray for hearts after God's own heart.

Thursday

Read through the Bible: 1 Samuel 17
Family Worship: 1 Samuel 17:1–11, 17–27, 31–51

Who was the Philistine champion? Who should have been Israel's? *1 Sam. 9:2; 10:1.* How did Saul respond to Goliath's taunts? How did David? How had God prepared David for this battle? How was God glorified in it? Who is our Champion, who defeated Satan, sin, and death? *Heb. 2:14-15.* What kind of giants do we face? How can you glorify God when facing these giants? Let's pray for the grace to trust and obey our Champion no matter the size of the enemy.

Friday

Read through the Bible: 1 Samuel 18
Family Worship: 1 Samuel 18:6–16

Who is in control of everything—even evil spirits? How did the women celebrate after David's victory? How did Saul respond? Why? What did Saul try to do to David? Why? What does envy do to people? **Prov. 14:30.** Reflect: Have you ever struggled with envy? How should you respond when a sibling is especially honored? *1 Cor. 12:26; 13:4.* Let's pray for hearts filled with love and free from envy.

Saturday

Read through the Bible: 1 Samuel 19
Family Worship: 1 Samuel 19:9–24

Who is in control of evil spirits, kings—and everything? How did God protect David? How did God humble Saul? Does the fact that Saul prophesied mean he was a true believer? *Matt. 7:21-23.* Who was Saul ultimately fighting against? *1 Sam. 18:12.* How do Saul's actions show the irrationality of sin? *Eph. 4:18.* How can we keep our minds from being darkened by sin? *Eph. 4:22-24; Rom. 12:2.* Let's ask the Holy Spirit to renew our minds through the truth of God's Word.

Year 1   Week 46

Sunday

Read through the Bible: Psalm 46
Family Worship: Psalm 46:1–11

Who will be exalted in all the earth? Does God promise that life will be easy for believers? What is God for His people in times of trouble? How is God like a mighty fortress? What should we do when faced with difficult times? Let's be still and know that He is God—praying that He would indeed be our mighty fortress and be exalted! *Hymn: "A Mighty Fortress Is Our God" (inspired by this psalm).*

Monday

Read through the Bible: 1 Samuel 20
Family Worship: 1 Samuel 20:12–17, 27–34

If God had allowed Saul's kingdom to continue, who would've been the next king? Was he jealous that God had chosen David? How was his response different from Saul's? *1 Sam. 18:1–4.* How did Saul's rage affect his family? Which greater Son of David did earthly rulers rage against? *Acts 4:24–27.* How should you respond when someone else receives a special gift or promotion? *Rom. 12:15.* Let's pray for magnanimous hearts that rejoice when others are blessed.

Tuesday

Read through the Bible: 1 Samuel 21
Family Worship: 1 Samuel 21:1–3, 6–7

Was David telling the truth? Was this right? What did David need? Was he normally allowed to have holy bread? Which was more important for the priests: providing for David or the ceremonial requirement of the law? **Matt. 12:1–4, 7.** Who desires mercy above sacrifice? If we were on the way to church and came upon an accident where people needed our help, would it be better to help them or go to church? Let's pray for hearts to value mercy above sacrifice.

Wednesday

Read through the Bible: 1 Samuel 22
Family Worship: 1 Samuel 22:6–19

David intended to protect Ahimelech by his lie, but what resulted instead? What greater Priest was slain—though innocent? Why wouldn't Saul's guards kill the priests? If the government tells us to do something sinful, what should we do? Who did Saul's dirty work? What kind of man was he? *Ps. 52:1-7*. What was Saul's jealousy doing to the kingdom? Can we keep our sin from harming others? Let's pray for the grace to walk in integrity and quickly repent when we sin.

Thursday

Read through the Bible: 1 Samuel 23
Family Worship: 1 Samuel 23:1–14

Who knows everything that will or could happen? *Isa. 46:9-10*. When David needed to make an important decision, what did he do? In the OT, God sometimes revealed His will through the ephod. How does God reveal His will to us? *Ps. 119:105; Deut. 29:29*. How do you make important decisions? How can we learn to make wise decisions? **James 1:5; 3:13-17**. Let's ask God for lives characterized by "wisdom from above"—from which flow wise decisions.

Friday

Read through the Bible: 1 Samuel 24
Family Worship: 1 Samuel 24:1–22

What did David's men believe God was leading him to do? Why didn't David kill Saul? *Ex. 20:13*. What did he do instead? How did David show integrity and faith? **Prov. 20:22**; *Rom. 12:19*. Whom did he trust to give him the kingdom? How did this affect Saul? Does the fact that you're able to do something mean you should? Let's pray for the integrity to do what's right instead of what's easy.

Saturday

Read through the Bible: 1 Samuel 25
Family Worship: 1 Samuel 25:2–35

What was Nabal like? How did he treat David? How did "hotheaded" David respond to "foolish" Nabal? Was what he planned to do right? Which Son of David was angry yet never sinned? What was Abigail like? How did she protect her family? How did she show great discretion? If your siblings are about to get into a fight, how can you show discretion? Let's pray for hearts of discretion.

Year 1 — Week 47

Sunday

Read through the Bible: Psalm 47
Family Worship: Psalm 47:1–9

Who is "the King of all the earth"? What kind of "kingly" things does He do? How is King Jesus subduing the nations? *Matt. 28:18–20; Eph. 1:20–22; Phil. 2:9–11.* How should subjects treat their king? How should we treat ours? Let's worship the King, praying He would indeed conquer the nations—and our hearts—by His grace. *Hymns: "All Peoples Clap Your Hands for Joy" (Ps. 47) and "O Worship the King."*

Monday

Read through the Bible: 1 Samuel 26
Family Worship: 1 Samuel 26:1–12

What "open door" did God give David? Why didn't David take the opportunity to kill Saul? What did David believe the Lord would do to Saul? A popular evangelical song goes, "When God closes a door, look for a window." Is this a good idea? Where should you look first before trying to interpret providence? **Ps. 119:35; Prov. 3:5–6.** Let's ask God to lead us in the path of His Word and give us discretion in discerning providence.

Tuesday

Read through the Bible: 1 Samuel 27
Family Worship: 1 Samuel 27:1–4

Whom or what did David consult for guidance before going to the Philistines? Whom did he fail to seek? *1 Sam. 23:9–14; Ps. 1:1–2.* How had God just protected David? Was David motivated by fear or faith? Until called to do something else, what should he have done? *1 Sam. 22:5.* Until God calls us to something new, what should we do? Let's pray that God would help us to be faithful in what He has already called us to do.

Wednesday

Read through the Bible: 1 Samuel 28
Family Worship: 1 Samuel 28:3–20

Who is Lord of the living and the dead? Why didn't God answer Saul? If God doesn't answer us, what is normally the problem? **Isa. 59:1–2.** What should we do about it? What did Saul do? Should we ever dabble in the occult? **Isa. 8:19-20**; *Deut. 18:9–14.* How does God speak to us? Why did the witch cry out? Can witches normally talk to the dead? Why did God bring up Samuel? How did Saul respond to his message? What should he have done? Let's pray for ears to hear God in His Word and for hearts to quickly repent.

Thursday

Read through the Bible: 1 Samuel 29
Family Worship: 1 Samuel 29:1–11

Why did the Philistine commanders not want David with the army? What dilemma would David face if he joined the battle? Who providentially protected David? *1 Cor. 10:13.* How? How could David have avoided this situation altogether? How can we avoid being tempted with God's enemies? *2 Tim. 2:22.* Let's pray as our Lord taught us: "Lead us not into temptation, but deliver us from evil" (Matt. 6:13).

Friday

Read through the Bible: 1 Samuel 30
Family Worship: 1 Samuel 30:1–10, 16–25

What happened to the men's families? What did the people talk of doing to David? Why? How did he respond? Who gave the Israelites the victory? What did the wicked men complain about? How did David respond? When God blesses our family, who should be able to share in it? Let's pray for the grace to enjoy God's blessings as a family without complaint, competition, or condescension.

Saturday

Read through the Bible: 1 Samuel 31
Family Worship: 1 Samuel 31:1–7

Why did Saul ask his armor-bearer to kill him? Why didn't he do as Saul asked? What did Saul do? Is it ever right to kill yourself? *No! Ex. 20:13.* What should he have done? During his life, who was Saul focused on: himself or God? In his death? Who should we focus on? In life, Saul either ignored God or tried to fight His will—how can you be different? Let's pray for hearts focused on God and fully submitted to His will.

Year 1   Week 48

Sunday

Read through the Bible: Psalm 48

Family Worship: Psalm 48:1–3

Who is "the great King"? Where is His city? What is Mount Zion like? How does it reflect God? What is the fulfillment of this earthly Mount Zion? **Heb. 12:22–24.** Who worships at the heavenly Mount Zion? How do we worship with them? How can we prepare for this? Let's pray that God would fit us to be His worshipers "in the city of our God."

Monday

Read through the Bible: 2 Samuel 1

Family Worship: 2 Samuel 1:1–16

What did the Amalekite say he did to Saul? Was this true? *1 Sam. 31:4–6.* What did he think he would gain from this lie? What did he get instead? Have you ever exaggerated or embellished something to make yourself look good? What is the difference between exaggerating and lying? Who is the Truth? *John 14:6.* How can you honor God when recounting an incident? Let's pray for the grace to be people of integrity who do not exaggerate our own importance.

Tuesday

Read through the Bible: 2 Samuel 2

Family Worship: 2 Samuel 2:1–11

What did David do after mourning for Saul and Jonathan? What did the men of Judah do? Who was Abner? What did he do? Why? Was this his place? Who had chosen David to be king? How was Abner's attitude different from David's? Who was more like Christ? *Heb. 2:8–9.* How can you be more like David? *1 Peter 5:6.* Let's pray for the grace to be Christlike in meekness, patience, and God-centeredness.

Wednesday

Read through the Bible: 2 Samuel 3

Family Worship: 2 Samuel 3:1, 6, 17–30

What did Abner do? How did David receive him? Who was Joab? How did he respond to Abner's change of allegiance? Was his killing of Abner justifiable? Why not? *1 Kings 2:5.* How was it morally different from Abner's killing of

Joab's brother? Who gave civil governments the power of judicial death? *Rom. 13:4.* When would it ever be right for a Christian to kill someone? *BCF 24:1–2.* Let's pray for the grace to handle conflict morally and redemptively.

Thursday

Read through the Bible: 2 Samuel 4
Family Worship: 2 Samuel 4:5–12

Who was Ish-bosheth? What did Rechab and Baanah do to him? Did they believe they were doing God's will? Were they? Where do we find God's will? Does the end ever justify the means? *AC: Would a Christian be justified to kill an abortion doctor? Ex. 20:13.* Is it right to do evil so that good may result? *Rom. 3:8; 12:21; 1 Peter 2:15.* Let's pray for the grace to do what's right and trust God with the results.

Friday

Read through the Bible: 2 Samuel 5
Family Worship: 2 Samuel 5:1–5, 10–12

What did the elders of Israel do? Who established David's kingdom? Who made him great? How long did David wait for God's promise to make him king? Does God always fulfill His promises? Does He fulfill them on our timetable or His? What are some promises of God we are waiting for? *2 Peter 3:9; 1 Thess. 5:23; 1 Cor. 15:24–26.* What should we do until God fulfills them? *Heb. 6:12.* Let's pray for the faith and patience to inherit God's promises.

Saturday

Read through the Bible: 2 Samuel 6
Family Worship: 2 Samuel 6:1–15

How did David try to transport the ark the first time? What happened? Why? *Num. 4:15.* How had the Philistines transported the ark? *1 Sam. 6:11.* How does the Bible say to carry the ark? *Ex. 25:14; Num. 7:9.* How did David transport the ark the second time? What happened? Should we look to the world for ideas on how to worship God? *BCF 22:1.* Where should we look? *John 4:24.* Let's pray for the wisdom to worship according to the Word instead of the world.

Year 1 — Week 49

Sunday

Read through the Bible: Psalm 49
Family Worship: Psalm 49:5–9, 15–17

What is a ransom? In what sense do we need to be ransomed? Can we ransom ourselves? Can one man ransom another? Who ransomed us? **Mark 10:45.** At what price? Can we take our riches with us to heaven? How should we handle the riches God provides? **1 Tim. 6:17-19.** What are you setting your hope on? Let's praise God for ransoming us by the riches of His grace in Christ! *Eph. 2:4-7.*

Monday

Read through the Bible: 2 Samuel 7:1–17
Family Worship: 2 Samuel 7:1–17

What did David want to do for God? What did God say He would do instead for David? What kind of "house" would God build for David? In whom is this promise fulfilled? *Luke 1:31-33; Heb. 1:5.* Whose plans were better: David's or God's? How has God changed your plans? Whose plans are always best? Let's praise God for King Jesus and pray He would indeed change our plans as He pleases for His glory.

Tuesday

Read through the Bible: 2 Samuel 7:18–29
Family Worship: 2 Samuel 7:18–29

What covenant had God made with David? How did David respond to God? What did he ask God to do? What covenant has God made with us? *Heb. 8:8-12.* Who is the fulfillment of both covenants? Why did God covenant with David—and with us? How should we respond to God for His covenants? Let's praise God and pray He would indeed fulfill all He has spoken that His name would be magnified.

Wednesday

Read through the Bible: 2 Samuel 8
Family Worship: 2 Samuel 8:3–14

What did David do? What did the Lord give David? How was this an initial fulfillment of God's covenant with him? *2 Sam. 7:9-10.* Who is David's greater Son? In what sense is God giving Jesus a far greater name and victory over the nations? *Phil. 2:9–11; Rev. 7:9–10.* How can we exalt the name of Christ in our home? Let's pray as our King taught us: "Hallowed be your name. Your kingdom come . . ." (Matt. 6:9–10).

Thursday

Read through the Bible: 2 Samuel 9–10
Family Worship: 2 Samuel 9:1–13

Who was Mephibosheth? **2 Sam. 4:4.** Why might he have been afraid of David? David could have been vindictive (since Jonathan's son was a potential rival to the throne), but what did he do instead? Why? *1 Sam. 20:15.* In his graciousness to the weak, who was David like? *Matt. 12:20.* How can older siblings be gracious with their younger siblings? Let's pray for hearts to be gracious with those who are "weaker."

Friday

Read through the Bible: 2 Samuel 11
Family Worship: 2 Samuel 11:1–4a, 14–17, 26–27*

*AC v. 4b. What was David doing while the ark and army were in battle? What should he have been doing? How did he try to cover up his sin? How did a "man after God's own heart" become an adulterer and murderer? *Jer. 17:9.* Who was displeased with David? How can we protect ourselves from the slippery slope of sin? *2 Tim. 2:22; Prov. 28:13.* Let's pray that God would help us stay busy doing what He's called us to and that He would "deliver us from evil" (Matt. 6:13).

Saturday

Read through the Bible: 2 Samuel 12
Family Worship: 2 Samuel 12:1–10, 13–14

Who sent Nathan to David? How did David respond to Nathan's story? How was David like the rich man? How did he respond to Nathan's rebuke? *Ps. 51.* How did God show His grace to David? *Ps. 32.* Did God's forgiveness remove the consequences of David's sin? When you sin, what do you need to do to be forgiven? Does forgiveness erase the consequences? Let's pray that God would graciously use His Word to bring us quickly to repentance.

Year 1 — Week 50

Sunday

Read through the Bible: Psalm 51*

Family Worship: Psalm 51:1–17

Psalm 51 is moved ahead to match the timeline in 2 Samuel. Who is "merciful and gracious, slow to anger, and abounding in steadfast love" (Ex. 34:6)? What did David confess? Whom did he blame? What did he ask God for? What would he do after God forgave and restored him? What kind of sacrifices did he offer? How is his prayer of repentance a model for us? Reflect: Is there any sin you need to confess? Is your heart broken or hardened over it? Let's pray for hearts broken over our sin and restored with the joy of salvation.

Monday

Read through the Bible: 2 Samuel 13

Family Worship: 2 Samuel 13:23–29, 37–39

Summarize vv. 1–22 as appropriate, e.g., "Amnon was very mean to his sister Tamar and hurt her." What did Absalom do to Amnon? Why? What did David do about the sin in his family? Who commanded parents to discipline their children? *Prov. 13:24.* How did the lack of discipline result in more sin? If one of your siblings hurts another, what should you do? How can we protect our family from the destructive spread of sin? Let's pray that God would help us deal redemptively with sin and cultivate friendships among siblings.

Tuesday

Read through the Bible: 2 Samuel 14

Family Worship: 2 Samuel 14:25–33

What did Absalom deserve for murdering his brother? Did David's lack of discipline lead him to repentance? Who disciplines us for our holiness? *Heb. 12:7–11.* How does the Bible describe Absalom? What is conspicuously missing from this description? When he didn't get his way, what did he do? What do you do when you don't get your way? Let's pray for hearts made beautiful through loving discipline.

Wednesday

Read through the Bible: 2 Samuel 15
Family Worship: 2 Samuel 15:1–14

How did Absalom steal the hearts of Israel? Was he giving justice to people? Was he being loyal to his father? To his country? To God? Which greater Son of David is always loyal to His Father? *John 8:29.* How can you show loyalty to God? To our family? To our country? Let's pray for hearts that stay loyal to God, our family, and our nation.

Thursday

Read through the Bible: 2 Samuel 16
Family Worship: 2 Samuel 16:5–14

Who was Shimei? What did he do? Why? Was he right? How did David respond? In being reviled but not reviling in return, who was David like? **1 Peter 2:23.** How do you typically respond to a rude comment? How should we? **1 Peter 3:9–12.** *Verses 10–12 are cited from Ps. 34:12–16, written by David.* Let's pray for the faith to return blessing for cursing.

Friday

Read through the Bible: 2 Samuel 17
Family Worship: 2 Samuel 17:1–14

What advice did Ahithophel give Absalom? What advice did Hushai give? Whose advice was better for Absalom? Whose advice did Absalom follow? Why? *2 Sam. 15:31.* Who foreordained this turn of events? Why? *BCF 5:1, 6.* How can the knowledge of God's absolute sovereignty comfort believers in distress like David? *BCF 5:5.16.* Let's praise God for ordaining all things for His glory and our good.

Saturday

Read through the Bible: 2 Samuel 18
Family Worship: 2 Samuel 18:1–15

Who won the battle? What happened to Absalom? Who can even use trees to defeat His enemies? What were the consequences of Absalom's rebellion for Israel? How can a breakdown in the family negatively affect the state? How can our family instead be a blessing? Let's pray for the grace to be a blessing (rather than a burden) to our community.

Year 1   Week 51

Sunday

Read through the Bible: Psalm 50
Family Worship: Psalm 50:7–23

Who owns "the cattle on a thousand hills"? Was God pleased with Israel's worship? Why not? What would God think of a family of complainers who argued and disobeyed parents on the way to church? How can we prepare to glorify God in our worship? What kind of sacrifices does God desire? What are some things you can thank God for today? Let's get right with God and each other—confessing our sin and offering a sacrifice of thanksgiving.

Monday

Read through the Bible: 2 Samuel 19
Family Worship: 2 Samuel 19:16–23

What had Shimei done to David? *2 Sam. 16:5-13*. Is it right to revile political leaders we don't like? *Ex. 22:28*. What did Abishai want to do to him? What did David do instead? In forgiving his enemies, who was David like? *Luke 23:34; 6:27-28; cf. 1 Kings 2:8-9*. Reflect: Is there anyone you need to forgive? How can you make it right? Let's pray for hearts quick to forgive those who wrong us.

Tuesday

Read through the Bible: 2 Samuel 20
Family Worship: 2 Samuel 20:1–2, 14–22

What did Sheba do? What kind of man was he? Was it a good idea for Israel to follow him? Why not? What kind of character traits should we seek in our leaders? *Ex. 18:21; Mark 10:42-45*. Reflect: Which of these needs the most development in your life? Who is the perfect Leader? Let's pray for the grace to grow in Christlike character.

Wednesday

Read through the Bible: 2 Samuel 21
Family Worship: 2 Samuel 21:15–17

Where was David? What happened to him? Who helped him? Would he necessarily have been "safer" had he stayed home? *2 Sam. 11*. Are spiritual warriors invincible? Do they get weary? Who never grows weary? *Isa. 40:28-31*. How can we encourage one another in spiritual combat? *Eccl. 4:9–10, 12;*

Eph. 6:18-20; Heb. 10:24-25. Let's pray for the strength to encourage and help one another in spiritual battle.

Thursday

Read through the Bible: 2 Samuel 22
Family Worship: 2 Samuel 22:1, 31–36, 47–51

What had God done for David? What has God done for us? Whose way and Word is perfect? How had the word of the Lord proved true for David? How has it proved true for us? To whom did David give the credit for all he had accomplished? Who gets the credit for what you do? How did David respond to God for all He had done for him? How should we? Let's sing praises to His name!

Friday

Read through the Bible: 2 Samuel 23
Family Worship: 2 Samuel 23:1–5

Who was "the sweet psalmist of Israel"? Who spoke through David? *Acts 4:25*. What did the Holy Spirit say through him? How was David's reign like sun and rain for Israel? How is Christ's reign greater? *Isa. 55:10–11; John 1:1; 8:12; Rev. 21:23; 22:1–5*. How should we respond to God for giving us the sweet psalms of David and the greater kingdom of His Son? Let's praise Him and pray: "Your kingdom come . . ." (Matt. 6:10).

Saturday

Read through the Bible: 2 Samuel 24
Family Worship: 2 Samuel 24:1–4, 9–17

Who governs all His creatures and all their actions? *BCF 5:1*. With whom was God angry? Why? What means did God use to judge Israel for their recent rebellions? **1 Chron. 21:1**; *BCF 5:4*. How did the census expose David's pride? *BCF 5:5*. What would the world be like if God was not sovereign over all events? How did God use the evil of the cross for His glory and our good? *Acts 4:27–28; John 10:15*. How should we respond to the innocent King who gave Himself for guilty sheep like us? *Rom. 11:33–36*. Let's worship Him!

Year 1   Week 52

Sunday

Read through the Bible: Psalm 52
Family Worship: Psalm 52:1–9

Who is the truth? Whose word is truth? Who was Doeg? What did he do? *1 Sam. 22:9-10, 18-19.* What were his words like? How can words be "like a sharp razor"? *James 3:5-10.* Reflect: What have your words to your siblings been like? How can you use your words to build up rather than cut down? *Eph. 4:29.* Let's pray for hearts so filled with love for one another that they overflow with words of love.

Monday

Read through the Bible: 1 Kings 1
Family Worship: 1 Kings 1:5–10

Who was Adonijah? What was he like? What did he do? What did David fail to do for him? **Prov. 22:6, 15; 29:15.** What were the consequences? Who disciplines every son He loves? *Heb. 12:6.* What would happen if we failed to discipline you? Would this be loving? *Prov. 13:24.* How can we please God in our discipline? Let's pray for the grace to "train up [our children] in the way [they] should go."

Tuesday

Read through the Bible: 1 Kings 2
Family Worship: 1 Kings 2:10–25

What was Adonijah's request? Do you think his motives were pure? How did Solomon deal with this "back door" claim to the throne? Who commanded us to "honor your father and your mother" (Ex. 20:12)? How did Solomon honor his mother? Did honoring her mean he had to obey her unwise advice? How does a child's application of the fifth commandment change when he becomes an adult? How can you honor your mother? Let's pray for the grace to do so.

Wednesday

Read through the Bible: 1 Kings 3
Family Worship: 1 Kings 3:16–28*

*AC v. 16. What happened between these women? How could Solomon tell which one was telling the truth? Who gave him this wisdom? What was the

root cause of this dispute? What causes quarrels among us? *James 4:1–2*. How can we "divide the baby"—that is, use wisdom to solve disputes? *James 1:5*. Let's pray for the grace to avoid disputes in the first place and the wisdom to resolve them when they do occur.

Thursday

Read through the Bible: 1 Kings 4:1–28
Family Worship: 1 Kings 4:20–21, 24–25

What did Solomon rule over? How did this fulfill God's promise to Abraham? *Gen. 15:18*. How were the peace and joy of his kingdom pictured? Who is Solomon's greater Son? How will His reign be even greater? *Mic. 4:3–4; Luke 13:29*. How do we already enjoy a foretaste of these blessings? *Rom. 14:17*. How should we live as members of Christ's greater kingdom? Let's pray for hearts filled with "righteousness and peace and joy in the Holy Spirit" (Rom. 14:17).

Friday

Read through the Bible: 1 Kings 4:29–5:18
Family Worship: 1 Kings 4:29–34

What did God give Solomon? What did Solomon compose? On which subjects did God give him wisdom? Who is wisdom? *1 Cor. 1:30; Col. 2:3*. On which subjects should we seek wisdom? How can our study of God's world enhance our worship of Him? *Pss. 19:1; 104:24*. Let's pray for growth in wisdom and wonder as we study God's Word and His world.

Saturday

Read through the Bible: 1 Kings 6
Family Worship: 1 Kings 5:17; 6:11–13

What kind of stones did Solomon use to build the temple? What kind of stones is God using to build His temple? **1 Peter 2:4–6.** Who is the precious cornerstone? What purpose did Solomon's temple serve? *A place of worship*. What purpose does God's temple serve? *A people of worship!* How can we fulfill our purpose as "living stones"? Let's ask God to fashion us into a beautiful house of worship for His glory.

"And these words that I command you today shall be **on your heart**."
– Deuteronomy 6:6

Year 2   Week 1

Sunday

Read through the Bible: Psalm 53
Family Worship: Psalm 53:1–3

What did God look down from heaven to see? Did He find anyone who seeks God (on his own)? **Rom. 3:9–12.** Why not? *Eph. 2:1–3.* Why do God's people seek Him? *Eph. 2:4–5; Luke 19:10.* Who has commanded, "Seek my face"? **Ps. 27:8.** How should we respond? Let's pray for hearts like David's, which cry out, "Your face, Lord, do I seek."

Monday

Read through the Bible: 1 Kings 7
Family Worship: 1 Kings 7:13–14

Who was Hiram? What was special about him? From whom did he learn his skill? Who is the ultimate giver of all skill? *Ex. 31:1–6.* How much effort do you think he had to put into becoming such a renown bronze craftsman? How did he glorify God? *1 Cor. 10:31.* How can you glorify God in your future vocation? How can you glorify God now? Let's pray that God would be glorified in our home through hard work and excellent craftsmanship.

Tuesday

Read through the Bible: 1 Kings 8
Family Worship: 1 Kings 8:37–40, 46–53

Who knows the hearts of all mankind? Who does not sin? How do you feel after you realize you've sinned? How is this like an affliction of the heart? How is this affliction like the pain that warns us of the danger of a hot stove? What should you do when your heart afflicts you? What does God promise those who repent with their whole mind and heart? Let's pray for hearts afflicted when we sin and quick to repent.

Wednesday

Read through the Bible: 1 Kings 9
Family Worship: 1 Kings 9:1–9

Who appeared to Solomon? What did God promise to do for the temple? What does it mean to consecrate something? What warning did He give? What greater temple has God made holy with His Spirit? **1 Cor. 3:16–17.** What warning did He give? How can we honor God's church as holy? Let's pray for the Spirit's power to honor God and His church through obedience.

Thursday

Read through the Bible: 1 Kings 10
Family Worship: 1 Kings 10:1–10

Why did the Queen of Sheba come to see Solomon? What did she find? How did she respond? What King is greater than Solomon? **Matt. 12:42.** How? **Col. 2:3.** How was Israel's response to Jesus different from the Queen's response to Solomon? *John 1:11.* How should we respond to the One far greater than Solomon? Let's pray for hearts hungry to seek Wisdom personified in Christ.

Friday

Read through the Bible: 1 Kings 11
Family Worship: 1 Kings 11:1–13

What had God warned Israel against? Why? Did Solomon obey God? What happened to his heart? What were the consequences? Who gave us His commandments to protect us? Should Christians marry unbelievers? *1 Cor. 7:39.* Why not? *2 Cor. 6:14.* How could unbelieving friends also turn our hearts away? *1 Cor. 15:33.* How can we keep our hearts from turning away from God? *Ps. 119:9–11; 2 Tim. 2:22.* Let's pray for "undivided devotion to the Lord" (1 Cor. 7:35).

Saturday

Read through the Bible: 1 Kings 12
Family Worship: 1 Kings 12:1–20

What did the people ask Rehoboam? What did the older men counsel him to do? What did the young men counsel? Whom did he listen to? What happened? Whom should you go to for advice? What greater King came to serve His people? *Mark 10:42–45.* How can you lead by serving in our family? Let's pray for hearts to be servant-leaders like Christ.

Year 2 — Week 2

Sunday

Read through the Bible: Psalm 54
Family Worship: Psalm 54:1–7

What enemies did David face? *1 Sam. 23:19; 26:1.* Whom did he trust to be his "helper"? Why did he believe God would answer his prayer? Did He? What kind of enemies do we face? Who is our Helper? **Heb. 13:6.** How has God been our Helper? How can recalling these times strengthen our faith? Let's praise God for being our Helper and pray He would continue to "deliver us from evil" (Matt. 6:13).

Monday

Read through the Bible: 1 Kings 13
Family Worship: 1 Kings 12:28, 33–13:6

What kind of worship did Jeroboam institute? From where did it originate? Was it pleasing to God? How can we ensure our worship is pleasing to God? Who alone institutes acceptable worship? *Deut. 12:32; BCF 22:1.* What did the prophet say would happen to Jeroboam's altar? How did God authenticate His word? Did His word come true? *Three hundred years later!* **2 Kings 23:15–16.** Will God's word ever fail? Let's worship God for His word—according to His Word.

Tuesday

Read through the Bible: 1 Kings 14
Family Worship: 1 Kings 14:1–18

Was Jeroboam a good or bad king? Why? What did he tell his wife to do? Who was physically blind in this story? Who was spiritually blind? In what sense could the blind man see better than the king? What did he "see" would happen? Who gives us spiritual sight? What has God caused you to see in His Word? *Ps. 119:18.* How have you responded? Let's pray for eyes to see and hearts to obey God's Word.

Wednesday

Read through the Bible: 1 Kings 15
Family Worship: 1 Kings 15:25–30

Who was Nadab? Was he a good or bad king? Why? What happened to him?

How was he affected by the sin of his family? Who judges idolatrous families? **Deut. 5:8–10.** Apart from grace, what will the children of God-hating idolaters grow up to be? What can we do to keep sin from being passed down in our family like this? *Deut. 6:4-9.* Let's plead for the grace to instead pass down wholehearted love for God.

Thursday

Read through the Bible: 1 Kings 16
Family Worship: 1 Kings 16:25, 29–33

Who was Ahab? Was he a good or bad king? Why? Whom did he provoke to anger? How was he like his father? How was he worse? How can sin be like a contagious disease in a family? Instead of sin, what should grow and increase in our home? **2 Thess. 1:3; 2 Peter 3:18.** Name an area where you need to grow. Let's ask God to help us grow in faith, love, and "in the grace and knowledge of our Lord and Savior."

Friday

Read through the Bible: 1 Kings 17
Family Worship: 1 Kings 17:1–16

Who is Lord over rain, ravens, and our daily bread? How did God judge Ahab and Israel for idolatry? How did He provide for Elijah? How did His provision require humility and faith? How was God's strength glorified in weakness? *2 Cor. 12:9-10.* In what sense are we poor and weak? *Matt. 5:3; 1 Cor. 1:26-29.* Name an area of weakness where you need God's strength. How can we glorify God in our weakness? Let's pray for the humility to recognize our weakness and for the faith to trust in God's strength.

Saturday

Read through the Bible: 1 Kings 18
Family Worship: 1 Kings 18:17–40

How many Gods are there? How were the people "limping between two different opinions"? How did Baal answer his prophets? Why didn't he? How did God answer Elijah? Do you think this turned the people's hearts back to God? How do people today limp between two opinions? Are you? How can we stay devoted to Christ? *Jer. 23:29.* Let's pray that God would use the fire of His Word to consecrate our hearts fully—and exclusively—to Christ.

Year 2   Week 3

Sunday

Read through the Bible: Psalm 55
Family Worship: Psalm 55:12–21

What problem did David face? *2 Sam. 15:12*? Why was it especially painful? Which greater Son of David was also betrayed by a friend? *Matt. 26:47–50.* What did David do about it? *2 Sam. 15:31.* When did David pray? When should we pray? *1 Thess. 5:17.* How can we cultivate loyal friendship in our family? Our church? Let's pray for loyal hearts to be true friends to each other—and to God.

Monday

Read through the Bible: 1 Kings 19
Family Worship: 1 Kings 19:1–18

How did Jezebel respond to the display of God's power on Mount Carmel? Do miracles alone change people's hearts? *Rom. 10:17.* What did Elijah do? Why? How did God display His power on Mount Horeb? How is the "low whisper" of God's Word even more powerful? *Jer. 23:29; Heb. 4:12.* Have you ever felt like Elijah? Who is responsible for the results of His Word? *Isa. 55:11.* What is our responsibility? Let's pray that God would use His Word powerfully in our home—helping us to be obedient and trust Him with the results.

Tuesday

Read through the Bible: 1 Kings 20
Family Worship: 1 Kings 20:1–21

Who was Ben-hadad? What was he like? Whom did he boast in? How did Ahab respond to him? What did the Lord promise? Why? What happened? How are many sports figures today like Ben-hadad? Are you a "trash talker"? Whom should we boast in? **2 Cor. 10:17–18.** How can we be commended by the Lord (instead of ourselves)? *Matt. 25:21.* Let's pray for humble hearts that "boast in the Lord."

Wednesday

Read through the Bible: 1 Kings 21
Family Worship: 1 Kings 21:1–24

Why was Ahab "vexed and sullen"? Do possessions bring lasting happiness? *Phil. 4:11–13.* Who said, "Be content with what you have" (Heb. 13:5)? What did Jezebel do? What would be the consequences for Ahab's family? What are you tempted to covet? Will getting it make you content? What more does God have to give you for you to be content? *1 Tim. 6:6-10.* Let's pray for hearts free from covetousness and content with what God has blessed us with.

Thursday

Read through the Bible: 1 Kings 22
Family Worship: 1 Kings 22:1–36

Who is lord over arrows and evil spirits? *BCF 5:4, 6.* Why did Ahab hate Micaiah? What did Micaiah say he would speak? What did he prophesy? How was this different from Ahab's "prophets"? Why did Ahab disguise himself? Did it help? Why not? If you had a disease and went to the doctor, would you want him to lie to make you feel good or tell the truth? How can we be like Micaiah and not Ahab? Let's pray for hearts to seek and speak the truth—even if it hurts.

Friday

Read through the Bible: 2 Kings 1
Family Worship: 2 Kings 1:1–17

What was wrong with Ahaziah? Where did he seek the truth of his condition? To what source of truth should he have gone? *John 17:17.* How did he respond to the truth of God's word? *Rom. 1:18.* What happened to the soldiers sent to arrest Elijah? How did the third captain of fifty show discretion and fear of God? What truth(s) has God revealed to you in His Word this week? How have you responded? Let's pray for hearts to seek and submit to the truth in reverent fear.

Saturday

Read through the Bible: 2 Kings 2
Family Worship: 2 Kings 2:1, 11–12a

What happened to Elijah? Where did he go? Did he die? Who is going to return in glory to bring us to heaven? *1 Thess. 4:16–18; 1 Cor. 15:51–52.* How will this resurrection be even greater than Elijah's? How can looking forward to our resurrection change how we live today? *1 Cor. 15:58.* Let's pray for the faith to work and worship with the end in sight.

Year 2   Week 4

Sunday

Read through the Bible: Psalm 56
Family Worship: Psalm 56:1–11

What problem was David facing? What did David do when he was afraid? What happened to his fear when he trusted in God? Are you ever afraid? What should we do when we're afraid? What does God use to build our trust or faith in Him? *Rom. 10:17.* How did David treat God's word? How can we show reverence for His Word? Let's praise God for His Word and pray He would use it to build our trust in Him.

Monday

Read through the Bible: 2 Kings 3
Family Worship: 2 Kings 3:1–20

What problem did the army face? What did Jehoshaphat propose? Whose word did he seek? What did Elisha tell Jehoram to do at first? Why? Why did he agree to inquire of the Lord? What did God do? The army was blessed because of Jehoshaphat; how can our family be a channel of blessing to others? Let's pray that God would pour out His grace on us—and through us to others.

Tuesday

Read through the Bible: 2 Kings 4
Family Worship: 2 Kings 4:8–17

What did the Shunammite woman do for Elisha? What did Elisha want to do for her? Who is sovereign over the womb? How did the Lord bless her in a way that kings and riches couldn't? How precious are children? *Ps. 127:3–5. Parents: Hug your children and tell them they are blessings from the Lord.* Let's praise God for the heritage of children.

Wednesday

Read through the Bible: 2 Kings 5
Family Worship: 2 Kings 5:1–14

Who was Naaman? Who made him a great leader? What was wrong with him? Who told him about Elisha? How can you honor God like she did when away from home? What did Elisha tell Naaman to do? How did he respond? What kind of spiritual leprosy did he have? What happened when he humbled himself? What kind of spiritual leprosy do you need to be healed from? Let's pray that God would use the water of His Word to cleanse us from the leprosy of sin.

Thursday

Read through the Bible: 2 Kings 6:1–23
Family Worship: 2 Kings 6:8–23

Who tried to capture Elisha? Why? How did God protect him? *Matt. 26:53; Rev. 19:11–16.* What did Elisha pray for his helper? What did he pray for the Syrians? What are the two kinds of sight and blindness pictured in this story? How do we obtain spiritual sight? *Ps. 119:18.* Who is "the light of the world" (John 8:12)? Let's ask the Light of the World to open our spiritual eyes to behold wondrous things.

Friday

Read through the Bible: 2 Kings 6:24–7:20
Family Worship: 2 Kings 6:24–25; 7:3–9

What problem did Israel face? Why did the lepers go to the Syrian camp? What did they find there? Who defeated the Syrian army? Why did the lepers say they weren't doing right? What did they do? How are we like those lepers? *Eph. 2:1–3.* What riches has God given us? *Eph. 2:4–9.* What good news can we share? How? Let's thank God for His grace and pray for His help to "go and tell" with lips and lives.

Saturday

Read through the Bible: 2 Kings 8
Family Worship: 2 Kings 8:1–6

Who called for a famine? How did Elisha help the Shunammite's family? What happened when they came back to Israel? Who providentially arranged the timing of the king's question? *Prov. 21:1.* Can you think of a time when God caused something to happen in your life at just the right time? How did you respond? Can we always see the perfection of God's timing? Let's praise God for sovereignly timing all things—even when we can't see it.

Year 2   Week 5

Sunday

Read through the Bible: Psalm 57
Family Worship: Psalm 57:1–11

What trouble was David facing? *1 Sam. 22:1*. What did he know about God that gave him faith? *Ex 34:6*. How do we need God to send out His steadfast love and faithfulness? What was the chief end of his prayer? Which greater Son of David is highly exalted to the glory of God the Father? *Phil. 2:9–11*. How can Christ be exalted in our home? Let's pray that God would send out his steadfast love and faithfulness and be exalted in our family—and over all the earth!

Monday

Read through the Bible: 2 Kings 9
Family Worship: 2 Kings 9:30–37

What did God say would happen to Jezebel? *1 Kings 21:23*. What happened? Who always fulfills His word? How did Jezebel prepare for judgment? What kind of "adornment" did she focus on? What kind of adornment should women focus on? *1 Peter 3:3–6*. How should we prepare for the judgment seat of Christ? *2 Cor. 5:10*. Let's pray for the grace to reflect the true beauty of Christlikeness.

Tuesday

Read through the Bible: 2 Kings 10
Family Worship: 2 Kings 10:10–11, 17, 28–31

What did the Lord say would happen to Ahab's family? *1 Kings 21:21*. What happened? Who always fulfills His word? *Isa. 55:11*. How is Jehu a good role model for dealing with sin or causes to sin in our lives? *Matt. 5:29–30*. How is he a poor role model? Reflect: What sin or cause to sin do you need to ruthlessly remove from your life? Let's pray for the passion to remove any sin or causes to sin from our lives.

Wednesday

Read through the Bible: 2 Kings 11
Family Worship: 2 Kings 11:1–4, 12–20

Who was Athaliah? *2 Kings 8:26*. What did she do? Why? Was she the rightful ruler? Who was? Is the king law or the law king? *Deut. 17:14–20*. Who created law? How did Jehoiada restore the rightful ruler? What did he institute afterward? What covenant do we have between our government and the people? What should we do if our leaders disobey the Constitution? Let's pray that God would give us leaders who uphold the rule of law.

Thursday

Read through the Bible: 2 Kings 12
Family Worship: 2 Kings 11:21–12:16

Was Joash a good or bad king? What was the crucial factor in his doing "what was right in the eyes of the Lord"? How did his discipleship result in devotion? How did the workmen show their devotion? Who is your "Jehoiada"? Who commanded parents to teach their children? *Deut. 6:6-7.* What is the goal of our instruction? How can you show your devotion to the Lord? *Eph. 6:1-3.* Let's pray that God would enable our discipleship to result in true devotion.

Friday

Read through the Bible: 2 Kings 13
Family Worship: 2 Kings 13:1–6, 22–23

Was Jehoahaz a good or bad king? How did God judge Israel? Then what did Jehoahaz do? How did God respond? Did Israel deserve God's grace? Do we? Why was He gracious to them? What greater covenant has God given us? What greater Savior? Are you in need of God's favor and grace? Is there a particular need? What should we do? Let's seek "the favor of the Lord."

Saturday

Read through the Bible: 2 Kings 14
Family Worship: 2 Kings 14:1–3, 7–14

Was Amaziah a good or bad king? What did he want to do after defeating Edom? What did Jehoash warn him about? Did he listen? How does Amaziah illustrate the truth of this proverb? **Prov. 16:18.** Who "opposes the proud, but gives grace to the humble" (James 4:6)? Reflect: What will it take for you to humble yourself? Let's pray for hearts to humble ourselves (before we have to be humiliated).

Year 2   Week 6

Sunday

Read through the Bible: Psalm 58
Family Worship: Psalm 58:1–5

Who is the righteous Judge? What problem did David face? *Ps. 82.* What are judges supposed to do? What did these do instead? How were they like deaf, poisonous snakes? When did they (and we) become sinners? *Ps. 51:5.* How are we sometimes like these unjust judges? How can we instead be like Christ? *Eph. 4:15, 25.* Let's pray that God would make us those who uphold justice by speaking the truth in love.

Monday

Read through the Bible: 2 Kings 15
Family Worship: 2 Kings 15:1–4, 8–9, 32–35

Who was Azariah (Uzziah)? What did he do? Who was Jotham? What did he do? Who was Zechariah? What did he do? What pattern do you see with all three of these? How influential was each king's father? *Fathers: Do you need to ask forgiveness for anything you don't want passed down?* Who is the perfect Father? **Matt. 5:48.** How can we be more like Him? Let's pray for the grace to be more like our Heavenly Father.

Tuesday

Read through the Bible: 2 Kings 16
Family Worship: 2 Kings 16:1–4, 10–14

What kind of king was Ahaz? What pattern did he use for his altar? Who designed the original altar? *Ex. 25:9; Heb. 8:5.* What pattern did he use for worship? What did God think of it? *Deut. 12:31-32.* What pattern should we use for worship? *John 4:24; Rom. 12:1.* How can we know we're following God's pattern? *Rom. 12:2.* Let's pray for renewed minds to follow the pattern of the Word rather than the world.

Wednesday

Read through the Bible: 2 Kings 17
Family Worship: 2 Kings 17:6–18

What happened to Israel? Why? How did God warn them? How did they respond? What did their actions reveal about their faith? *James 2:17.* How has

God warned us? *Heb. 2:1-4*. What has He warned us about? *Heb. 10:23-36*. What will happen if we refuse to listen? Are you listening? Do your actions show it? Let's pray that God would expose any stubborn defiance in our hearts and lead us to repentance.

Thursday

Read through the Bible: 2 Kings 18
Family Worship: 2 Kings 18:1–8

What kind of king was Hezekiah? What kind of family did he grow up in? *2 Kings 16:1-4*. Who called him by grace out of an ungodly family? Was his faith dead or living? *James 2:17*. How can you tell? How can you exercise living faith? (Be specific.) Why did he break the bronze serpent? Are there any good things we have which could become snares to sin? *BCF 30:4, 6*. If so, what should we do? Let's pray for the grace to be passionate in our obedience like Hezekiah.

Friday

Read through the Bible: 2 Kings 19
Family Worship: 2 Kings 19:10–20, 32–37

Who is the only "living and true God" (1 Thess. 1:9)? What did the Assyrian king write to Hezekiah? How did he respond? How should we respond to those who mock our faith? *1 Peter 3:15-16; Matt. 7:6*. Are you able to defend what you believe? What was the goal of his prayer? How did God respond? Why? Is God's glory the goal of your prayers? Let's pray that God would be glorified in His church and in our family as we stand in humble faith against mockers.

Saturday

Read through the Bible: 2 Kings 20
Family Worship: 2 Kings 20:12–21

What did Hezekiah show the Babylonians? What did Isaiah say would happen? How did he respond? How is this picture of Hezekiah different from the last chapter? *2 Chron. 32:25-26, 31*. Note: *This chapter is a "flashback" to before the Assyrian invasion (20:6; cf. 18:15-16)*. Which is the biggest struggle for you: indiscretion, pride, or selfishness? Who is the only perfect king? How can you be more like King Jesus in these areas? Let's pray for the grace of discretion, humility, and selflessness.

Year 2   Week 7

Sunday

Read through the Bible: Psalm 59
Family Worship: Psalm 59:1–10, 16–17

What problem did David face? *1 Sam. 19:11*. What did he do about it? Who never slumbers or sleeps? *Ps. 121:4*. Why did David ask God to "awake" and "rouse" Himself? What would he do until he saw God's answer? Have you ever felt like God wasn't answering your prayers? What should we do in those times? Let's ask God to meet with us in steadfast love then worship Him while we wait.

Monday

Read through the Bible: 2 Kings 21
Family Worship: 2 Kings 20:21–21:9

What kind of king was Manasseh compared to his father? Where did he learn such wickedness? Does being in a Christian family make you a Christian? What can we do to help multiple generations of our family faithfully serve the Lord? *Deut. 6:4–9*. Who commanded parents to disciple their children? Who will disciple your children? Let's pray for the grace to faithfully disciple each new generation of our family.

Tuesday

Read through the Bible: 2 Kings 22
Family Worship: 2 Kings 22:1–20

What did Josiah command concerning the temple? What did the priest find there? How did it get lost? What did Josiah do when he heard God's Word? Why? How did God respond? What happens when people don't have God's Word? *Prov. 29:18*. What place should God's Word have in our home? Our hearts? *Deut. 6:6–9*. Does it? How can we show our gratitude for God's Word? Let's praise God for His Word and pray He would cause it to be on our hearts.

Wednesday

Read through the Bible: 2 Kings 23:1–30
Family Worship: 2 Kings 23:1–5, 21–25

What did Josiah read to the people? Were God's words on his heart? How can you tell? As a part of his reform, what did he remove? What did he reinstitute? What do you need to remove from your life to more fully obey God's Word?

What do you need to replace it with? Let's pray for the passion of Josiah to fully obey God's Word.

Thursday

Read through the Bible: 2 Kings 23:31–24:20
Family Worship: 2 Kings 23:36–24:20a

What kind of kings reigned after Josiah? What happened to Judah? Who cast them out from His presence? Why? How had God been patient with Judah? Was He patient forever? Will God be patient with man forever? **2 Cor. 6:1-2; 2 Thess. 1:6-10.** What do we need to do during this "favorable time"? *Heb. 2:1-3a.* Let's praise God for His patience with us and pray He would make this "a day of salvation" for our family.

Friday

Read through the Bible: 2 Kings 25
Family Worship: 2 Kings 24:20b-25:12

What kind of king was Zedekiah? What kind of leadership did he provide for his people? What greater King does he show us the need for? Why did all this happen to God's people? *Deut. 28:15, 36.* How does Judah's judgment show us the need for a greater obedience? *Heb. 2:1-3.* In what do you need greater obedience? Let's praise God for our greater King and pray He would lead us to greater obedience.

Saturday

Read through the Bible: Matthew 1
Family Worship: Matthew 1:18–24

Whom was Joseph descended from? What is the significance of his royal ancestry? What was he was initially concerned about? How did the angel reassure him? By whose power was the baby conceived? What was he to name Him? Why? How would King Jesus be greater than any of the kings of Israel or Judah? Why do we need King Jesus? How should we respond to His Majesty King Jesus, our Savior and Lord? Let's worship Him! *Hymn:* "O Come, O Come, Emmanuel."

Year 2   Week 8

Sunday

Read through the Bible: Psalm 60
Family Worship: Psalm 60:9–12

What problem did David face? What did he do about it? Whom did he trust to tread down his foes? Who is our chief foe? What did God promise to do to him? **Gen 3:15; Rom. 16:20.** How did Jesus bruise Satan's head? *Heb. 2:14.* How will He finally crush him? *Rev. 20:10.* Until then, how can we face our terrible foe? *Rev. 12:11.* Let's ask God to "grant us help against the foe," and soon crush him under the church's feet. *Hymn: "A Mighty Fortress Is Our God."*

Monday

Read through the Bible: Matthew 2
Family Worship: Matthew 2:1–12

Who is the King of Kings and the bright morning star? *Rev. 19:16; 22:16.* How did King Herod respond to the news of King Jesus? How did the people of Jerusalem? The chief priests and scribes? The wise men? How can we joyfully seek Him today? *2 Peter 1:19.* How can we joyfully worship Him? What can we joyfully give Him? *Rom. 12:1.* Let's joyfully seek, worship, and give ourselves to King Jesus.

Tuesday

Read through the Bible: Matthew 3
Family Worship: Matthew 3:11–17

Why did John baptize people? Did Jesus ever sin? Why then was He baptized? *2 Cor. 5:21.* How many Gods are there? Who are the three persons in the one true God? What did the Holy Spirit do at Jesus's baptism? *1 Sam. 16:13.* What did God the Father do at His baptism? *2 Sam. 7:14.* Though a great king with great power, Jesus showed great humility—how can you follow His example? Let's pray for the Spirit's power to follow the Son in obeying the Father.

Wednesday

Read through the Bible: Matthew 4
Family Worship: Matthew 4:1–11

What did the Spirit lead Jesus to do? Why? **Heb. 4:15.** What did the devil tempt Him to do? Why? *Heb. 7:26–27.* How was Jesus (the second Adam) greater than the first Adam? *Rom. 5:19.* How was King Jesus greater than King David? What did Jesus use to defeat temptation? *Ps. 119:11.* How can you defeat temptation? Let's pray for the power of the Spirit and the Word to be obedient and resist temptation. *Hymn: "A Mighty Fortress Is Our God."*

Thursday

Read through the Bible: Matthew 5
Family Worship: Matthew 5:14–16

What would our house be like at night with no lights? What would the world be like without the church? What makes Christians shine? Are we saved by good works? *Titus 3:5.* Who is glorified when believers do good works? What can you do to shine? How can our family be "a city set on a hill"? Let's pray that God would cause our lights to so shine that He would be glorified.

Friday

Read through the Bible: Matthew 6
Family Worship: Matthew 6:25–34

Do birds worry? Why not? Are they lazy? Who provides for them? How are we to be like birds? What is something you're tempted to worry about? Will worrying help? What should we do instead? *Phil. 4:6-7.* Let's ask the King to give us hearts of simple faith to seek first His kingdom and righteousness and trust Him with the results.

Saturday

Read through the Bible: Matthew 7
Family Worship: Matthew 7:1–5

Who is "the Judge of all the earth" (Gen. 18:25)? What did Jesus tell us not to do? What would it be like if a person, with a log in his own eye, tried to take a speck out of his brother's eye? *Use a pencil to demonstrate.* How does this picture a hypocrite who tries to correct his brother? Is it always wrong to point out a sin in a brother? *Matt. 18:15-17; John 7:24; 1 Cor. 5:12; Gal. 6:1.* What do we need to do first? Let's pray that God would show us any logs in our own eyes.

Year 2   Week 9

Sunday

Read through the Bible: Psalm 61
Family Worship: Psalm 61:1–3

What did David do when his heart was faint? What did he ask God to do for him? Who is "the rock that is higher than I"? *Pss. 18:2; 27:5; 1 Cor. 10:4.* How would a strong tower on a high rock plateau protect a warrior? How is Jesus like that? Is there something for which you need Christ the Rock? What should we do? Let's ask God to "lead [us] to the rock that is higher than [we are]."

Monday

Read through the Bible: Matthew 8
Family Worship: Matthew 8:5–13

What is a centurion? Why did he come to Jesus? What did he recognize about Jesus that many Jews did not? Who has "all authority in heaven and on earth" (Matt. 28:18)? How did the centurion show great humility? Great faith? How is he an example of those who will recline at table in heaven? How can you follow his example today? Let's ask our King for the humility and bold faith of the centurion.

Tuesday

Read through the Bible: Matthew 9
Family Worship: Matthew 9:35–38; John 4:35–38

Who is "the Lord of the harvest"? What does a farmer need to harvest large fields of grain? How are believers like laborers in a field? **1 Cor. 3:5–9.** How can we work together with the Lord of the harvest in world missions? In our church? In our home? Let's "pray earnestly to the Lord of the harvest to send out laborers into his harvest." (Then let's roll up our sleeves and get to work.)

Wednesday

Read through the Bible: Matthew 10
Family Worship: Matthew 10:28–33

Whom are we not to fear? Why not? Whom are we to fear? Why? *The consequences of unbelief (Luke 19:27; Heb. 10:26–31).* How is fearing God like fearing a fierce lion? How is it different? What should the fear of God look like in everyday life? What is God sovereign over? How can the knowledge of His sovereignty comfort us? How can it embolden us? Let's ask our Almighty King for hearts to fear Him in love.

Thursday

Read through the Bible: Matthew 11
Family Worship: Matthew 11:25–30

Who is sovereign in salvation? Whom has God hidden Himself from? Whom has He revealed Himself to? Why? How are little children different from the worldly wise? Which are you more like? Whom does Christ invite to come to Him? What does He promise? Is this a rest of inactivity? Are you burdened with your sin? What should we do? Let's come to King Jesus now, confessing our burden of sin and taking His love-lined yoke of service and peace of soul.

Friday

Read through the Bible: Matthew 12
Family Worship: Matthew 12:33–37

How can you know the type of a tree? How are words like fruit? Why are careless words dangerous? Who will judge our words? If the walls of our home had ears, what kind of words would they hear? What do they reveal about your heart? What kind of evidence will they provide at the judgment? What kind of words should we speak instead? Let's pray that our home would be filled with loving words flowing from grace-filled hearts.

Saturday

Read through the Bible: Matthew 13
Family Worship: Matthew 13:44–46

What did the men who found the treasure and the pearl do? Why? How valuable is the kingdom of God? How do these men picture a proper response to the riches of God's kingdom? *Isa. 55:1.* In what sense is salvation free? Who paid the full price of our salvation? Yet in what sense does it cost everything? *Matt. 16:24; Phil. 3:8.* How have you responded to God's riches "hidden" in His Word? Let's ask our King for hearts willing to joyfully give up all for the treasure of Christ.

Year 2 — Week 10

Sunday

Read through the Bible: Psalm 62
Family Worship: Psalm 62:1–7

What problem did David face? What did he do about it? Why? Who alone was his salvation? *Acts 4:12*. Many false doctrines begin with trusting "Christ plus ___" for salvation. What are some things that fill in the blank? Whom are you trusting for salvation? Plus anything? Whom do you turn to in your time of need? Let's pray for hearts that trust in Christ alone for salvation—and keep trusting Him in all of life.

Monday

Read through the Bible: Matthew 14
Family Worship: Matthew 14:22–33

Who created the wind and the waves? How did Jesus show His power? How did the disciples respond? How did Peter? What happened when he looked at the wind instead of Jesus? Have you ever taken a bold step of faith then wavered when seeing the difficulties around you? What do we need to do when that happens? Let's pray for bold and enduring faith that will keep our eyes "looking to Jesus" (Heb. 12:2).

Tuesday

Read through the Bible: Matthew 15
Family Worship: Matthew 15:21–28; 5:3

Who is the Savior of Jews and Gentiles? What did the Canaanite woman ask for? How did Jesus test her faith? How did she show great faith? How does she picture what it means to be "poor in spirit"? How might a proud person have responded? *Matt. 15:12*. A spoiled child? Which are you more like? What should poverty in spirit look like in our family? Let's pray for hearts poor in spirit.

Wednesday

Read through the Bible: Matthew 16
Family Worship: Matthew 16:13–18

Who did people say that Jesus was? What did Peter confess? Who revealed this truth to Peter? How was Peter (Greek: *Petros*) like a rock (Greek: *petra*)? *Eph. 2:20; Rev. 21:14*. Was he always like a rock? *Compare Matthew 16:23, where he is literally a stumbling block.* What is Jesus building? Will death (the gates of hell) stop the church? Who do you say Jesus is? Let's pray that God would make us "living stones" (1 Peter 2:5) in His church who boldly confess the truth of Christ.

Thursday

Read through the Bible: Matthew 17
Family Worship: Matthew 17:1–8

What happened to Jesus? *Rev. 1:16.* Who appeared to Him? How is Jesus greater than Moses the lawgiver? *John 1:17.* How is He greater than Elijah the prophet? *John 1:18.* Who fulfilled the law and the prophets? What did the Father declare about Jesus? How did the disciples respond to this glimpse of the glorified Christ? How might your attitude be different if you thought more about Christ in His glory? Let's pray for hearts focused on the glory of Christ.

Friday

Read through the Bible: Matthew 18
Family Worship: Matthew 18:21–35

How much did the servant owe his king? How did the king show him mercy? How did he then treat his fellow servant? How did the king respond? How does this story show the ugliness of unforgiveness? Who is our King? How much do we owe Him? Reflect: Are you treating others with the same mercy God has shown you? Let's pray as our King taught us: "Forgive us our debts, as we forgive our debtors" (Matt. 6:12).

Saturday

Read through the Bible: Matthew 19
Family Worship: Matthew 19:13–15; Mark 10:13–16

Who loves children? Who came to Jesus? What did the disciples do? How did Jesus respond? Did the children come to Jesus to test Him, like the Pharisees did? *Matt. 19:3–15.* Did they come thinking they could save themselves like the rich young ruler? *Matt. 19:16–22.* How are these children a model for how to receive the kingdom? Are you coming to Jesus like an independent adult or a dependent child? Let's pray for humble hearts to receive God's kingdom like these children.

Year 2 — Week 11

Sunday

Read through the Bible: Psalm 63
Family Worship: Psalm 63:1–8

Who is the Water of Life? *John 4:14*. What would it be like to be in "a dry and weary land where there is no water"? What would you want more than anything else? How does this picture David's relationship with God? Reflect: Does this picture your relationship with God? How could you more earnestly seek Him? Let's pray for souls thirsty for God and satisfied with the Water of Life.

Monday

Read through the Bible: Matthew 20
Family Worship: Matthew 20:1–16

Who did the most work? What did they do when paid? Why did they grumble? Did they have a right to? Who does what He chooses with what belongs to Him? What aspect of salvation is pictured by the same wage for all? How do the grumbling workers picture spiritual pride? Reflect: Do you think of yourself as better than others because of something you do better or more? Let's pray that God would expose any spiritual pride in our hearts and lead us to repentance.

Tuesday

Read through the Bible: Matthew 21
Family Worship: Matthew 21:28–32*

**AC vv. 31–32*. Who always obeyed His Father the first time? What did the first son do? The second? How does the first son picture repentance? How does the second picture hypocrisy? Reflect: Which one pictures you when told to do something you don't want to do? Is there anything you've promised to do but haven't? Let's pray for hearts that immediately obey—and that repent quickly when we don't.

Wednesday

Read through the Bible: Matthew 22
Family Worship: Matthew 22:1–14

Who is this King? Who is His Son? What did the King prepare for His Son? How did those first invited respond? How do they picture Israel? Who did the King invite next? How does this picture the Great Commission? What clothes did the King provide for His chosen? **Isa. 61:10**. How does the man without a wedding garment picture one who trusts in his own righteousness? **Isa. 64:6**; BCF 10:4. How should we respond to the King's invitation? Let's come to Him now and exchange our filthy rags for His righteousness.

Thursday

Read through the Bible: Matthew 23
Family Worship: Matthew 23:23–24

Who is glorious in justice and mercy? What did the Pharisees focus on? What did they neglect? In what sense were they "straining out a gnat and swallowing a camel"? *Matt. 27:6; John 18:28*. How might we be like them? What are some "weightier matters" we need to focus on more in our home? Let's pray for hearts focused on what is truly important.

Friday

Read through the Bible: Matthew 24
Family Worship: Matthew 24:29–31, 36–44

Who is coming back "with power and great glory"? What was it like in the days of Noah? How will it be like this when Jesus returns? If we knew that someone were going to break into our house tonight, what would we do? How does this picture readiness for the Lord's return? How can we get ready? **Matt. 24:45–46; 25:14–46**. Let's pray for the grace to be "faithful and wise servant[s]" who stay spiritually awake and alert.

Saturday

Read through the Bible: Matthew 25
Family Worship: Matthew 25:31–46

Who is this glorious King? Who are the sheep? Was their faith living or dead? How can you tell? *James 2:17-18; BCF 11:2; 16:2*. Who are the goats? Was their faith living or dead? How can you tell? What will happen to the sheep and the goats? How can we minister to King Jesus *in* our family? How can we minister to Him *as* a family? Let's ask the King for hearts of living faith to serve Him by serving others.

Year 2   Week 12

Sunday

Read through the Bible: Psalm 64
Family Worship: Psalm 64:1–10

What kind of arrows were being shot at David? What kind of words are like arrows? How can a person's tongue be like a sword? *James 3:5–10.* Did David respond in kind? What did he trust God to do? Who judges all people with the sword of His Word? *Heb. 4:12; Rev. 19:15.* How should we respond when others shoot bitter arrow-words at us? Have you shot any of these arrows recently? Let's pray for the grace to speak words that heal and help rather than hurt.

Monday

Read through the Bible: Matthew 26
Family Worship: Matthew 26:6–16

Who gave His life for us? How did Mary show her devotion to Jesus? How did the disciples respond? Which did Judas love more: Jesus or money? *John 12:4–6.* What is our family worship like: extravagant (Mary), pragmatic (the disciples), or cheap (Judas)? How can we show true devotion to our King? *Rom. 12:1.* Let's pray for hearts so filled with love for our Savior that they overflow with extravagant worship.

Tuesday

Read through the Bible: Matthew 27
Family Worship: Matthew 27:15–26

Who will sit on the judgment seat in glory to judge Pilate—and all people? *Matt. 25:31–46; 2 Cor. 5:10.* Why did Pilate wash his hands? Was he truly innocent of Jesus's blood? In what sense are we guilty of Jesus's blood? *Isa. 53:6.* What can wash away our sin? *Rom. 5:9; 1 John 1:7.* Are you washed in the blood of Jesus or condemned by it? For our cleansing, let's make this our only plea: "Nothing but the blood of Jesus." *Hymn: "Nothing but the Blood."*

Wednesday

Read through the Bible: Matthew 28
Family Worship: Matthew 28:1–15

Who is no longer in the grave? What does the resurrection prove about our Lord? *Rom. 1:4.* How did the guards respond to the resurrection? How did the chief priests and elders respond? How can sleeping men know what happened? How did the women respond? What did they do when they saw Jesus? How should we respond to the resurrection of our Lord? Let's worship our risen King—with great joy! *Hymn: "Christ the Lord Is Risen Today."*

Thursday

Read through the Bible: 1 Chronicles 1–5
Family Worship: 1 Chronicles 1:1–4; Acts 17:24–27

Who made all people from one man? Who was that one man? How does this truth condemn racism? Did God create us because He needed us? Why did He create us? *Isa. 43:7*. What are all people responsible to do? Does anyone have an excuse for not seeking God? *Rom. 1:19-20*. How can we do what we were created for? Let's seek God now—praising Him for giving us "life and breath and everything."

Friday

Read through the Bible: 1 Chronicles 6–10
Family Worship: 1 Chronicles 9:1; 10:13–14

Whose is the kingdom? *1 Chron. 29:11*. Why did God remove Judah from the kingdom? Why did God remove the kingdom from Saul? How did Saul commit a "breach of faith"? How did Judah? What is the relationship between faith and obedience? *James 2:17-18; Rom. 1:5*. What does your level of obedience show about your faith? Let's pray for the grace to exercise the obedience of faith rather than a breach of faith.

Saturday

Read through the Bible: 1 Chronicles 11
Family Worship: 1 Chronicles 11:12–14

How was Eleazar a mighty man? What did the Lord do through him? What does the Lord call us to do in spiritual battle? **Eph. 6:13**. What should you do if you are away from us and everyone around you wants to do something sinful? Who gives us the strength to stand firm? Let's ask our Commander for the strength to be mighty men and women who will stand firm (and alone if necessary).

Year 2 — Week 13

Sunday

Read through the Bible: Psalm 65
Family Worship: Psalm 65:1–8

Who is sovereign in salvation? Whom does God draw near to Himself? *Eph. 1:4–5.* Did we choose God, or did He choose us? **John 15:16.** How are we enabled to draw near to Christ in faith? **John 6:44;** *3:3.* How does the doctrine of election humble man and exalt God? *Jonah 2:9.* How should we respond to our Sovereign Savior? Let's draw near in awe to praise God for His glorious grace. *Hymn: "'Tis Not that I."*

Monday

Read through the Bible: 1 Chronicles 12
Family Worship: 1 Chronicles 12:23, 32

What was noteworthy about the men from Issachar? What has God given to help us understand the times and know what we ought to do? *2 Tim. 3:16–17.* How does the Bible help us properly understand the times? *Prov. 14:12; Rom. 12:2; 1 Cor. 2:12–16.* How can we cultivate a biblical worldview? *Deut. 6:6–7; Ps. 119:98–100.* Let's pray for minds renewed by the Word to think biblically about the world.

Tuesday

Read through the Bible: 1 Chronicles 13
Family Worship: 1 Chronicles 13:5–14

Who "dwells in unapproachable light" (1 Tim. 6:16)? How did God say to carry the ark? *1 Chron. 15:13–15.* What did Israel do instead? What did the ark symbolize? *Ex. 25:22.* What does Uzzah's death teach us about how to approach the presence of God? *Lev. 16:1–3; Heb. 12:28b–29.* How can you show more respect for the presence of God in family worship? In church? Let's pray for hearts filled with reverence and awe as we approach the presence of God.

Wednesday

Read through the Bible: 1 Chronicles 14
Family Worship: 1 Chronicles 14:1–2, 8–12

Whom did David give credit to for the establishment of his kingdom? Whom did he give credit to for his defeat of the Philistines? How has God blessed you?

Our family? Who gets the credit? How can we publicly give glory to God for His work in us? Let's praise Him now and pray for hearts quick to give credit where credit is due.

Thursday

Read through the Bible: 1 Chronicles 15
Family Worship: 1 Chronicles 15:2–3, 11–15, 25–28

How was this attempt to transport the ark different from the last (ch. 13)? Where did they learn how to do this? Was David sincere in his worship both times? *1 Chron. 13:8.* Is sincerity enough? Who decides how we should worship God? How must the Father be worshiped? **John 4:24.** How can we ensure we are worshiping God "in spirit and truth"? Let's worship God now—in sincerity—according to the truth of His Word.

Friday

Read through the Bible: 1 Chronicles 16
Family Worship: 1 Chronicles 16:1–4, 7–13, 23–27

Where do we learn how to rightly worship God? How did David demonstrate worshiping God "in spirit and truth" (John 4:24)? How did he express joy in worship? Was David's joy hindered because he worshiped according to God's Word instead of his imagination? How can you express joy in your worship? Let's worship God now, with joy, according to the truth of His Word.

Saturday

Read through the Bible: 1 Chronicles 17
Family Worship: 1 Chronicles 16:43; 17:1–15

What play is there on the word *house*? In what sense did David's son build a house for God? In what sense did God build a house for David? Who is the fulfillment of the Davidic covenant? How is this imagery fulfilled in Christ? *Luke 1:31–33; Heb. 1:5.* In what sense are we a part of God's house? *Eph. 2:19–22.* How should we respond to King Jesus for making us a part of His house/family/temple? Let's praise Him and pray He would make ours a faithful house.

Year 2 — Week 14

Sunday

Read through the Bible: Psalm 66

Family Worship: Psalm 66:1–4, 16–20

Who hears and answers prayer? What had God done for the psalmist? When will God *not* listen to prayer? *Isa. 59:1-2; 1 Peter 3:7.* What does it mean to cherish something? Can we enjoy God and sin at the same time? Why not? *Matt. 6:24.* What can you do so that God will listen to your prayers? *Prov. 28:13.* Let's ask God to show us any sin we're enjoying in our hearts and to lead us to repentance so we can glorify and enjoy Him forever. *Hymn: "Love Divine, All Loves Excelling."*

Monday

Read through the Bible: 1 Chronicles 18

Family Worship: 1 Chronicles 18:14

What did David do for his people? What is justice and equity? What greater Son of his will administer justice and equity to all people? *Isa. 9:6-7; 42:1-4; cited Matt. 12:18-21.* What happens when nations are ruled with justice and equity? **Prov. 21:15.** How can we work for justice and equity in our nation? Our home? Let's pray for the grace to practice Christlike justice and equity in our home and society.

Tuesday

Read through the Bible: 1 Chronicles 19–20

Family Worship: 1 Chronicles 19:10–15

What problem did Joab face? What was his strategy for victory? On whom did the outcome of the battle depend? How does Joab model the balance between human responsibility and divine sovereignty? *Phil. 2:12-13.* What are you responsible to do in the spiritual battles of life? *Eph. 6:10.* On whom do the results depend? Let's pray that God would help us do our best, then let's trust Him with the results.

Wednesday

Read through the Bible: 1 Chronicles 21

Family Worship: 1 Chronicles 21:14–27

Summarize 21:1-13, compare Family Worship 2 Sam. 24. What did God command David to do to make atonement? What did Ornan offer to do? Why didn't David accept? What does true worship cost? *Rom. 12:1.* Who paid the cost of our forgiveness with His life? What can you give the Lord in costly worship? Let's praise God for giving His best for us and pray for the grace to give Him our best in worship.

Thursday

Read through the Bible: 1 Chronicles 22
Family Worship: 1 Chronicles 22:5–16

Who called Solomon to build a house for His name? What did David do to prepare Solomon to build the temple? What do you think God might call you to do when you grow up? What can we (your parents) do to help you prepare for your calling? What can you do to prepare yourself? Let's pray that God would enable us to prepare you for whatever He calls you to do.

Friday

Read through the Bible: 1 Chronicles 23
Family Worship: 1 Chronicles 23:2–6, 25–32

Who "is not a God of confusion but of peace" (1 Cor. 14:33)? What did David do to ensure the work of God's house would "be done decently and in order" (1 Cor. 14:40)? What would have happened had the gatekeepers quit because they wanted to do something more "spiritual"? What are some mundane tasks you can do to help our home run in an orderly fashion? How can you do it to the glory of God? *1 Cor. 10:31.* Let's pray for the grace of an orderly home.

Saturday

Read through the Bible: 1 Chronicles 24
Family Worship: 1 Chronicles 24:1–3, 19

Who "is not a God of confusion but of peace" (1 Cor. 14:33)? What did David do to ensure worship would "be done decently and in order" (1 Cor. 14:40)? What would a church service be like if there was no order or leadership? What can you do to ensure our times of corporate worship will "be done decently and in order"? Our times of family worship? Let's pray for the grace of orderly worship.

Year 2   Week 15

Sunday

Read through the Bible: Psalm 67
Family Worship: Psalm 67:1–5

Who "ransomed people for God from every tribe and language and people and nation" (Rev. 5:9)? Why did the psalmist want God to bless Israel? Whom did he want to praise God? When will all peoples praise Him? *Rev. 7:9–10.* How has the psalmist's prayer been partially fulfilled in us? *Eph. 2:12–13.* How should we respond to God for calling us to be His worshipers? Let's praise God and pray He would make His saving power known among all nations.

Monday

Read through the Bible: 1 Chronicles 25
Family Worship: 1 Chronicles 25:1, 5–7

Who gives children as a heritage and reward? *Ps. 127:3–5.* How did God exalt Heman? How did his family exalt God? *Ps. 88.* How can those who lead worship exalt God? *Ps. 33:3.* How has God exalted our family? How can we exalt God in worship? In our work? *Prov. 22:29.* Let's praise God for blessing us with children and pray for the grace to exalt Him through skillful worship and work.

Tuesday

Read through the Bible: 1 Chronicles 26
Family Worship: 1 Chronicles 26:1a, 4–8

Who gives children as a heritage and reward? *Ps. 127:3–5.* How did God bless Obed-edom? Why? *1 Chron. 13:14.* What quality did his sons and grandsons possess? Where are children trained to become "able men" (and women)? What leadership can you exercise now as training for greater responsibility? Let's pray that God would bless us by making our children and grandchildren people of great ability.

Wednesday

Read through the Bible: 1 Chronicles 27
Family Worship: 1 Chronicles 27:25–31

What is a steward? What did David's stewards do? Who lavished on us the riches of His grace? *Eph. 1:7–8.* What are we stewards of? **1 Peter 4:10–11.** What kind of grace-gifts has God given us? *Rom. 12:6–8; James 1:17.* How can you be a good steward of these? *1 Cor. 4:2*. Let's pray for hearts to be "good stewards of God's varied grace"—for His glory.

Thursday

Read through the Bible: 1 Chronicles 28
Family Worship: 1 Chronicles 28:9

What did David charge Solomon to do? How do you get to know someone? How can we know God? With what kind of heart and mind are we to serve God? Why can't God be fooled by external show? Who searches all hearts and minds? How can you seek and serve God with a whole heart and willing mind? *Isa. 55:6–7.* Let's pray for whole hearts and willing minds to seek, know, and serve the Lord.

Friday

Read through the Bible: 1 Chronicles 29
Family Worship: 1 Chronicles 29:3, 6, 9–17, 22

Whose "is the kingdom, and the power, and the glory" (Matt. 6:13, KJV)? What belongs to God? How did David and the people respond to the greatness and glory of God? With what kind of hearts and minds did they worship God? How can we worship God with whole hearts and willing minds? *2 Cor. 9:7; Rom. 12:1.* Let's pray for whole hearts and willing minds to give ourselves freely in joyful, costly worship.

Saturday

Read through the Bible: 2 Chronicles 1
Family Worship: 2 Chronicles 1:7–12

"In whom are hidden all the treasures of wisdom and knowledge" (Col. 2:3)? What did God ask Solomon? What did Solomon ask for? **1 Kings 3:9.** What would most people ask for? How did God respond? **1 Kings 3:10–14.** Why did Solomon's request please God? How does what we pray for reflect what's in our hearts? *James 4:3.* What should we ask God for? *Matt. 6:9–13; Rom. 12:2.* Let's ask for understanding minds to discern and desire what is good and pleasing to God.

Year 2   Week 16

Sunday

Read through the Bible: Psalm 68
Family Worship: Psalm 68:4–6

Some say, "God helps those who help themselves." What's wrong with this? Who helps the helpless? What are some examples in this psalm of how God helps the helpless? How does God help the solitary? In what sense are all helpless before God? *Eph. 2:1–9; Job 12:10.* How has God helped us? How should we respond? Let's praise God for helping helpless sinners like us and thank Him for giving us a family.

Monday

Read through the Bible: 2 Chronicles 2
Family Worship: 2 Chronicles 2:5–6

Who is everywhere present all the time? How big is God? *2 Chron. 6:18; Jer. 23:24.* Where is He? Is there anywhere where God isn't? **Ps. 139:7–12.** How can the knowledge of God's omnipresence comfort us? *Ps. 23:4.* How can it enlarge our view of God? How might your actions change if you really believed that God was wherever you are? Let's pray for a larger view of God and lives that are changed as a result.

Tuesday

Read through the Bible: 2 Chronicles 3–4
Family Worship: 2 Chronicles 3:1–7

Who "has made everything beautiful in its time" (Eccl. 3:11)? In what ways was the temple beautiful? Does artistic beauty come from man or God? *Ps. 27:4; Rev. 21:10–21.* How can we glorify and enjoy God through artistic beauty? How can you reflect God's beauty through your attitude and actions? *1 Peter 3:4; Rev. 19:7–8.* Let's pray for the grace to glorify and enjoy God by reflecting His beauty.

Wednesday

Read through the Bible: 2 Chronicles 5–6:11
Family Worship: 2 Chronicles 5:7, 11–14; 7:1–3

What happened when the priests brought the ark into the temple and again after Solomon prayed? How did the people respond? Who "is the radiance of the glory of God" (Heb. 1:3)? In what temple is God's glory now manifest? *1 Cor. 3:16.* How might you act differently in church if you could see the glory of Christ? Let's pray for eyes to see the glory of God—and lives that are changed as a result.

Thursday

Read through the Bible: 2 Chronicles 6:12–42
Family Worship: 2 Chronicles 6:36–39

Which greater Son of Solomon never sinned? *1 Peter 2:22.* Is there anyone else who has not sinned? *Eccl. 7:20.* What do we need to do to be forgiven when we sin? What is repentance? *BCF 15:3.* Why do you think Solomon mentions repentance with both mind and heart? Have you sinned? What should we do? Let's confess our sin and repent with all our mind and all our heart.

Friday

Read through the Bible: 2 Chronicles 7
Family Worship: 2 Chronicles 7:11–14

Who is "good and forgiving, abounding in steadfast love to all who call upon [Him]" (Ps. 86:5)? What had Solomon prayed for? How did God answer him? What are the elements of true repentance mentioned here? Which needs the most emphasis in your life? What does God promise to do when His people repent? Let's humble ourselves, pray, seek God's face, and turn from our wicked ways.

Saturday

Read through the Bible: 2 Chronicles 8
Family Worship: 2 Chronicles 8:1–10

What did Solomon do after completing the temple and his palace? How does he model the principle of industry (the work ethic)? What greater King is building a greater kingdom? How can you honor God in your work? *1 Cor. 10:31; Col. 3:23-24; Prov. 6:6-8.* What military preparations did Solomon make? When should our nation prepare for war? When should we prepare for spiritual battle? Let's pray for the grace to honor God by hard work and wise preparation.

Year 2 — Week 17

Sunday

Read through the Bible: Psalm 69
Family Worship: Psalm 69:9a

Who fulfilled this verse? **John 2:13–17.** What is "zeal"? What are you zealous for? What was Jesus zealous for? How did He show it? What do you think the money changers were zealous for? *1 Tim. 6:10.* How can you show zeal for God's house today? Let's pray that God would give us a holy zeal for His house.

Monday

Read through the Bible: 2 Chronicles 9
Family Worship: 2 Chronicles 9:22–24

What did the kings of the earth seek? How important was it to them? How important is it for us to get wisdom? **Prov. 4:5–8.** What kind of effort does seeking wisdom require? *2 Tim. 2:15.* How can you diligently seek wisdom? *Ps. 19.* In "whom are hidden all the treasures of wisdom and knowledge" (Col. 2:3)? Let's pray for hearts to diligently seek God's wisdom in His Word and His world.

Tuesday

Read through the Bible: 2 Chronicles 10
Family Worship: 2 Chronicles 10:1–19

When Solomon began his reign, whom did he seek wisdom from? What did the people ask Rehoboam? Whom did he ask for advice? What advice did the older men give? The young men? Who gave him the best advice? *1 Kings 12:7; Mark 10:42–45.* Whom did he listen to? To whom should you go for advice? What is the ultimate standard for evaluating advice? *Acts 17:11.* Let's pray for the discernment to listen to wise advice.

Wednesday

Read through the Bible: 2 Chronicles 11
Family Worship: 11:13–17

What did the priests and Levites do? Why? What did it cost them? What did the other faithful Israelites do? Why? For whom did they "set their hearts to seek"? When you're in a crowd that is doing something sinful, what should you do? *2 Tim. 2:22.* What may it cost you? *Luke 14:27–33.* Let's pray for hearts set to flee sin and seek the Lord no matter the cost.

Thursday

Read through the Bible: 2 Chronicles 12
Family Worship: 2 Chronicles 12:1–8

What did Rehoboam do when he was strong? Which greater Son of his endured in faithfulness? *Heb. 12:2*. What did God do? How did Rehoboam respond? Was this temporary or saving faith? **2 Chron. 12:14**; *BCF 14:3*. Rehoboam abandoned God when he felt strong—when is your heart prone to wander? How can we keep our hearts from wandering? Let's humble ourselves and ask God to bind our wandering hearts to Christ. *Hymn: "Come, Thou Fount."*

Friday

Read through the Bible: 2 Chronicles 13
Family Worship: 2 Chronicles 13:1–18

How was Israel fighting against the Lord? How might so-called Christians be fighting against the Lord today? How much bigger was Israel's army than Judah's? Who defeated Israel? Why? How did Abijah and Judah show overcoming faith? *1 John 5:4*. How can we follow their example (and not Israel's)? Let's pray for hearts of obedient, overcoming faith.

Saturday

Read through the Bible: 2 Chronicles 14
Family Worship: 2 Chronicles 14:1–4, 8–13.

What kind of king was Asa? What did he do? How much bigger was the Ethiopian army than Judah's? Who is able to help the weak against the mighty? How is Asa an example of overcoming faith in worship? *1 John 5:3–4*. In war? How can we exercise overcoming faith in worship? In spiritual war? Let's pray for hearts of obedient, overcoming faith.

Year 2 — Week 18

Sunday

Read through the Bible: Psalm 70
Family Worship: Psalm 70:1–5

Have you ever wanted to ask God to hurry up? Can we? Should we? *Luke 18:1–8; Rev. 6:10*. What did David ask the Lord to do? What does he show us about honesty in prayer? Whose timing is always perfect, even when we don't see it? How can you be both honest and reverent in your prayers? Let's "rejoice and be glad in [God]," while also honestly and reverently bringing our petitions to Him.

Monday

Read through the Bible: 2 Chronicles 15
Family Worship: 2 Chronicles 15:1–15

Who said, "Seek, and you will find" (Matt. 7:7)? What promise and warning did the prophet give Asa? How did Asa lead the people to seek the Lord? What elements of genuine repentance do you see? *BCF 15:3*. What was the result of their repentance, reform, and covenant renewal? How can we seek the Lord today? Let's pray for renewed hearts and whole desire to "seek the LORD while he may be found" (Isa. 55:6).

Tuesday

Read through the Bible: 2 Chronicles 16
Family Worship: 2 Chronicles 16:1–10

Whose eyes "run to and fro throughout the whole earth"? What is God seeking? Why? Was Asa that kind of person? Whom did he rely on for help? How was this different from when he was younger? *2 Chron. 14:11*. How did he respond to God's rebuke? How do you typically respond to discipline? What can we do to grow in faith as we grow older? *Heb. 12:1–11*. Let's pray that God would give us what He is seeking: hearts that "still bear fruit in old age" (Ps. 92:14).

Wednesday

Read through the Bible: 2 Chronicles 17
Family Worship: 2 Chronicles 17:1–9

Whom did Jehoshaphat seek? What did he send certain men to do? What did they teach the people? Whom has God appointed to teach His Word in the family? *Deut. 6:6–7.* In the church? *Eph. 4:11–16.* What can you do so that the teaching of the Word is fruitful in your life? *2 Chron. 7:14; James 1:22.* Let's pray for lives that bear fruit from the teaching of God's Word in our home and church.

Thursday

Read through the Bible: 2 Chronicles 18
Family Worship: 2 Chronicles 18:1–22, 28–34

What/whom did Jehoshaphat seek before battle? Why did he ask for another prophet? Why did Ahab tell him to wear his royal robes? How was God gracious to Jehoshaphat? How could he have shown greater discernment? **2 Chron. 19:2.** How can you show greater discernment? How can you train your powers of discernment? *Heb. 5:14.* Let's pray for the discernment to be godly but not gullible.

Friday

Read through the Bible: 2 Chronicles 19
Family Worship: 2 Chronicles 19:4–7

With whom is there no injustice? *Deut. 32:4.* What did Jehoshaphat do for his people? Why is it important for judges to be just? How can we model God's justice in our home? What can we do to see His justice reflected in our nation? Let's praise God for His justice and pray it would be reflected more clearly in our home and nation.

Saturday

Read through the Bible: 2 Chronicles 20
Family Worship: 2 Chronicles 20:1–6, 12–24

Who "rule[s] over all the kingdoms of the nations"? What problem did Judah face? How did Jehoshaphat and Judah fight their enemies? What did God do? What kind of enemies do we face? *Eph. 6:10–12.* How should we fight them? *Eph. 6:13–18.* Let's ask God to "deliver us from evil" (Matt. 6:13) as we pray and praise Him.

Year 2 — Week 19

Sunday

Read through the Bible: Psalm 71
Family Worship: Psalm 71:4–6, 15–18

Upon whom had the psalmist leaned since before birth? In what sense had he leaned on God from the womb? How did this encourage him in his present distress? How did it help him hope for the future? How can remembering God's providential care encourage our faith? Let's praise God for His lifelong care for us and pray He would help us exercise lifelong faith that we can pass to the next generation.

Monday

Read through the Bible: 2 Chronicles 21
Family Worship: 2 Chronicles 21:1–6

Who was Jehoram? How was he different from his father? Which greater King died for His brothers? *Matt. 25:40.* Who influenced Jehoram to such evil? *2 Chron. 22:10.* What responsibility does godly Jehoshaphat bear for this? *2 Chron. 18:1.* What are some evil influences that could harm our faith and family? *1 Cor. 15:33.* How can we protect against these? *2 Cor. 6:14.* Let's pray for the discretion to avoid anyone or anything that could destroy our faith or family.

Tuesday

Read through the Bible: 2 Chronicles 22
Family Worship: 2 Chronicles 22:1–4, 10–12

Who was Athaliah? What did she do to her family? Who was Jehoshabeath? What did she do for her family? Which greater Son of Joash was also saved from death as a baby? How do these women demonstrate the impact a woman can have for good or evil? Daughters: How can you prepare to be a godly woman? Sons: Why is it important to marry a godly woman? Let's pray that God would empower our daughters and future daughters-in-law to be godly women.

Wednesday

Read through the Bible: 2 Chronicles 23
Family Worship: 2 Chronicles 23:1–3, 8–18

Who was Jehoiada? What did he lead his nation to do? Whose word did he lead the nation to obey? How does he demonstrate the impact one godly leader can have? Sons: How can you prepare to be godly leaders in your future family? Church? Nation? Daughters: Why is it important for your future husband to be a godly leader? Let's pray that God would empower our sons and future sons-in-law to be godly leaders.

Thursday

Read through the Bible: 2 Chronicles 24
Family Worship: 2 Chronicles 24:1–2, 15–25

What kind of king was Joash? How was he influenced by others? Who sent prophets to warn him? How did he respond to God's word? How do you respond to correction: with humility or hardness of heart? Both Joash and Zechariah were discipled by Jehoiada, yet how were they different? Who is your "Jehoiada"? How can you prepare to be a Zechariah and not a Joash? Let's pray for the grace to be disciples who endure—and become disciple-makers.

Friday

Read through the Bible: 2 Chronicles 25
Family Worship: 2 Chronicles 25:1–4, 14–16, 27

What kind of king was Amaziah? How did God warn him? How does God warn us? *Heb. 4:12.* How did he respond to God's word? What are ways we might say, "Stop!" when being corrected? How should we respond when God corrects us? *Heb. 12:5–6; Isa. 55:6–7.* How should children respond when corrected by their parents? Let's pray for open ears to listen to and whole hearts to obey God's Word.

Saturday

Read through the Bible: 2 Chronicles 26
Family Worship: 2 Chronicles 26:1–5, 8, 15–21

What kind of king was Uzziah? What happened when he became strong? *Prov. 16:18.* What was wrong with what he did? Who only is both King and Priest? How did God "cure" Uzziah of his pride? What should we do so we don't need this type of "medicine"? *1 Peter 5:5–6.* In what area do you need to humble yourself? Let's pray for the grace to humble ourselves before we need to be humiliated.

Year 2   Week 20

Sunday

Read through the Bible: Psalm 72
Family Worship: Psalm 72:1–11

Whom is Solomon ultimately praying about? How is King Jesus already fulfilling this prayer? *Matt. 28:18–20; Eph. 1:19–23; Col. 1:13–14.* How will He completely fulfill it? *1 Cor. 15:24–26.* How can you show that King Jesus is reigning in your life? Let's praise our King for calling us into His kingdom of grace, and pray He would prepare us for His kingdom of glory. *Hymn: "Jesus Shall Reign."*

Monday

Read through the Bible: 2 Chronicles 27–28
Family Worship: 2 Chronicles 27:1–6

What kind of king was Jotham? How was he like his father? How was he different? *2 Chron. 26:16.* What kind of spiritual family resemblance do you have? *Dad: What is one way you don't want your children to be like you?* Who is the perfect role model? Why did Jotham become mighty? How can you order your ways before the Lord? *Ps. 119:1–3.* Let's pray for the grace of greater family resemblance with Christ.

Tuesday

Read through the Bible: 2 Chronicles 29
Family Worship: 2 Chronicles 29:1–11, 15–16

What kind of king was Hezekiah? What did he command the priests and Levites to do? Why? *2 Chron. 28:22–24.* What kinds of cleansing were required? How is physical washing a picture of repentance? *Isa. 1:16.* Is there any moral filth we need to carry out of our house? Our hearts? Who or what can wash away our sin? Let's confess the filth of our sin and be cleansed. *Hymn: "Nothing but the Blood."*

Wednesday

Read through the Bible: 2 Chronicles 30
Family Worship: 2 Chronicles 30:1–12

Whom did Hezekiah invite to the Passover? Why did he invite the northern tribes? *2 Chron. 6:36–39; 7:14.* How did they respond? How did Judah respond? Why? What did Jesus commission His church to do with the good news of

God's grace? *Mark 16:15-16*. How will people respond? Whom do we trust with the results? Let's pray for opportunities to tell others of God's grace and for the faith to trust God with the results.

Thursday

Read through the Bible: 2 Chronicles 31
Family Worship: 2 Chronicles 31:2–10

How were the priests and Levites provided for? Who commanded us to give the tithe? What happened when the people gave the tithe as commanded? How is our pastor provided for? **1 Cor. 9:13–14.** If he is well provided for, what will he be able to focus on more? **Acts 18:1–5.** What can we do to help? Let's pray that God would so bless our church that we could bless our pastor with an abundance and free him to focus more on the Word.

Friday

Read through the Bible: 2 Chronicles 32
Family Worship: 2 Chronicles 32:24–31

Who tested Hezekiah? How did God test him? *2 Kings 20:12-19*. Why? What did it reveal? How can God's blessing test us? How can the testing itself be a blessing? *BCF 5:5*. How has God blessed you? How have you responded? Let's thank God for how He has blessed us—including the blessing of exposing our sin so we can humble ourselves.

Saturday

Read through the Bible: 2 Chronicles 33
Family Worship: 2 Chronicles 33:1–17

What did God initially do to call Manasseh to repentance? How did he respond? When he ignored His word, what did God do? How did Manasseh respond then? *1 Tim. 1:13-15; BCF 15:1*. What marks of true repentance did he show? *BCF 15:3*. What has God given us to call us to repentance? *BCF 15:5; Luke 24:44-47*. How have you responded? Let's pray for the grace to repent at the hearing of the Word before needing the rod of the world. *Hymn:* "Amazing Grace."

Year 2   Week 21

Sunday

Read through the Bible: Psalm 73
Family Worship: Psalm 73:1–8, 11–26

What bothered the psalmist? What helped him change his way of thinking? What did he remember when he went into God's sanctuary? *Luke 16:19-25.* Who *is* God's sanctuary? *John 1:14.* How should corporate worship change how we think during the week? *Col. 3:1-4.* How can you be more heavenly-minded this week? Let's worship God now, praying for hearts and minds transformed to live with the end in sight.

Monday

Read through the Bible: 2 Chronicles 34
Family Worship: 2 Chronicles 34:1–2, 8, 14–28

What did Hilkiah find in the temple? How did Josiah respond to the reading of God's Word? Why? What marks of true repentance do you see here? How was his response different from Manasseh's? *2 Chron. 33:10.* What has God given us to call us to repentance? *2 Tim. 3:16; BCF 15:5.* When corrected by God's Word, is your heart typically humbled or hardened? How can you be more like Josiah? Let's praise God for His Word and pray for tender hearts to humble ourselves when we hear it.

Tuesday

Read through the Bible: 2 Chronicles 35
Family Worship: 2 Chronicles 35:1–2, 6, 12–13, 16–18

What did Josiah lead the people to do? Where did they learn how to keep the Passover? How do we know what we need to do to obey God? *2 Tim. 3:16-17; Josh. 1:8.* Sin is not only doing what God forbids but also failing to do what He requires. Reflect: Is there something God has commanded that you are not doing? Let's ask God to show us in His Word—and lead us to repentance.

Wednesday

Read through the Bible: 2 Chronicles 36
Family Worship: 2 Chronicles 36:11–21

What kind of king was Zedekiah? What did God do to call him and the people to repentance? How did they respond? What were the consequences? What remedy is there for those who refuse to listen to God? How does God speak to us? *2 Peter 1:19-21.* How can you keep from becoming like Zedekiah? *Heb. 12:25.* Let's pray for hearts to repent quickly and never "refuse him who is speaking" (Heb. 12:25).

Thursday

Read through the Bible: Ezra 1–2
Family Worship: Ezra 1:1–5

Who is sovereign over pagan kings? How did He show this? *Isa. 44:28.* Who is faithful to keep His promises? How did He show this? **Jer. 25:11-12; 29:10.** How are we like the exiles? *1 Peter 1:1, 17; 2:11; Heb. 11:13-16.* How can God's sovereign faithfulness to the exiles stir up our hearts today? Let's pray for hearts stirred up to live like exiles—with our true homeland in sight.

Friday

Read through the Bible: Ezra 3
Family Worship: Ezra 3:8–13

What did the people do when the foundation of the temple was laid? Why were some of the people so joyful? Why were some so sad? **Hag. 2:2-9.** Who is the greater and more glorious temple? *Rev. 21:22.* Why should we be joyful in worship? Are you? When should we be somber in worship? *BCF 15:3.5.* Are you? Let's pray for hearts to be passionate worshipers—joyful for God's grace and contrite because of sin and its effects.

Saturday

Read through the Bible: Ezra 4
Family Worship: Ezra 4:1–5

What did the people of the land say they wanted to do? Do you think they were genuine? What did they do next? Why didn't the returned exiles want their help? **2 Kings 17:24, 33-34, 41.** Whom alone are we to worship? *Syncretism* is the mixture of true worship with that which is false. Are there people who do this today? Should we worship with them? What if they say we are "intolerant"? Let's pray for hearts passionate for true worship—unmixed with anything false.

Year 2   Week 22

Sunday

Read through the Bible: Psalm 74
Family Worship: Psalm 74:1–17

What frustrated the psalmist? What did he ask God? What did he remember about God? Who is our King from of old? Did God answer his prayer? *Ezra 1.* What should we do when we don't see God working as we think He should? Is it okay for us to pray, "How long"? *Rev. 6:10.* Let's pray for hearts to remember the majesty and mercy of our King, even when we don't understand His ways.

Monday

Read through the Bible: Ezra 5
Family Worship: Ezra 4:4–5, 24–5:2

What did the people of the land do to discourage the returned exiles? What effect did it have on the rebuilding of the temple? What encouraged them to begin building again? What has God given to encourage us? **Rom. 15:4.** How can what is written in Ezra encourage us today? Let's pray for "the encouragement of the Scriptures" to give us hope and endurance—even in the midst of difficulty.

Tuesday

Read through the Bible: Ezra 6
Family Worship: Ezra 6:13–16, 22

Who turns the heart of kings to do His will? *Prov. 21:1.* By whose decrees was the building completed? Whom did God work through to accomplish His decree? What work has God called you to do? How can the truth of His sovereignty empower you to complete it? *Phil. 2:12-13.* What did the people do when the work was done? What should we do when God does something through us? Let's pray that God would move our hearts to work and worship with joy.

Wednesday

Read through the Bible: Ezra 7
Family Worship: Ezra 7:1–10

Who was Ezra? Whose good hand was on him? What did he set his heart to do? Why is it important to study God's Word? *2 Tim. 2:15.* Why is it important to do God's Word? *James 1:22.* Why is it important to teach God's Word?

2 Tim. 3:15–17. How can we follow Ezra's example in our home? *Deut. 6:6–9.* Let's pray for hearts set to study, to do, and to teach God's Word.

Thursday

Read through the Bible: Ezra 8
Family Worship: Ezra 8:21–23, 31–32

Why did Ezra proclaim a fast? Why didn't he ask the king for protection? Is it wrong to seek human means of physical protection? *Neh. 2:9; BCF 5:3.* How did God respond to Ezra's prayer? Whose good hand was on them? As exiles en route to the heavenly Jerusalem *(1 Peter 1:1, 17; 2:11),* how can we be protected from the spiritual "dangers, toils, and snares" of this life? Let's seek God for the grace which "will lead [us] home." *Hymn: "Amazing Grace."*

Friday

Read through the Bible: Ezra 9
Family Worship: Ezra 9:1–6, 13–15

At whose word should we tremble? *Isa. 66:2.* What was the problem? What did Ezra do about it? Why is intermarriage with unbelievers so serious? *1 Kings 11:1–8.* How does your attitude toward sin compare with Ezra's? How can you show greater reverence for God's Word? Let's pray for hearts that tremble at God's Word and are therefore broken over our sin.

Saturday

Read through the Bible: Ezra 10
Family Worship: Ezra 10:1–5

Who commands us to only marry believers? How did the returned exiles deal with the problem of intermarriage with pagans? Why? *Compare Ezra 6:21; 9:1 with Deut. 7:2–4; 13:6–10. Idolaters (even family members) were to be executed. They did not have civil authority to do so, therefore, divorce was their most biblical option.* How should we treat this situation today? *1 Cor. 7:12–16.* How can we avoid this situation altogether? *1 Cor. 7:39; 2 Cor. 6:14.* Let's pray for godly, believing spouses for our children.

Year 2 — Week 23

Sunday

Read through the Bible: Psalm 75
Family Worship: Psalm 75:1–3

In Psalm 74, what question did Asaph ask God? *Ps. 74:10.* In this psalm, how does God answer him? When we think God's timing isn't right, what should we remember? Who has appointed a time for everything? *Eccl. 3:1; Acts 1:7.* When it seems sin is out of control, what should we remember? Whose "ways are justice" (Deut. 32:4)? Let's praise God for His perfect timing and perfect justice—and thank Him that His name is always near.

Monday

Read through the Bible: Nehemiah 1
Family Worship: Nehemiah 1:1–11

What was the problem? What did Nehemiah do about it? What did he pray? What did he remind God of? *Deut. 30:1–6.* Where do we find God's promises? In whom do "all the promises of God find their Yes" (2 Cor. 1:20)? What are some of God's promises? *John 10:28; Heb. 13:5; 1 John 1:9.* How can we pray more like Nehemiah? Let's pray for hearts to be passionate pray-ers of God's promises.

Tuesday

Read through the Bible: Nehemiah 2
Family Worship: Nehemiah 2:1–8

Whose good hand was upon Nehemiah? What did he ask the king for? Note how specific his requests are—in addition to praying during the four months between chapters 1 and 2, what else had Nehemiah done? Two farmers prayed for rain, but only one prepared his fields to receive it—which one prayed in faith? Which was Nehemiah like? Which one are you? How can we "prepare for rain"? Let's pray for hearts to pray and prepare in faith.

Wednesday

Read through the Bible: Nehemiah 3
Family Worship: Nehemiah 2:17–18; 3:1–5

Whose good hand was upon Nehemiah? How did he show wise leadership in motivating the people? In organizing the people? How did the people respond?

Why wouldn't some of the nobles help? What would happen if there was no leadership in our home? What if some family members acted like the nobles? What can you do to help our family? Let's pray for the grace to work together in our home with wise leadership and unity of effort.

Thursday

Read through the Bible: Nehemiah 4
Family Worship: Nehemiah 4:6–20

What did Nehemiah's enemies plan to do? How did he respond? How did he show both prudence and piety? Who worked through his prudent plans to frustrate the enemies' evil plans? What kind of enemies do we face? How can we work with one hand while holding a weapon in the other? *Eph. 6:10-18; Matt. 26:41; 1 Peter 5:8–9.* Let's pray for the grace to watch and pray with prudence and piety.

Friday

Read through the Bible: Nehemiah 5
Family Worship: Nehemiah 5:14–19

What was Nehemiah entitled to as governor? Why didn't he demand his right? What did he do instead? Who said, "It is more blessed to give than to receive"? **Acts 20:35.** How did Nehemiah exemplify our Lord's teaching? How can you be more like Nehemiah? Let's pray for generous hearts which rejoice in giving rather than demanding.

Saturday

Read through the Bible: Nehemiah 6
Family Worship: Nehemiah 6:1–14

What are three ways Nehemiah's enemies tried to deceive him? How did he show discretion in responding to each? *Compare Neh. 6:11 to Num. 1:51.* Should you believe everything you hear? *1 John 4:1.* What should you do if you hear something that you're not sure is right? Against what standard should we test truth claims? *John 17:17.* How can you grow in discretion? *Eph. 4:11-16; Heb. 6:14.* Let's pray for the grace to grow in maturity and discretion so that we are not deceived by "craftiness in deceitful schemes" (Eph. 4:14).

Year 2   Week 24

Sunday

Read through the Bible: Psalm 76
Family Worship: Psalm 76:7–9

Who "can stand before [God] when once [His] anger is roused?" Who faced God's anger for our sins on the cross? *1 John 4:10; Rom. 5:9.* What will Jesus do for the "humble" on judgment day? *1 Thess. 1:10.* In view of God's anger and His grace, how is He to be treated? How can you show a proper fear of God in worship? In everyday life? Let's praise God for His grace and pray for hearts to fear Him in love.

Monday

Read through the Bible: Nehemiah 7
Family Worship: Nehemiah 6:15–16

How many days did it take to build the wall? Why were the nations afraid? Who helped the people? How had God helped them? *Neh. 2:8, 12, 18, 20; 4:15, 20; 7:5.* What would have happened had the people not worked diligently? If Nehemiah hadn't provided wise leadership? Does God's providence give us an excuse for laziness? Why not? *Phil. 2:12–13; BCF 5:2.* Let's pray for hearts to be hard workers through whom God works.

Tuesday

Read through the Bible: Nehemiah 8
Family Worship: Nehemiah 8:1–12

What did Ezra read to the people? What did the Levites do? How did the people respond? Why did they rejoice? *Ps. 119:130.* How might their response have been different if they hadn't understood the Word? Who helps you understand God's Word? *Deut. 6:6–7.* How should we respond when God speaks to us through His Word? Let's pray for understanding and joy at the unfolding of God's Word.

Wednesday

Read through the Bible: Nehemiah 9
Family Worship: Nehemiah 8:13–18

What did the fathers study? What did they learn? How did they respond? What have you learned recently from studying God's Word? How have you responded? What should happen as we continue to study God's Word? *Ps. 119:34; 2 Peter 3:18.* Let's pray for growth in grace, knowledge, and joyful obedience as we study God's Word.

Thursday

Read through the Bible: Nehemiah 10
Family Worship: Nehemiah 9:1–3

What were the people continuing to read and study? What did they do in response? *2 Chron. 7:14.* How was their relationship with God deepening? Which of these needs more emphasis to deepen your relationship with God: fasting, separation, confession, Bible study, or worship? Let's pray for the grace to grow deeper in our relationship with God.

Friday

Read through the Bible: Nehemiah 11
Family Worship: Nehemiah 9:38; 10:28–29

What did the people do? What did they promise in this covenant renewal? What sacrament has God given the church for covenant renewal? *1 Cor. 11:23-26.* Who are we to remember in the Lord's Supper? How can we prepare for our covenant renewal? *1 Cor. 11:27-28.* Since we are in covenant with God, how should we live? *Luke 9:23; John 14:15.* Let's pray for hearts ready for covenant renewal and recommitted to follow our Lord.

Saturday

Read through the Bible: Nehemiah 12
Family Worship: Nehemiah 12:27, 43

After the wall and the covenant community were rebuilt, what did the people do? Who "made them rejoice with great joy"? What had God done for them? Who were included in this celebration? What has God done for us? How should we respond? Let's pray that God would give our family a joy that can be seen and heard far away.

Year 2 — Week 25

Sunday

Read through the Bible: Psalm 77
Family Worship: Psalm 77:1–15

What was wrong with the psalmist? Had God "forgotten to be gracious"? Who is "full of grace and truth" (John 1:14)? When the psalmist felt like that, what did he do? What happened when he meditated on God's mighty deeds of old? Have you ever felt like this? What should we do when we doubt God's graciousness? Let's pray that God would continually remind us of His mighty deeds in the Scriptures and in our lives.

Monday

Read through the Bible: Nehemiah 13
Family Worship: Nehemiah 13:1–9

What did the people read? What did they rediscover as they read the law? What did they do about it? What violation of this law did Nehemiah discover when he returned? What did he do about it? *Matt. 21:12.* What does this show us about the need for regular Bible study? Continual reformation? *Compare Neh. 9:2; 10:39.* Spiritual leadership? What can we do to keep reforming? *Josh. 1:8; James 1:22–25.* Let's pray that God would keep us always reading His Word and always reforming.

Tuesday

Read through the Bible: Esther 1
Family Worship: Esther 1:1–5, 8, 10–22.

What did the king reign over? What reigned over the king? *Rev. 17; John 8:34.* How does he show us the need for self-government? Which greater King is a greater husband to His bride? *Eph. 5:25–33.* How can you be more like Christ and less like Ahasuerus? *Mark 10:42–45.* Let's pray for hearts free to serve others (and not enslaved to our passions).

Wednesday

Read through the Bible: Esther 2
Family Worship: Esther 2:1–9, 15–17

Who was Mordecai? Who was Esther? How was she exalted from obscurity to royalty? Who was working by His providence behind the scenes? *1 Sam. 2:7–8.*

How does the plan to provide a new queen contrast with God's plan for marriage? *Mark 10:7–9.* Is God's providence hindered by sin? *BCF 5:4.* How have you seen God's providence in our family? Let's praise God for His providence in Esther's life and in ours—whether we can see it or not.

Thursday

Read through the Bible: Esther 3–4
Family Worship: Esther 3:1–15

Who was Haman? What was his ancestry? *Deut. 25:17-19; 1 Sam. 15:2-3, 32-33.* What was Mordecai's ancestry? *Est. 2:5-6.* How does the conflict between Haman and Mordecai reflect the conflict between Agag and Saul? What did Haman plan to do? Had he succeeded, what would have happened to the lineage of Christ? Whose plans can never be thwarted? What should we do when people are hostile to the church? *1 Peter 4:12-19.* Let's pray for the faith to "entrust [our] souls to a faithful Creator while doing good" (1 Peter 4:19).

Friday

Read through the Bible: Esther 5–6
Family Worship: Esther 4:1–17

What did Haman plan to do? How did Mordecai respond? How did he see God's providence at work? Who had raised Esther to royalty? What dilemma did Esther face? How did she rise to the occasion? Esther learned that with rank comes responsibility. *Luke 12:48.* How can you serve others instead of yourself in the place God has put you? Let's pray for the faith to rise to the occasion to serve others.

Saturday

Read through the Bible: Esther 7–8
Family Worship: Esther 5:1–14

Why had the people been fasting and praying for three days? How did God begin to answer their prayers? Why do you think Esther delayed asking her petition? Whose timing is always perfect? How did Esther show humility? Selflessness? Discretion? How was Haman the opposite of these? What are some ways you can practice the qualities Esther displayed? Let's pray for the grace to be humble, selfless, and discreet.

Year 2 — Week 26

Sunday

Read through the Bible: Psalm 78
Family Worship: Psalm 78:1–8

What has God commanded fathers to teach? What is the goal of this teaching? How can we obey this commandment? *Deut. 6:6-9.* How will your children learn to "set their hope in God"? How will their children? How can you prepare to teach them? Let's pray for the grace to teach God's Word to the yet unborn generations of our family.

Monday

Read through the Bible: Esther 9–10
Family Worship: Esther 6:1–14

How was the timing of these events an example of God's providence? Who said, "Whoever exalts himself will be humbled, and whoever humbles himself will be exalted" (Matt. 23:12)? Who exalted himself and was humbled? Who humbled himself and was exalted? What are some ways you can humble yourself this week? Let's pray for the grace to humble ourselves before we need to be humbled.

Tuesday

Read through the Bible: Song of Songs 1–2
Family Worship: Esther 7:1–10

Whose "ways are justice" (Deut. 32:4)? What did Esther request? How did the king respond? How did Haman? What happened to him? How is this an example of poetic justice? **Prov. 26:27.** How might this proverb be fulfilled when one sibling tries to get another in trouble? How can we help one another out of pits instead of digging them? Let's pray for the grace to help rather than hurt.

Wednesday

Read through the Bible: Song of Songs 3–4
Family Worship: Esther 8:1–17

Who is able to radically reverse situations that seem hopeless? How did God do so in Mordecai's life? Esther's? His people's? Has God ever reversed a situation in your life? *1 Tim. 1:12-16.* Is there a situation in our family, church, or nation that needs to be reversed? Let's come before the King of Kings and ask Him to do what only He can do.

Thursday

Read through the Bible: Song of Songs 5–6
Family Worship: Esther 9:1–6, 16

Who is able to radically reverse situations that seem hopeless? How did God do so for His people? How will God radically reverse the last battle for His church? *Rev. 20:7-10.* What are some enemies the church faces now? *Eph. 6:10-12.* How can we prepare to fight? *Eph. 6:13-18.* Let's go to arms—by praying for the strength to stand firm against the spiritual forces of evil.

Friday

Read through the Bible: Song of Songs 7–8
Family Worship: Esther 9:20–22

Who gave the Jews relief from their enemies? What did Mordecai do in response? How is this like our national holiday of Thanksgiving? What are some things God has done in our family that we can celebrate with "feasting and gladness"? Let's thank and praise God for His work in our family—and on suitable occasions, let's have a feast!

Saturday

Read through the Bible: Job 1
Family Worship: Job 1:1–5

Who blessed Job? What material riches did God give him? *Prov. 10:22.* What spiritual riches? *Eph. 1:7.* What kind of person was Job? What kind of father? How did his children interact? How is this godly family different from many we've seen in Scripture? What can we do so that our family is more like Job's? Let's pray for the riches of grace in a loving, godly family.

Year 2   Week 27

Sunday

Read through the Bible: Psalm 79
Family Worship: Psalm 79:8–9

What did the psalmist ask God to do? On what basis did he ask God to act? How would answering this prayer glorify God? Who glorified God by atoning for our sins? *John 13:31.* How does our salvation glorify God? *Eph. 1:6, 12, 14; 2:7.* How can answering our prayers glorify God? What is something we need God to do for us? Whatever our needs, let's ask God to answer "for the glory of [His] name."

Monday

Read through the Bible: Job 2
Family Worship: Job 1:6–22

Who is sovereign over Satan? *BCF 5:1, 4.* What did God say about Job? How did Satan slander him? *Rev. 12:10.* Was it true? How did Job respond to Satan's attack? How did his response show great faith? How did Job's view of God help him respond in faith? How can Job's point of view help us when facing hardship? *Rom. 8:28.* Let's pray for the faith to worship God when He gives and when He takes away.

Tuesday

Read through the Bible: Job 3
Family Worship: Job 2:1–10

Who is sovereign over all things—including evil? *Isa. 45:7.* What did God say about Job? How did Satan slander him? Was it true? Reflect: Do you typically honor or slander others? Trials either make us bitter or better—how was this true in Job's family? How can you become better rather than bitter in trials? *James 1:2-4; 5:11.* Let's pray for the grace to grow better instead of bitter in trials.

Wednesday

Read through the Bible: Job 4–5
Family Worship: Job 2:11–3:2, 11; 4:1, 7–8; 5:27.

How did Job's continued suffering affect him? What did Eliphaz think the problem was? Is his assertion in 4:7 correct? Who was perfectly innocent—yet suffered? *1 Peter 2:22-23.* Where did Eliphaz get his "wisdom"? How is this human wisdom different from what God had said about Job? *Job 1:8, 22; 2:3, 10.* How can you discern whether someone is giving you human or divine wisdom? *Acts 17:11.* Let's pray for the discernment to evaluate all truth claims against *the* truth: God's Word.

Thursday

Read through the Bible: Job 6–7
Family Worship: Job 6:24–25; 7:11, 17–21

What did Job think of Eliphaz's counsel? Finding no help from this so-called friend, whom did Job turn to? How is his prayer like the "how long?" petitions in the Psalms? What does it show about his faith? Though "friends may fail [us]" who can we always turn to—"even when [our hearts are] breaking"? Let's go to Him now, thanking God for "Jesus! What a Friend for Sinners" *(and singing the hymn by that name).*

Friday

Read through the Bible: Job 8–9
Family Worship: Job 8:1–4, 8–10; 9:1, 32–33

What did Bildad say the problem was? Was it true? What was his standard for truth? *Matt. 15:6, 9.* What did Job say he needed in order to present his case before God? What is an arbiter? Who is the only Arbiter/Mediator between God and man? *1 Tim. 2:5.* How can we present our petitions before God? *John 16:23–24.* Let's do so now in the name of Jesus, praising God for Christ the Mediator.

Saturday

Read through the Bible: Job 10–11
Family Worship: Job 11:1–6

What was Zophar's message to Job? Is his last statement true? Was it helpful? Though heartless and not applicable to Job, is there a grain of truth there? *Ezra 9:13; Ps. 103:10; 2 Cor. 5:21.* How can you be a better friend than Zophar? *Rom. 12:15.* Who is the best Friend for sinners? *John 15:12–13.* Let's thank God for not treating us as our sins deserve, and pray that He would help us be Christlike friends.

Year 2 — Week 28

Sunday

Read through the Bible: Psalm 80
Family Worship: Psalm 80:1–7, 18–19

What did the psalmist ask God to do? Why? What does it mean to restore something? Do you need to be restored from the ravages of sin? What is a shining face like? Make a shining face. What does God's shining face express? *Num. 6:25.* Who experienced God's stern face of judgment so we could know the smile of His grace? Do you need the smile of God's grace? What should we do? Let's pray: "Restore us, O God; let your face shine, that we may be saved!"

Monday

Read through the Bible: Job 12
Family Worship: Job 12:7–10

Who "gives to all mankind life and breath and everything" (Acts 17:25)? Who ultimately caused Job's suffering? *Isa. 41:20.* Why is blaming Satan only partially true and not really helpful? *BCF 5:1–4.* Imagine for a minute a universe where God is not sovereign over all things—could we have faith that "all things work together for good" (Rom. 8:28)? How should we respond to the One who holds our life and breath in His hand? *Rom. 11:33–36.* Let's worship Him!

Tuesday

Read through the Bible: Job 13
Family Worship: Job 13:1–5, 15

How helpful were Job's "friends"? In what sense were they "worthless physicians"? Finding no help from them, to which Physician did he turn? How did Job show great faith in the Great Physician? What do you need the Great Physician to do for you? *Matt. 9:12–13.* Let's go to Him now for the medicine of grace and truth.

Wednesday

Read through the Bible: Job 14
Family Worship: Job 14:13–17

Having received no help from his "friends," to whom did Job turn? What did he ask for? What is the answer to his question in verse 14? *1 Cor. 15:20–23.* How is Job a model for those struggling with doubt? What do we have to build our faith that Job didn't? *Rom. 10:17*. What should we do when tempted to doubt? Let's praise God for His Word and pray He would work through it to strengthen our faith.

Thursday

Read through the Bible: Job 15
Family Worship: Job 15:1–6, 17–20

According to Eliphaz, why was Job suffering? Was he right? What did he say always happens to the wicked? Was he right? *Luke 16:19-25*. What were his truth claims based on? Why are human wisdom and experience insufficient to explain Job's suffering? To explain life in general? What, then, do we need? *2 Tim. 3:16-17*. How should we respond to God for revealing things to us in His Word that we could not otherwise know? Let's thank and praise Him!

Friday

Read through the Bible: Job 16–17
Family Worship: Job 16:1–2, 19–21

What did Job think of his "friends"? Having found no comfort from them, whom did he appeal to? What is a witness? Who is our heavenly Witness? *Rom. 8:34; Heb. 7:25*. Who is our heavenly Comforter? *John 14:16-17 (KJV)*. How can we be better comforters than Job's "friends"? *2 Cor. 1:3-4*. Let's praise God for our heavenly Witness and heavenly Comforter and pray for His grace to be merciful comforters.

Saturday

Read through the Bible: Job 18–19
Family Worship: Job 19:23–27

What did Job wish for his words? Where are his words written? What did he know? Who is Job's—and our—risen Redeemer? How had his faith grown? *Job 14:14*. How can the truth of the resurrection encourage us? *1 Thess. 4:16-18*. How can it help us persevere like Job? *1 Cor. 15:58*. Let's praise God for the resurrection of our Redeemer and pray He would help us live with our own resurrection in sight. *Hymn: "I Know that My Redeemer Lives."*

Year 2 Week 29

Sunday

Read through the Bible: Psalm 81
Family Worship: Psalm 81:8–16

Who commands us to listen to Him? What is the first commandment? *Deut. 5:7.* Did Israel listen to God? What is the connection between listening to God and walking in His ways? How do I know if you are really listening to me? How can you show you're really listening to God? *James 1:22; Matt. 7:24-27.* Let's pray for ears to listen, hearts to submit, and feet to walk in God's ways.

Monday

Read through the Bible: Job 20
Family Worship: Job 20:1–5

What was Zophar's basic message? What was it based on? Whose "understanding" did he need? What had he learned since his last speech? *Job 11:6.* In contrast, how had Job grown in his faith? *Job 19:25-27.* Reflect: How have you grown in your faith this year? How can we keep growing in our faith? *1 Peter 2:2; James 1:22; Prov. 27:17.* Let's pray that God would cause us to "grow in the grace and knowledge of our Lord and Savior Jesus Christ" (2 Peter 3:18).

Tuesday

Read through the Bible: Job 21
Family Worship: Job 21:7–9, 22–26, 34

What did Job think of Zophar's human wisdom? Did Job understand why God often allows the wicked to prosper in this life? *Ps. 73:3.* In spite of his perplexity, whom did he trust? Do you understand all God's ways? *Isa. 55:8-9.* Do we need to understand before we trust Him? *Heb. 11:1.* How can we exercise faith when we have questions? Let's pray for the grace to trust and obey God whether or not we understand.

Wednesday

Read through the Bible: Job 22
Family Worship: Job 22:1, 4–11

According to Eliphaz, why was Job suffering? Did he have any substantiation for his accusations? Were they true? How serious is it to falsely accuse someone? *Ex 20:16.* Reflect: Have you ever accused a sibling of doing something without proof that later turned out false? *Parents: Have you done this to your children?* Who is "the faithful and true witness" (Rev. 3:14)? How can you be more like Christ and not Eliphaz? Let's pray for the integrity to bear true witness.

Thursday

Read through the Bible: Job 23–24
Family Worship: Job 23:1–17

Whom was Job seeking? Where was God? What should we do when we don't "feel" God's presence? How did Job view God's word? How can you treasure God's Word? How did he view God? Though afraid, what did he want to do? How does Job picture a real and reverent relationship with God? How can you be both real and reverent with God? Let's be reverent as we approach God and His Word and bring Him the real issues and concerns of our hearts.

Friday

Read through the Bible: Job 25–26
Family Worship: Job 25:1–6

What is man like compared to God? *Isa. 41:14.* How then "can man be in the right before God"? *Rom. 3:28.* Do you think Bildad and his friends understood justification by faith? Who "was delivered up for our trespasses and raised for our justification" (Rom. 4:25)? How was Abraham made right before God? *Rom. 4:3.* How was Job? *Job. 1:8.* How should we respond to God for His amazing grace to worms such as us? Let's worship Him! *Hymn: "Alas! and Did My Savior Bleed?"*

Saturday

Read through the Bible: Job 27–28
Family Worship: Job 27:1–6

Whose "words are trustworthy and true" (Rev. 22:6)? What did Job refuse to do? What is integrity? How would agreeing with his "friends" compromise his integrity? How can you practice integrity when you see money on the counter and no one is looking? When you did something wrong and are later questioned by your parents? Let's pray for hearts of integrity and lips that speak the truth.

Year 2 — Week 30

Sunday

Read through the Bible: Psalm 82
Family Worship: Psalm 82:1–4

Whose "ways are justice" (Deut. 32:4)? What was God displeased with? What did He command? What would a country be like if there were no justice? What would happen to the weak and needy? How can we practice the principle of helping the weak in our family? How can we work to "give justice to the weak" in society? Let's pray for hearts of compassion to help the weak and work for justice.

Monday

Read through the Bible: Job 29–30
Family Worship: Job 29:1–17

What did Job long for? Who was his true Friend? *James 2:23.* How did his friendship with God affect how he treated others? *Ps. 82:3-4.* Job implies that his friendship with God was past *(Job 30:20-21)*—was it? Do we have friendship with God? *John 15:13-15.* How should our friendship with God affect how we treat each other? *John 15:12.* Let's pray for the grace of friendship with God and one another.

Tuesday

Read through the Bible: Job 31
Family Worship: Job 31:5–8

Why had Job's "friends" said he was suffering? What was Job's final response? How can our hearts go after our eyes? *Matt. 6:21.* What kind of things do our eyes see that would be bad to set the affections of our hearts on? *Discuss Job 31:1 and Matt. 5:27-29 with older boys, and the need for modesty with older girls.* How can we guard our eyes? *2 Cor. 4:18.* Who should we fix our eyes on? *Heb. 12:2.* Let's pray for eyes fixed on Jesus.

Wednesday

Read through the Bible: Job 32
Family Worship: Job 32:1–9

Where did Elihu get wisdom? *Prov. 2:6.* Where do we find wisdom? *Ps. 119:98-100; Col. 2:3.* How did Elihu exercise wisdom (i.e., why did he wait to speak)?

How can you exercise wisdom when adults are having a serious discussion? When you know something that an adult doesn't? Is true wisdom merely knowledge? *Job 28:28.* How can you show true wisdom by your actions? *James 3:13–17.* Let's pray for the grace to "show [our] works in the meekness of wisdom" (James 3:13).

Thursday

Read through the Bible: Job 33
Family Worship: Job 33:1–12

What did Elihu rebuke Job for? *Job 13:24.* Was God his enemy? Who is Job's (and our) best Friend? Job had been careful to guard his eyes *(31:1)*, but what had he failed to guard? *Ps. 39:1; Prov. 13:3.* Why is it important to guard our mouths? *Matt. 12:36–37.* How can you guard your mouth? Let's pray for the grace to guard our mouths.

Friday

Read through the Bible: Job 34
Family Worship: Job 34:1–15

What did Elihu rebuke Job for? Had God been unjust with Job? *Rom. 9:20–21; Matt. 20:15.* Whose "ways are justice" (Deut. 32:4)? Sometimes when tragedy strikes, people say, "That's not fair!" How is this slandering God? If God treated man with strict fairness and no grace, what could He do? *Ps. 130:3–4.* How should we respond when we don't understand the justice of God's ways? Let's thank God for this reminder that He is God and we are not—and praise Him for it.

Saturday

Read through the Bible: Job 35–36:21
Family Worship: Job 36:1–2, 10, 15

Who sometimes uses adversity to open our ears? *Ps. 119:67, 71, 75.* How can affliction or adversity help people better listen to God? How can affliction deliver the afflicted? *BCF 5:5.* What remaining sin did Job's afflictions expose? *Job 35:16; 38:1–2.* How has God used affliction to draw you closer to Him? Let's pray that God would "deliver us from evil" (Matt. 6:13)—but if not, that He would provide the grace to draw closer to Him through it.

Year 2   Week 31

Sunday

Read through the Bible: Psalm 83
Family Worship: Psalm 83:1–4, 13–18

Who is "the Most High over all the earth"? What were God's enemies doing to God's people? What did Asaph ask God to do about it? According to Ps. 83:16–17, what are two different ways God conquers His enemies? Which enemy of the church did Jesus conquer by His grace? *1 Tim. 1:13.* How should we pray about those who persecute God's people? Let's pray that God would conquer His enemies—to the praise of His glorious grace or His glorious justice.

Monday

Read through the Bible: Job 36:22–37:24
Family Worship: Job 37:1–5, 14–24

Who created thunderstorms? Do you understand everything about a thunderstorm? Can you create one? If we can't do these, do you think we can understand everything about the Creator? When we don't understand God's actions, should we teach Him or be taught by Him? What should our attitude be toward Him? **Job 36:22–26.** Let's pray for humble, teachable hearts to fear God rather than question Him.

Tuesday

Read through the Bible: Job 38
Family Worship: Job 38:1–11

Who spoke to Job? Did God answer any of Job's questions? What did He do instead? Did He tell him what He had done or why? Does He have to? What did He rebuke Job for? When you don't know what you're talking about, what should you do? How do we know what we know about God? *Deut. 29:29.* Let's pray for the faith to obey what God has revealed, and quietly trust Him for what He hasn't.

Wednesday

Read through the Bible: Job 39–40:5
Family Worship: Job 39:13–18; 40:1–5

Who created the ostrich? Why would God make a bird that doesn't fly but runs like a horse? Why would He make their mothers cruel? How could a holy and loving God allow evil and suffering? Are these questions of faith or faultfinding? What's the difference? *Compare Ps. 8:4 and Rom. 9:19-20.* How had Job been a faultfinder? How did he respond to God? How do you ask questions: as a humble learner or as a faultfinder? Let's pray for hearts of faith rather than faultfinding.

Thursday

Read through the Bible: Job 40:6–41:34
Family Worship: Job 40:6–8; 41:1–34

Who created Leviathan? What is Leviathan like? Can you stand before a beast like that? If not, can we stand before its Creator? Did God owe Job an explanation for what He did? Does He owe us salvation? When confronted with truths in the Bible that are hard to understand (like the problem of evil or sovereign election), how should we respond? *Rom. 11:33–36.* Let's pray for the grace to worship our glorious Creator—rather than try to judge Him.

Friday

Read through the Bible: Job 42
Family Worship: Job 42:1–17

How did Job respond to God? What did he repent for? Did God reveal the purpose for Job's suffering? What (whom) did He reveal instead (that was even better)? How did God respond to Job? What has Job taught you about how to handle suffering? Let's pray that God would "deliver us from evil" (Matt. 6:13)—but if we "suffer according to God's will," that He would give us the grace to "entrust [our] souls to a faithful Creator while doing good" (1 Peter 4:19).

Saturday

Read through the Bible: Proverbs 1
Family Worship: Proverbs 1:1–7

What is the purpose of Proverbs? In "whom are hidden all the treasures of wisdom and knowledge" (Col. 2:3)? What is the beginning of knowledge? **Job 28:28;** *Ps. 111:10.* How do the wise respond to wisdom and instruction? How do fools? How do you? How can you grow in wisdom? Let's pray for hearts to fear the Lord and cherish knowledge.

Year 2   Week 32

Sunday

Read through the Bible: Psalm 84

Family Worship: Psalm 84:1–4, 10

What did the psalmist long for? Which would he choose: living in tents of wickedness or being a servant in God's house? Why? Who is God's "dwelling place"? *Col. 1:19.* In Christ, who is being "built together into a dwelling place for God" (Eph. 2:22)? Where is your heart longing to be today? Let's pray for hearts which yearn for God's house and shun the tents of wickedness.

Monday

Read through the Bible: Proverbs 2

Family Worship: Proverbs 2:1–6

In "whom are hidden all the treasures of wisdom and knowledge" (Col. 2:3)? Where do we find God's wisdom? How is wisdom like hidden treasure? *Prov. 3:13–15.* How can we "mine" this treasure? *2 Tim. 2:15 (KJV).* Once we find it, what will we understand? What are you doing to seek this treasure? Let's pray for hearts that treasure God's wisdom and diligently seek it.

Tuesday

Read through the Bible: Proverbs 3

Family Worship: Proverbs 3:11–12; Heb. 12:5–11

Whom do fathers discipline? Why do they discipline their children? Who is "the Father of spirits"? Whom does God discipline? What is the goal of His discipline? What would it mean if God didn't discipline us? What does discipline produce in those trained by it? Reflect: How do you typically receive discipline? Let's pray for hearts to humbly receive our Father's loving discipline and share in His holiness.

Wednesday

Read through the Bible: Proverbs 4

Family Worship: Proverbs 4:20–27

What are we to keep within our hearts? *Ps. 119:11.* Why? *Deut. 32:46–47.* What are we to do with our hearts? Why is this important? According to verses 24–27, how do we guard our hearts? *Matt. 12:34–37; Job 31:7; 1 Peter 1:22.* What are some things you need to guard your mouth, eyes, and feet from? What are some positive things you should do with these instead? Let's pray that God would help us guard our hearts.

Thursday

Read through the Bible: Proverbs 5
Family Worship: Proverbs 5:1–14

What are we to pay attention to? *2 Peter 1:19.* What are we to avoid? *For young disciples, use the "forbidden woman" as a symbol of temptation.* Why? How can temptation be both sweet and bitter? How can you avoid temptation? *Prov. 6:28; 2 Tim. 2:22.* What should you do when tempted? *Matt. 4:1–11.* What are the consequences of spurning this wisdom? Let's pray for hearts to flee temptation and humbly receive instruction.

Friday

Read through the Bible: Proverbs 6
Family Worship: Proverbs 6:6–11

Who created ants? What are ants like? *1 Thess. 4:10–12; Col. 3:23–24.* How is the sluggard different? How is the fruit of his life different? What are some specific ways you can be more like the ant? Let's pray for the grace to be diligent and self-governed like the ant.

Saturday

Read through the Bible: Proverbs 7
Family Worship: Proverbs 7:1–3

What should be on our hearts? *Deut. 6:6* From whom do children primarily learn God's words? **Prov. 1:8–9; 6:20–22;** *Deut. 6:7.* What do we need to do with God's words? How can we write them on our hearts (i.e., our affections)? How can we bind them on our fingers (i.e., our actions)? *Deut. 6:8.* Let's pray for affections and actions transformed by God's words.

Year 2   Week 33

Sunday

Read through the Bible: Psalm 85
Family Worship: Psalms 85:1–7

Who alone can give dead sinners spiritual life? *Eph. 2:4–5*. What did the psalmist ask God to do? What does it mean to physically revive someone? What then is spiritual revival? What will God's people do as a result of revival? What do we need to do to experience revival? *2 Chron. 7:14*. Let's humble ourselves, confess our sin, and ask God to "revive us again, that [we] may rejoice in [Him]."

Monday

Read through the Bible: Proverbs 8
Family Worship: Proverbs 8:1–13

Who "became to us wisdom from God" (1 Cor. 1:30)? What does the woman speaking here represent? What does she offer? Which is better: her instruction or precious jewels? Does she ever lie? What does she hate? Reflect: Would she love or hate what you've said lately? How should we respond to wisdom's call? Let's pray for hearts to treasure and lips to speak wisdom from God.

Tuesday

Read through the Bible: Proverbs 9
Family Worship: Proverbs 9:7–10

Who "became to us wisdom from God" (1 Cor. 1:30)? What is a "scoffer"? How does he respond to correction? How does the wise man? Think about the last time you were corrected; which were you more like? What is the beginning of wisdom? How should the fear/knowledge of the Lord affect the way we respond to correction? Let's pray for humble, teachable hearts.

Wednesday

Read through the Bible: Proverbs 10
Family Worship: Proverbs 10:19; 17:27

As a visual aid, have children squeeze toothpaste out of the tube, and then challenge them to put it back in. How are words like this toothpaste? What normally results from talking too much? What does the wise man do instead? Have you ever said something you later regretted? What do you wish you had done instead? How can you be more prudent with your lips? Who was silent when falsely accused? *Isa. 53:7*. Let's pray for the grace to "be quick to hear, slow to speak" (James 1:19).

Thursday

Read through the Bible: Proverbs 11
Family Worship: Proverbs 11:12

What does it mean to "belittle" someone? What is a person like who belittles his neighbor? What does a wise man do instead? **Eph. 4:29**. Reflect: Have your words this week belittled or built up others? Finish this sentence: If you don't have something nice to say . . . *don't say anything at all*. Let's pray for the grace to say words that build up rather than belittle.

Friday

Read through the Bible: Proverbs 12
Family Worship: Proverbs 11:22; 12:4

What does a gold ring make you think of? What if it was in a pig's snout? How does this picture a woman without discretion? Daughters: How can you prepare to be the crown of your future husband? Sons: What kind of characteristics should you look for in a future wife? In whose sight is a woman's gentle and quiet spirit very precious? *1 Peter 3:4*. Let's pray that God would give our daughters and future daughters-in-law the beauty of discretion.

Saturday

Read through the Bible: Proverbs 13
Family Worship: Proverbs 13:13; 16:20; 19:16

What does it mean to despise something? How do some people despise God's Word? What do they end up doing to themselves? What does it mean to revere something? What are we to revere? What will happen to those who do? How can you revere God's Word? What have you learned this week in Proverbs? Have you been obeying what you've learned? Let's praise God for His Word and pray for hearts to revere and obey it.

Year 2 — Week 34

Sunday

Read through the Bible: Psalm 86
Family Worship: Psalm 86:8–13

Whom shall all nations come and worship? *Rev. 15:4.* What does it mean to be "halfhearted" about something? What would halfhearted worship be like? What did David ask God to do for his heart? *Jer. 32:39–40.* What are some things that could distract you from wholehearted worship today? How can we prepare for wholehearted worship? Let's ask God to unite our hearts to fear His name.

Monday

Read through the Bible: Proverbs 14
Family Worship: Proverbs 14:17, 29; 15:18; 16:32

What is the fruit of a quick temper? What are we to be instead? **James 1:19–20.** Is anger always sinful? *Eph. 4:26.* Who was angry yet never sinned? *Mark 10:14.* What typically makes you angry? What does your anger accomplish? How can you rule your spirit in those situations? Let's pray that God would help us be "slow to anger."

Tuesday

Read through the Bible: Proverbs 15
Family Worship: Proverbs 15:5, 20; 10:1; 17:25

What does a wise son bring his father? What does a foolish son bring his mother? How might a foolish child dishonor his parents when being corrected? When with friends away from home? How would a wise son act differently in those situations? Reflect: Which one are you? Who always honors His Father? *John 8:49.* How can you honor your parents this week? Let's pray for the grace to honor your father and mother.

Wednesday

Read through the Bible: Proverbs 16
Family Worship: Proverbs 16:1, 3–4, 9, 33

Who is sovereign over every detail? *Matt. 10:29–30.* Does this mean we should just sit back and do nothing? *BCF 5:2.* How should we make plans for the future? *James 4:13–15; Prov. 3:5–6.* Has there ever been a time when you made plans that God changed? Whose way was better? Let's pray for the wisdom to commit all our work and plans to God in obedience and for the faith to trust Him for the results.

Thursday

Read through the Bible: Proverbs 17
Family Worship: Proverbs 17:1; 15:17

If you could have anything money could buy, what would you want? If it caused fighting and hatred in our home, would it be worth it? Why not? Is the problem with things or with our hearts? Who "richly provides us with everything to enjoy" (1 Tim. 6:17)? What can you do to make our home more peaceful, quiet, and loving? Let's pray for hearts to value our relationships with each other more than things.

Friday

Read through the Bible: Proverbs 18
Family Worship: Proverbs 18:17

Whose word is truth? *John 17:17.* One sibling came to tattle on another, but when the second one came, the story changed—does this ever happen in our home? Why? How can we keep it from happening? *Ex. 20:16.* What should you do when you are third party to a dispute? Let's pray for hearts to love the truth, the whole truth, and nothing but the truth.

Saturday

Read through the Bible: Proverbs 19
Family Worship: Proverbs 19:18; 13:24; 22:15; 23:13–14

Who "disciplines the one he loves" (Heb. 12:6)? What would a child be like who was never disciplined? Why? What would be the ultimate consequences? What has God commanded parents to do to prevent this? A toddler was about to put his finger into an electrical outlet and refused to stop—what would be the loving thing to do? What if an older child smarts off to his parent? Let's pray that God would work through loving discipline to drive the foolishness out of our hearts.

Year 2 — Week 35

Sunday

Read through the Bible: Psalm 87
Family Worship: Psalm 87:1–6

Where were you born? What city of Israel was it a great privilege to be born in? Why? Where is the city of God today? *Heb. 12:22; Rev. 3:12*. Who has been born there? *Gal. 4:26*. Who causes us to be born from above? *John 3:3*. How should we respond to God for giving us heavenly birth? Let's praise God that, though to earthly Zion we are strangers, of heavenly Jerusalem it may be said, "This one was born there." *Hymn: "Glorious Things of Thee Are Spoken."*

Monday

Read through the Bible: Proverbs 20
Family Worship: Proverbs 20:29; 16:31

Is gray hair a curse or a crown? Why? Who was revealed to John with hair "white . . . like snow" (Rev. 1:14)? What did God command us to do for those with gray hair? **Lev. 19:32.** Do you think this happens very often in our day? Why not? What is valued in our culture above the wisdom of maturity? How can you honor the gray head this week? Let's pray for the grace to honor God by honoring our elders.

Tuesday

Read through the Bible: Proverbs 21
Family Worship: Proverbs 21:22; 2 Cor. 10:3–6

What kind of false strongholds do people trust in? What are we to do with strongholds? What kind of weapons has God given us to destroy them? Whom must all our thoughts obey? How can you become equipped to bring down these strongholds? *Deut. 6:4–9; Matt. 22:37*. Let's pray that God would make our family a training ground for wise men and women who would bring down the strongholds of the mighty.

Wednesday

Read through the Bible: Proverbs 22
Family Worship: Proverbs 22:29

What kind of man will be honored? What are some ways a skillful man might be honored today? A skillful woman? *Prov. 31:28–31*. Does God care about the quality of your work? *Ex. 31:1-6; Prov. 31:10-27.* Who gives able men ability? What work can you be skillful in? What do you need to work at to be more skillful? Let's pray for the grace to honor God through skillful work.

Thursday

Read through the Bible: Proverbs 23
Family Worship: Proverbs 23:29–35; 20:1; 9:1–6

Who turned water into wine? *John 2:1-11; Ps. 104:14-15.* Is wine good or bad? *Isa. 25:6; Mark 14:23-24.* When does drinking alcohol become sinful? *Eph. 5:18.* What are the dangers of alcohol, if abused? What are some of God's other gifts that are abused? How can we enjoy God's gift of alcohol without abusing it? Let's thank God for all His gifts and pray He would help us enjoy them in moderation.

Friday

Read through the Bible: Proverbs 24
Family Worship: Proverbs 24:27

Where do we find God's wisdom for faith and life? What should a man do first: get married or get established in his career? Why? Sons: What could happen to your career plans if you got married too soon? Daughters: Would it be wise to marry a man that was still in college? Why not? Let's pray that God would enable our sons and future sons-in-law to prepare their "fields" before building their household.

Saturday

Read through the Bible: Proverbs 25
Family Worship: Proverbs 25:21–22; Rom. 12:20–21

Who said, "Love your enemies" (Matt. 5:44)? *Rom. 5:10.* How can we love an enemy who is hungry? What will this do? How would you feel if you were mean to someone and he was kind in return? How would this be like having "burning coals" heaped on your head? How should you treat a sibling who does something mean to you? Let's pray for the grace to love our enemies and "overcome evil with good."

Year 2 — Week 36

Sunday

Read through the Bible: Psalm 88
Family Worship: Psalm 88:1–7, 13–18

Who faced God's wrath on the cross and was forsaken by His friends? What was troubling the psalmist? What did he do about it? Did he get a quick and easy answer? Have you ever doubted God's love? *Rom. 8:35.* Or your salvation? *BCF 18:4.* What should we do with feelings like that? What if it seems God isn't answering? Let's pray for the grace to keep trusting and seeking God no matter our feelings.

Monday

Read through the Bible: Proverbs 26
Family Worship: Proverbs 26:13–16

Who set the example of working for six days and resting on the seventh? What is a sluggard like? What kind of excuses have you heard people make to get out of work? Have you used any of these? What does a sluggard deserve to eat? *2 Thess. 3:10.* What should you be like instead? **1 Thess. 4:10–12.** How can you be a hard worker this week? Let's pray for hearts and hands joyful to do the work God has called us to.

Tuesday

Read through the Bible: Proverbs 27
Family Worship: Proverbs 27:17

Preparation: a knife and sharpening stone. What is a dull knife good for? How do you make a knife useful? How do you sharpen a knife? *Demonstrate.* How does this picture the effect of one godly man on another? Who is sharpening you? What is the sharpening stone of truth? *2 Tim. 3:16–17.* How can we sharpen one another? *Heb. 10:24–25.* Let's pray that God would sharpen us through our family and church so that we would be useful tools in His hand.

Wednesday

Read through the Bible: Proverbs 28
Family Worship: Proverbs 28:13

Do you like to play hide-and-go-seek? Have you ever hidden yourself so well that you couldn't be found? Can we hide our sins? What will happen if we try?

What should we do instead? What will happen then? **1 John 1:9.** Who died for our sins so that God would be just to forgive us? *Rom. 3:25-26.* Reflect: Have you tried to hide any sins from God? Let's confess and forsake our sins and praise God for being faithful and just to forgive us.

Thursday

Read through the Bible: Proverbs 29
Family Worship: Proverbs 29:18

Where do we find "prophetic vision"? *2 Peter 1:19; 3:2.* What would our country be like if we had no laws? What are people like without God's law/prophetic vision? *Ex. 32:25.* What are children like without their parents' rules and discipline? **Prov. 29:15.** Since we have the gift of God's law, what do we need to do with it? Let's praise God for His prophetic Word and pray He would help us keep it.

Friday

Read through the Bible: Proverbs 30
Family Worship: Proverbs 30:4–5

[Ask the questions in 30:4]. Which of these can you answer without the Bible? *Rom. 1:20.* We can know there is a Creator, but what do we need in order to know Him? What can we trust to tell us the truth about God and His world? How should we respond to God for giving us His inspired Word, which reveals the Incarnate Word? Let's praise Him!

Saturday

Read through the Bible: Proverbs 31
Family Worship: Proverbs 31:10–31

The "excellent wife" is a gift from whom? *Prov. 19:14.* What is she like? How does her wise and industrious home management benefit her family? How do they show their gratitude to her? How can you show appreciation for your mother? Girls: How can you prepare to be an excellent wife? Boys: What are the potential consequences of marrying a girl who is pretty but is ungodly and a poor home manager? Let's praise God for your mother and pray He would make our daughters and daughters-in-law excellent wives like her.

Year 2 — Week 37

Sunday

Read through the Bible: Psalm 89
Family Worship: Psalm 89:1–4, 20–37

How did God show His steadfast love to David? His faithfulness? In whom did God gloriously fulfill His covenant promises to David? *Col. 1:15–19.* How has God shown His steadfast love and faithfulness to us? *Col. 1:13–14.* How should we respond to Him? Let's "sing of the steadfast love of the LORD" and "make known [His] faithfulness."

Monday

Read through the Bible: Ecclesiastes 1
Family Worship: Ecclesiastes 1:1–3, 8–9, 12–14

Who is "the Preacher"? What repeated phrase clues us in that he is reasoning from a man-centered position in this passage? What would life be like if there was nothing more than what was "under the sun"? Instead of focusing "under the sun," what are we to set our minds on? **Col. 3:1–4.** Who is above the sun? Reflect: What is your mind set on? How does what you focus on affect your attitude? Let's pray for minds to "seek the things that are above, where Christ is."

Tuesday

Read through the Bible: Ecclesiastes 2
Family Worship: Ecclesiastes 2:1–11, 24–26

What did Solomon do to try to find happiness and meaning in life under the sun? Did it work? Why not? In whom did he find true meaning and enjoyment? *1 Tim. 6:17.* If you had everything money could buy, would it make you happy? *Eccl. 5:10; 1 Tim. 6:9–10.* How can we find true enjoyment and meaning in life? *1 Cor. 10:31; 15:58.* Let's pray for hearts to glorify God and enjoy Him in all of life.

Wednesday

Read through the Bible: Ecclesiastes 3
Family Worship: Ecclesiastes 3:1–13

Who created time? Who "has made everything beautiful in its time"? Who has our times in His hand? *Ps. 31:15.* Is it always the proper time to laugh? Cry?

Play? Work? What is wrong with this statement: "I'll finally enjoy life when ___"? What is something you need to spend more time on? What is something you need to spend less time on? Let's pray for the grace to glorify and enjoy God with the gift of time.

Thursday

Read through the Bible: Ecclesiastes 4
Family Worship: Ecclesiastes 4:7–12

What would it be like to be all alone with no family or friends? Who said, "It is not good that the man should be alone" (Gen. 2:18)? Why is it not? Which is stronger: a cord with two strings or three? How is this a picture of Christian marriage? Who is the third cord? Do you typically lift others up or cut them down? How can you lift up another in our family? Our church? Let's thank God for the gift of our family and pray He would help us lift one another up.

Friday

Read through the Bible: Ecclesiastes 5
Family Worship: Ecclesiastes 5:1–3, 7

Whom must we fear? *Matt. 10:28.* When we draw near to God, which is more important: listening or speaking? Why? *Isa. 55:8–9; Matt. 6:7–8.* How does God speak to us today? *Isa. 55:11.* Are you listening? How can you show proper reverence for God in family worship? In church? Let's pray for reverent hearts, attentive ears, and prudent lips—at all times—but especially when approaching God.

Saturday

Read through the Bible: Ecclesiastes 6
Family Worship: Ecclesiastes 5:18–6:2

Do money and possessions automatically bring happiness? Who gives us the power to make wealth? *Deut. 8:18.* Who gives us the power to enjoy wealth? *1 Tim. 6:17.* Is it necessary to have lots of money and possessions to be happy? *Phil. 4:11–13.* What gifts has God given you? Are you enjoying them or wishing for more? Let's praise God for the gifts He's given us and pray for contented hearts to enjoy them.

Year 2 — Week 38

Sunday

Read through the Bible: Psalm 90
Family Worship: Psalm 90:1–4, 10–14

Who "alone has immortality" (1 Tim. 6:16)? How old is God? What is one thousand years like to Him? Regarding time, how are we different from Him? In light of our mortality, how should we live? **Eph. 5:15–16.** How can you make "the best use of the time"? *1 Cor. 10:31; 15:58; Eccl. 3:1–13.* Let's pray for hearts of wisdom to use every day to glorify and enjoy God forever. *Hymn: "Our God, Our Help in Ages Past."*

Monday

Read through the Bible: Ecclesiastes 7
Family Worship: Ecclesiastes 7:1a; Proverbs 22:1

For 7:1b, compare Phil. 1:21. Why don't most people name their daughters *Jezebel* or their sons *Judas*? What would happen to our family name if I had a reputation as a liar? How can we honor our family name? How can we honor the name *Christian*? *1 Peter 4:16.* Whose name are we to hallow? *Matt. 6:9.* Let's pray for the grace to honor our family name and glorify our Savior's name.

Tuesday

Read through the Bible: Ecclesiastes 8
Family Worship: Ecclesiastes 8:10–13

Whom are we to fear? Why? *Matt. 10:28; Heb. 10:26–31.* Does God immediately punish all evil? Why not? *Rom. 2:4; 2 Peter 3:9.* What effect does the delay of final justice have on the wicked? *Rom. 2:5.* How should we respond to God in light of His patience toward us? Let's praise Him and pray His patience would lead us to repentance and holy fear.

Wednesday

Read through the Bible: Ecclesiastes 9
Family Worship: Ecclesiastes 9:7–10

How would you feel if you gave someone a gift and he tossed it aside and never used it? What if instead he took it joyfully and constantly used it? Who gave us the gift of life? *John 10:10.* What should we do with the gift of life? The gift of work? *Col. 3:23–24.* The gift of family? When can we enjoy these gifts?

Eccl. 9:6; 12:1, 7. Let's praise God for the gifts of life, work, and family and pray for a healthy zest to enjoy them with all our might.

Thursday

Read through the Bible: Ecclesiastes 10
Family Worship: Ecclesiastes 10:10

Where do we find God's wisdom for faith and life? Who will be able to chop more wood: one who takes time to sharpen his ax or one who just starts chopping? Who will be a better provider for his family: one who prepares himself with proper education and skills or one who just starts working? Boys: How can you prepare to be good providers? Girls: How can you prepare to be wise home managers? How can we prepare to be disciples who make an impact? Let's pray for the wisdom to sharpen our skills for success.

Friday

Read through the Bible: Ecclesiastes 11
Family Worship: Ecclesiastes 11:9

What should we do in our youth? Who "will bring every deed into judgment" (Eccl. 12:14)? How can remembering judgment day help us enjoy our youth responsibly? What are some things some people squander their youth on (that they will be judged for)? How can you instead enjoy youth in a way that honors God? Let's pray for the grace to glorify and enjoy God in the days of our youth—and forever.

Saturday

Read through the Bible: Ecclesiastes 12
Family Worship: Ecclesiastes 12:1, 13–14

Who is our Creator? What is the most important thing to do in our youth? Why? *Eccl. 12:2-7*. What's wrong with this statement: "I'm going to have fun now; I'll serve God when I get older"? What is the conclusion of all we've learned in Ecclesiastes: How do we find true meaning in life? What do you need to do to experience the fullness of life as God designed? Let's pray for the grace to glorify and enjoy God in the days of our youth—and forever.

Year 2 — Week 39

Sunday

Read through the Bible: Psalm 91
Family Worship: Psalm 91:1–8

Under whose wings do we find refuge? How is a mother bird a picture God's protection of His people? *Deut. 32:11*. Does God promise to protect us from all physical harm? *Matt. 10:28*. What do baby birds need to do to be protected? How are we protected from the doom and penalty of sin? What happens to those who refuse the Savior's protection? *Matt. 23:37–39*. Let's confess our need—and flee by faith for protection under the wings of Christ.

Monday

Read through the Bible: Isaiah 1
Family Worship: Isaiah 1:11–18

What did God think of Israel's worship? Why? What did He tell them to do? How is washing a picture of repentance? In addition to cleansing from sin, what does true repentance include? *Matt. 22:39*. What do you need to do to make your worship acceptable to God? Whose blood can make us "white as snow"? *1 John 1:7*. Let's confess our sin and be washed by the blood of Jesus. *Hymn: "Nothing but the Blood."*

Tuesday

Read through the Bible: Isaiah 2
Family Worship: Isaiah 2:1–3

What did Isaiah say would happen in the latter days? What would the nations come to Jerusalem to hear? Note their eagerness—how eager are you to be taught God's Word? How was this prophecy initially fulfilled at Pentecost? *Luke 24:47*. What "mountain" do people from many nations come to for worship today? *Heb. 12:22*. Having heard His Word, what are we responsible to do? Let's praise God for teaching us His ways and pray He would empower us to "walk in His paths."

Wednesday

Read through the Bible: Isaiah 3–4
Family Worship: Isaiah 3:5, 8

Whose presence is glorious? How did Judah defy God's glorious presence?

How did they treat one another? Think about how you've been treating others in our family; do your words and deeds honor or dishonor God? How can we honor God's glorious presence in our home? Let's pray for the grace to honor God with our speech and deeds.

Thursday

Read through the Bible: Isaiah 5
Family Worship: Isaiah 5:1–7

Who is the vineyard owner? Who is the vineyard? What kind of "grapes" did God look for? What did He find? What do the different grapes picture? What would God do to His vineyard? *Mark 12:1–9.* Who is the true vine? *John 15:1.* How can we produce grapes that are pleasing to God? *John 15:5.* Let's pray for the grace to abide in the true vine and to bear grapes pleasing to God.

Friday

Read through the Bible: Isaiah 6
Family Worship: Isaiah 6:1–7

Whom did Isaiah see? *John 12:41.* What was He like? After seeing Jesus in His glory, how did Isaiah see himself? What did an angel do to him? Why? Having seen a glimpse of God's glory in His Word, how should we view ourselves? How should we respond to our glorious God? Let's pray for eyes to see Jesus as He is—"high and lifted up"—and lips to humbly confess our sin and worship Him.

Saturday

Read through the Bible: Isaiah 7
Family Worship: Isaiah 7:14

Who is the virgin mother Isaiah spoke of? Who is "Immanuel"? **Matt. 1:18–23.** What does the name *Immanuel* mean? How is Jesus "God with us"? Some people think God is far off and not involved in people's lives—what does *Immanuel* teach us about this? How should we respond to our glorious God who became "God with us"? Let's worship Him! *Hymn: "O Come, O Come, Emmanuel."*

Year 2 — Week 40

Sunday

Read through the Bible: Psalm 92

Family Worship: Psalm 92:5–9, 12–15

Whose works are great? How are the wicked like grass? How are the righteous like a tree? How long does a true believer continue to bear fruit? Who receives the glory for this? Last Thursday we discussed bearing pleasing fruit—how has the fruit of your life been since then? Let's pray that God would make us like palm trees in His house, bearing fruit through all of life to His glory.

Monday

Read through the Bible: Isaiah 8

Family Worship: Isaiah 8:13; 1 Peter 3:14–16

Whom are we to fear and honor as holy in our hearts? Whom are we not to fear? What must we always be prepared to do? *Jude 3*. In what manner should we present a defense of our faith? What if people make fun of us or threaten us? Christian: What do you believe? How can you become better prepared to defend the faith? Let's pray for hearts to cherish and fear Christ and for minds prepared to explain why.

Tuesday

Read through the Bible: Isaiah 9

Family Worship: Isaiah 9:1–2, 6–7

Who is the Son born to us? *Matt. 4:13–16*. Is He God or man? *John 1:1, 14; Rom. 9:5; 1 Tim. 2:5; BCF 8:2*. What titles does He have? What do they tell us about Him? How is He our "Wonderful Counselor"? *Isaiah 28:29*. "Mighty God"? *John 1:18*. "Everlasting Father"? *1 Cor. 15:45–49*. "Prince of Peace"? *Eph. 2:14*. How should we respond to God for giving us His divine Son? Let's praise Him!

Wednesday

Read through the Bible: Isaiah 10

Family Worship: Isaiah 10:21–22

Who has chosen people for salvation from every nation? *Rev. 5:9*. How many Israelites were there? How many would be saved? **Rom. 9:27–28**. What is a "remnant"? How is the church a remnant? Should the remnant be proud of their place? Why not? **Rom. 11:5–6.** How should we respond instead? *Rom. 11:20, 33–36.* Let's humbly worship God for including us in His remnant.

Thursday

Read through the Bible: Isaiah 11
Family Worship: Isaiah 11:1–10

Who is the "root of Jesse"? What is He like? What is His delight? Reflect: What is your delight? What is His kingdom like? What aspects of His kingdom are being fulfilled *already*? **Rom. 15:12.** What aspects are *not yet*—that is, will be fulfilled at Christ's return? How should we live in anticipation of the final fulfillment? Let's ask our King for hearts to delight in the fear of the Lord and pray as He taught us: "Your kingdom come . . ." (Matt. 6:10).

Friday

Read through the Bible: Isaiah 12–13
Family Worship: Isaiah 12:1–6

How will God's people respond when He brings about the kingdom described in chapter 11? *Ex. 15:1–2.* Who gives us living water from the wells of salvation? *John 4:13–14.* Since Christ has opened the wells of salvation and begun the kingdom age, how should we live? Which is there more of in our home: complaining or singing? Shouting for joy or anger? Let's drink, shout, and sing for joy to our glorious Savior!

Saturday

Read through the Bible: Isaiah 14
Family Worship: Isaiah 14:12–15

Who tried to exalt himself and be like God? Was he able to? *Luke 10:18; John 12:31; Rev. 12:9.* What will ultimately happen to Satan? *Rev. 20:10.* What attitude is reflected in his words, "I will"? In contrast, who said to God, "Not as I will, but as you will" (Matt. 26:39)? How is Jesus different from Satan? *Phil. 2:5–11.* Whose words and attitude are more like yours? Let's confess our prideful defiance and pray as Jesus taught us: "Thy will be done" (Matt. 6:10).

Year 2 — Week 41

Sunday

Read through the Bible: Psalm 93
Family Worship: Psalm 93:1–5

Who reigns over the universe? Who is mightier than floods or storms—or anything? *Mark 4:37-41.* What kind of floods and storms do we have to go through in life? *BCF 17:1.2.* Are you going through one now? What do we need to remember during those times? *John 16:33.* Let's praise God that He is on the throne and pray He would remind us of that whenever we get caught in the storms and floods of life.

Monday

Read through the Bible: Isaiah 15–16
Family Worship: Isaiah 16:3–5

Who rules with steadfast love and righteousness on the throne in David's tent? *Acts 15:16-18.* Where do the outcasts of Moab find shelter from the destroyer? Where do we find shelter from the would-be destroyer of souls? Whom can we pray for who needs to find shelter in Christ? Let's pray that God would draw them to find shelter in Christ.

Tuesday

Read through the Bible: Isaiah 17–18
Family Worship: Isaiah 17:4–6

How many olives would be left on the tree after the harvest? How did this picture the coming judgment? *Rev. 14:14-20.* How is it like the road to salvation? **Matt. 7:13-14.** Who is the gate/door to life? *John 10:9.* In what sense is it "narrow" and "hard"? *John 14:6.* Where does the other road lead? In what sense is it "wide" and "easy"? How many are on each road? Which one are you on? Let's pray for hearts that flee the broad road and run to the narrow gate of Christ.

Wednesday

Read through the Bible: Isaiah 19
Family Worship: Isaiah 19:1, 21–25

Who will ride on the clouds and return in glory? *Rev. 1:7.* What would God do to Egypt? In what sense would He strike and heal them? *Ezek. 36:26-27, 31.* What would be the result? *Rom. 9:25.* Reflect: Are you struck with the knowledge of your sin? *Matt. 9:12-13*. How can you be healed? What does God graciously call us? Let's worship the Great Physician for striking, healing, and making us His People.

Thursday

Read through the Bible: Isaiah 20–21
Family Worship: Isaiah 21:9

Who is the living and true God? What did Babylon do to Judah? *2 Chron. 36*. What would God do to Babylon? How is the sinful world like Babylon? *1 Peter 5:13; Rev. 17–18*. What is God going to do to this Babylon? **Rev. 18:1-2, 4.** A remnant of Israel physically left Babylon *(Ezra 1)*—in what sense must we leave spiritual Babylon? *John 17:14-15*. Reflect: What is a specific aspect of "Babylon" you need to flee? Let's pray for eyes to see Babylon as she really is and hearts to flee her.

Friday

Read through the Bible: Isaiah 22
Family Worship: Isaiah 22:20–22

What do we use keys for? What key did God promise Eliakim? What "door" could he open? *Access to the Davidic king.* Who has the key of David now? **Rev. 3:7.** What door did Jesus open for His people? *John 10:9*. Can anyone else open or shut the door to eternal life? *John 14:6*. Have you gone through the door to salvation? How should we respond to Him who gives us open access to God? *Rom. 5:2*. Let's rejoice and worship our King!

Saturday

Read through the Bible: Isaiah 23
Family Worship: Isaiah 23:1, 8–9

What would happen to Tyre? Who purposed it? Why? What happens to everyone who exalts himself? *Matt. 23:12; James 4:6*. What should we do instead? *1 Peter 5:5-6*. Reflect: When are you most tempted to exalt yourself in "pompous pride"? How can you humble yourself during those times? Let's pray for the grace to humble ourselves (before we need to be humbled).

Year 2 — Week 42

Sunday

Read through the Bible: Psalm 94

Family Worship: Psalm 94:1–11, 22–23

Who is "the Judge of all the earth" (Gen. 18:25)? What is vengeance? *Note the word "repay" in Psalm 94:2.* In what sense is the Lord a "God of vengeance"? Does He repay the wicked what they deserve immediately? Does He repay us what we deserve? Should we try to avenge ourselves when we experience injustice? **Rom. 12:19.** What should we do instead? *Rom. 12:20–21; 13:3–4.* Let's run to our stronghold and pray He would "deliver us from evil" (Matt. 6:13). *Hymn: "God of Vengeance, O Jehovah."*

Monday

Read through the Bible: Isaiah 24

Family Worship: Isaiah 24:1–6, 13–16a

Who is "the Judge of all the earth" (Gen. 18:25)? What will the Lord do to all the earth? Why? Who will be left after the judgment? In what sense are they "few"? In what sense are they also many? *Mark 10:45; Rev. 7:9.* What will they do? Why? Where will they come from? *Matt. 8:11; 24:31.* What do we deserve for our sin? Knowing what we've been saved from, how should we respond to God? Let's worship Him with "songs of praise." *Hymn: "Amazing Grace."*

Tuesday

Read through the Bible: Isaiah 25

Family Worship: Isaiah 25:6–8

What will heaven be like? *Rev. 19:6–9.* Who will be there? *Matt. 8:11.* What will be there? What will never be there? **1 Cor. 15:54.** Who "will wipe away tears from all faces"? *Rev. 21:4.* What does the picture of a rich feast show us about our relationship with God? *1 John 1:3.* How can we prepare for the feast God is preparing for us? Let's pray for hearts hungry and thirsty for God.

Wednesday

Read through the Bible: Isaiah 26

Family Worship: Isaiah 26:8–9

How can you tell what a person is passionate about? What is the world passionate about? What or whom was Isaiah passionate about? How can you tell? What would others say you are passionate about? How can we fuel greater passion for God? What aspect of your devotional life needs more earnest effort? Let's pray for hearts passionate for God.

Thursday

Read through the Bible: Isaiah 27
Family Worship: Isaiah 27:13

What did Isaiah prophesy would happen when a trumpet sounded? Who will return for His people when a trumpet sounds? **Matt. 24:30-31; 1 Cor. 15:51-53;** *1 Thess. 4:16-17.* How are we like those lost in Assyria or Egypt? *1 Peter 1:1; Phil. 3:20.* How might our lives change if we thought of ourselves as "elect exiles" in a foreign land, waiting for our King to rescue us at His trumpet call? *Col. 3:1-4.* Let's pray for minds set on things above as we live with the end in sight.

Friday

Read through the Bible: Isaiah 28
Family Worship: Isaiah 28:16; 8:14

What is the purpose and importance of a cornerstone to a foundation? Who is the cornerstone of God's house? **1 Peter 2:4-8.** How is Jesus like a cornerstone? *Eph. 2:19-21.* How is He also like a stumbling stone? *Luke 20:17-18; Rom. 9:32-33.* How can we ensure that, to us, He is a cornerstone and not a stumbling stone? Let's pray for the grace to be "living stones" whose belief is evident by obedience to the Word.

Saturday

Read through the Bible: Isaiah 29
Family Worship: Isaiah 29:16; 45:9

Who is the Potter? Who is the clay? How is God like a potter? How are we like clay? Imagine making something out of clay that talks back and tries to correct you! What would you say to that clay? **Rom. 9:20-21.** How can we be like this with God? What should we be like instead? As God forms us for His glory, let's pray that He would help us remember that He is God and we are not.

Year 2   Week 43

Sunday

Read through the Bible: Psalm 95
Family Worship: Psalm 95:1–6

Who is the "great God"? How is He greater than false gods? Who is the "great King"? How is He greater than all other kings? *Rev. 19:16.* Who is "the rock of our salvation"? Who is "our Maker"? What should we bring when we come into the presence of our great God/King/Savior/Maker? What would you like to thank God for today? Let's go to Him now with thanksgiving and joyful praise!

Monday

Read through the Bible: Isaiah 30
Family Worship: Isaiah 30:8–11, 15, 18

What kind of "children" were the people of Israel? What were they unwilling to do? In what could they be saved? Who exalts Himself to show mercy to us? How did God exalt Himself in both grace and justice at the cross? *Rom. 3:23–26.* How do you typically respond to instruction? How should we respond to "the instruction of the LORD"? Let's pray for hearts willing to listen, trust, and obey the instruction of the Lord. *Hymn: "Trust and Obey."*

Tuesday

Read through the Bible: Isaiah 31–32
Family Worship: Isaiah 30:1–2; 31:1–3

Who "does not call back his words"? When Judah was threatened by Assyria, in whom did they trust? Why? Did God tell them to do that? Would Egypt be able to save them? What should they have done instead? **Ps. 20:7.** What do people trust in today instead of God? What should we do when facing difficulties in our lives? Are you facing a trial right now? How can we pray for you? Let's pray for hearts that "trust in the name of the LORD our God."

Wednesday

Read through the Bible: Isaiah 33
Family Worship: Isaiah 33:5–6

Who is our "salvation, wisdom, and knowledge"? *1 Cor. 1:30.* What is "Zion's treasure"? What makes something a treasure? How is the fear of the Lord a treasure? What riches does the fear of the Lord bring? *Ps. 31:19.* How can you tell what a person's treasure is? *Matt. 6:21; 13:44.* What do worldly people treasure? What would others say your treasure is? Let's pray for hearts which find their treasure in knowing and fearing the Lord.

Thursday

Read through the Bible: Isaiah 34–35
Family Worship: Isaiah 35:10

Who gave "his life as a ransom for many" (Mark 10:45)? What is a ransom? In what sense would those taken captive to Babylon be ransomed? What would they do? Was this promise completely fulfilled in Judah's return from Babylon? *Ezra 3:10-13.* How will it be completely fulfilled? *Rev. 5:9-10.* In what sense have we been ransomed? What should the ransomed do while en route to heavenly Zion? **Col. 3:16.** Let's praise our Redeemer with thankful and joyful singing!

Friday

Read through the Bible: Isaiah 36
Family Worship: Isaiah 36:1–2, 13–20

What did the king of Assyria say about the Lord? What had the Lord said about Assyria? **Isa. 30:31; 31:8.** Whose word should the people listen to? Whose word came true? **Isa. 37:36-38.** What should you do if someone tells you something different from God's Word? Let's pray for hearts to trust the word of the Lord over the word of man.

Saturday

Read through the Bible: Isaiah 37
Family Worship: Isaiah 37:26a; 25:1

Who planned everything that will ever happen? *BCF 3:1.* When did He make these plans? *Eph. 1:4.* Who ensures that what He has planned comes to pass? Do we always understand God's plans? Are they good or bad plans? How can knowing that God has planned all things help you face trials? Let's praise God for planning all things for His glory and our good. *BCF 5:5.16.*

Year 2 — Week 44

Sunday

Read through the Bible: Psalm 96
Family Worship: Psalm 96:1–9

Who is the "living and true God" (1 Thess. 1:9)? What are "the gods of the peoples"? How is God greater than "worthless idols"? Who "made the heavens"? What do all people owe God? *BCF 2:2.26.* How can we worship God today? *Col. 3:16.* Let's "ascribe to the LORD the glory due his name," praying for hearts which produce new songs of praise.

Monday

Read through the Bible: Isaiah 38–39
Family Worship: Isaiah 38:1–8, 21

What was wrong with Hezekiah? What did Isaiah tell him? What did Hezekiah do? How did God answer him? What means did God use to heal him? Who planned everything that will ever happen? *Isa. 37:26.* Does God's sovereignty mean we don't have to pray? Use medicine? *BCF 5:2-3.* Do you need something from God today? Let's ask God to supply our needs—and the wisdom to use the means He's provided.

Tuesday

Read through the Bible: Isaiah 40
Family Worship: Isaiah 40:28–31

Who is "the Creator of the ends of the earth"? According to this text, what is God like? How are we different from God? What happens to youths and young men who trust in their own strength? What happens to those who instead "wait for the LORD"? What do we need to "run with endurance the race that is set before us" (Heb. 12:1)? Let's wait on the Lord and pray for renewed strength.

Wednesday

Read through the Bible: Isaiah 41
Family Worship: Isaiah 41:8–10

What were some things the exiles in Babylon might have feared? How did God reassure them? What had He done for them? What did He promise to do? In what sense are we exiles? *1 Peter 1:1, 17; 2:11.* Who has chosen us and called us His friends? *John 15:15-16.* Is there something you fear? How can these promises reassure you? Let's praise God for His friendship, take our fears to Him in prayer, and receive His strength.

Thursday

Read through the Bible: Isaiah 42
Family Worship: Isaiah 42:1–4

Who is Isaiah describing? **Matt. 12:15–21.** How is Jesus different from pompous, powerful kings? How is He immeasurably more powerful? How has He been a gentle Savior to you? *Matt. 11:28–30.* How does God the Father feel about Him? How can we delight in our Savior? **Isa. 42:10–12;** *1 Cor. 10:31.* Let's praise God for our gentle Savior and pray for hearts that find our full delight in Him.

Friday

Read through the Bible: Isaiah 43
Family Worship: Isaiah 43:1, 7, 21, 25, 11, 15

Who is the only Savior? What else is God for us? What has He done for us? Did God create us because He was lonely and needed people to love? Why, then, did He create and redeem us? *1 Peter 2:9.* How can you do what you were created for today? *1 Cor. 10:31.* Let's pray for the grace to glorify God in all we do, and begin by declaring His praise.

Saturday

Read through the Bible: Isaiah 44
Family Worship: Isaiah 44:1–5

What did God promise to do for Israel's offspring? What would they say after receiving the Spirit? Who poured out the water of the Holy Spirit on the new Israel—the church? *John 7:37–39; Acts 2.* What effect does water have on dry land? How should the outpouring of the Spirit change our lives? *Gal. 5:22–23; Heb. 6:7–8.* How can you say by your actions, "I am the LORD's"? Let's pray that God would indeed pour His Spirit upon us and revive us.

Year 2 — Week 45

Sunday

Read through the Bible: Psalm 97
Family Worship: Psalm 97:1–12

Who is "the Judge of all the earth" (Gen. 18:25)? On judgment day, what will all people (including God's enemies and false gods) do? *Phil. 2:9–11.* What will happen to those who hate God and love evil? *Rev. 20:10, 14–15.* How will God's people respond when all evil is destroyed? *Rev. 18:20.* How then should we (God's former enemies conquered by grace) now live? *Rom. 5:9–10; 12:9.* Let's praise God for His grace to us and pray for hearts to love Him and hate evil.

Monday

Read through the Bible: Isaiah 45
Family Worship: Isaiah 45:22–23

What is God calling all the ends of the earth to do? Why not turn to Buddha or Muhammad or self? To whom will every knee bow and every tongue confess? **Phil. 2:9–11.** When will this happen? **Rom. 14:10-11.** How have you responded to God's gracious call? **Rom. 10:9.** How can you show by your actions that you have bowed the knee to Christ? *Luke 6:46.* Let's bow the knee to Him now and confess: "Jesus is Lord."

Tuesday

Read through the Bible: Isaiah 46–47
Family Worship: Isaiah 46:8–11

Who is like God? What are some things He can do that no one else can? Who knows the future? Who planned the future? *BCF 3:1.1.* Can anyone thwart God's plans? How can the truth of God's sovereignty strengthen our faith? What are some promises God has given us in His Word? Why can we be sure of His promises? *Heb. 6:17–18.* Let's praise God that (no matter how chaotic the world seems) He is sovereign.

Wednesday

Read through the Bible: Isaiah 48
Family Worship: Isaiah 48:10–11

What does refining do to silver or gold? How does this picture what trials do for our faith? **1 Peter 1:6-7**; *James 1:2-4, 12.* Which is more precious: pure gold or pure faith? Who gets the glory when our faith is refined and tested genuine? How have trials strengthened your faith? How should we face the next trial? *1 Peter 4:12–13.* Let's pray for faith that when tested is refined and found genuine to the glory of God.

Thursday

Read through the Bible: Isaiah 49
Family Worship: Isaiah 49:5–6

Whom did the Lord send to bring Israel back to Him? Whom else was Jesus sent to save? How did this begin to be fulfilled in the early church? **Acts 13:44–48.** How did the Gentiles respond? How is this prophecy being fulfilled today? How have you responded? How can we share the light of Christ with others? *Rom. 1:16.* Let's rejoice and glorify God—and pray that His salvation would indeed "reach to the ends of the earth."

Friday

Read through the Bible: Isaiah 50–51
Family Worship: Isaiah 50:5–9

Who is speaking in this passage? **Mark 10:32–34; 15:19.** What did people do to Jesus? Why? What does this show us about the ugliness of our sin? What does it show us about God's love for us? *John 3:16.* Reflect: Does sin ever look fun to you? How might thinking of Jesus's suffering change your view of sin? Your view of suffering? Let's praise our Lord for what He did for us and pray He would remind us of it whenever we think sin looks fun.

Saturday

Read through the Bible: Isaiah 52–53
Family Worship: Isaiah 53:1–6

Who is this "man of sorrows"? **1 Peter 2:24–25.** Some say they would believe in God if they could just see Him—but how did people treat God when He became man? What was Jesus punished for on the cross? In what sense are we healed by His wounds? How should we respond to the "Mighty God" (Isa. 9:6) who became the "man of sorrows" for us? Let's worship Him. *Hymn: "Man of Sorrows."*

Year 2 — Week 46

Sunday

Read through the Bible: Psalm 98
Family Worship: Psalm 98:1–3

What has the Lord done for His people? Is salvation just for the Jews? *Rom. 1:16.* How did the psalmist respond to his Savior? How will you? Who is our King? **Ps. 98:4–6.** How did the psalmist honor the King? How will you? *Luke 19:37-40.* Who is "the Judge of all the earth" (Gen. 18:25)? **Ps. 98:7–9.** How will creation respond when He comes to make all things right? *Rom. 8:19-22.* How will you? Let's worship our Savior, King, and Judge with joyful songs and praises!

Monday

Read through the Bible: Isaiah 54–55
Family Worship: Isaiah 55:1–3

What is God inviting people to do? How much does it cost? Who paid for this rich feast? Who is the Water and Bread of Life? *John 4:10; 6:35; 7:37.* How does this picture God's free grace in salvation? Whom is He inviting to this feast? What are you thirsty for? How have you responded? Let's pray for souls thirsty for and delighted with the Water of Life.

Tuesday

Read through the Bible: Isaiah 56–57
Family Worship: Isaiah 56:6–7

What shall God's house be called? Whom is it for? Who quoted this verse when cleansing the temple? *Mark 11:17.* Which is a more accurate name for our home: "house of prayer" or "house of complaining"? "House of joy" or "house of strife"? How can we make our home more conducive to prayer and joyful worship? *Col. 3:12-24.* Let's pray for a home filled with love, prayer, and joyful worship.

Wednesday

Read through the Bible: Isaiah 58–59
Family Worship: Isaiah 59:21

What did the Lord promise to do for Israel? Who is the true Israelite, in whom all Israel's promises are fulfilled? *2 Cor. 1:20; Gal. 3:16.* Who are now counted as Israel's "offspring"? *Gal. 3:29.* What can we do to see this promise fulfilled in our family? *Deut. 6:6-7.* (This is the purpose of *On Your Heart*!) Let's pray that God's Spirit and God's Word would never depart from our family.

Thursday

Read through the Bible: Isaiah 60–61
Family Worship: Isaiah 61:1–2

Whom is Isaiah writing about? **Luke 4:16-21.** What was Jesus sent to do? How did He fulfill this Scripture? In what sense are we poor? *Matt. 5:3.* Captive, or bound? *Rom. 6:17.* Blind? *Rev. 3:17.* How do we need Jesus to fulfill this Scripture in our home? Let's pray that God would indeed send Christ to us through His Spirit and His Word to free us from our spiritual poverty, blindness, and captivity to sin.

Friday

Read through the Bible: Isaiah 62–63
Family Worship: Isaiah 62:4–5

How does a bridegroom feel about his bride? *Dad: Are you being a good example?* How does this picture the relationship God promises with His people? Who is the church's Bridegroom? How is this prophecy fulfilled in Christ? *Eph. 5:25-33, Rev. 21:2, 9-10.* Think about God delighting in and rejoicing over us—how does that make you want to respond to Him? **Isa. 61:10.** Let's "greatly rejoice in the Lord."

Saturday

Read through the Bible: Isaiah 64–65
Family Worship: Isaiah 65:17–25

Who is the Creator? What is God going to create? When? *Rev. 21:1-27.* What will life be like in the new heaven and earth? *Rev. 22:1-5.* How is this word picture different from the popular view of people with wings floating on clouds strumming harps? How can you get ready to live in the new creation? **2 Cor. 5:17.** Let's pray that God would prepare us for the new creation by making us new creations in Christ.

Year 2 — Week 47

Sunday

Read through the Bible: Psalm 99
Family Worship: Psalm 99:1–5, 9

What is God like? *Isa. 6:3.* What does it mean to be holy? Who is "holy, innocent, unstained, separated from sinners, and exalted above the heavens" (Heb. 7:26)? What did Jesus do to make His bride holy? *Eph. 5:25–27.* How should we treat our holy God? *Matt. 6:9; 1 Peter 3:15.* How can we get ready to worship our holy God? *2 Cor. 7:1.* Let's pray for hearts passionate for holiness so we can "offer to God acceptable worship, with reverence and awe" (Heb. 12:28).

Monday

Read through the Bible: Isaiah 66
Family Worship: Isaiah 66:1–2

What kind of people does the world pay attention to? Why are people impressed with them? What kind of person does God look to? How are these different? What do they tremble at? How can you practice greater humility and brokenness of spirit in our family? How can you show greater reverence for God's Word? Let's pray for humble and contrite spirits and hearts that tremble at God's Word.

Tuesday

Read through the Bible: Mark 1
Family Worship: Mark 1:1–8

Whom is the gospel all about? What did Isaiah say would happen before the Lord appeared? *Isa. 40:3; Mal. 3:1.* How was this fulfilled? How did John "prepare the way of the Lord"? How does baptism picture repentance? *Acts 22:16; Isa. 1:16; BCF 29:1.* How can we be a people prepared for the Lord? Let's get prepared to meet the Lord in Mark's gospel by confessing and being washed of our sins.

Wednesday

Read through the Bible: Mark 2
Family Worship: Mark 2:1–12

How could Jesus see the faith of the four men? How can you make your faith visible? How did Jesus first heal the paralytic? What is the most important type of healing that people need? Why did the scribes get upset? Who alone can forgive sins? How did Jesus demonstrate His authority to forgive sins? Is there anyone we need to "carry" to Jesus in prayer? Let's do so—and pray for the grace to make our faith visible.

Thursday

Read through the Bible: Mark 3
Family Worship: Mark 3:13–21, 31–35

Who calls to Himself those He desires? *John 15:16.* How many apostles did Jesus appoint? How might the twelve apostles be the spiritual patriarchs of a new, spiritual Israel? *Matt. 21:43; Rom. 9:6–8; Gal. 3:29; 6:16.* How did Jesus's family respond to Him? How can you tell who is in Jesus's spiritual family? What part of your life needs to change so there is more of a "family resemblance" with Jesus? Let's pray for the grace to be more like Christ by doing the will of God.

Friday

Read through the Bible: Mark 4
Family Worship: Mark 4:35–41

What were the disciples (many of whom were experienced fishermen) afraid of at first? Who has authority over storms? What did Jesus do? How did the disciples' fear change? Why? How did their faith change? What should we do in the storms of life? How can faith change our fear? Let's pray for an increasing faith to fear God rather than the storms He guides us through.

Saturday

Read through the Bible: Mark 5
Family Worship: Mark 5:1–20

What was wrong with the man? Who has authority over demons? What did Jesus do? What did the people of the region beg Jesus to do? Why? What did the man beg Jesus to do? What important ministry did Jesus give him? How has Jesus had mercy on you? Whom does Jesus want us to tell? Let's praise God for His mercy to us in Christ, then show our gratitude by telling our family and friends.

Year 2 — Week 48

Sunday

Read through the Bible: Psalm 100
Family Worship: Psalm 100:1–5

What is all the earth commanded to do? Why? Who made us? How are we to enter His presence? Why? Name two things you would like to thank God for. In addition to thanking Him in prayer, how else can you show your gratitude? Let's enter His courts now with thanksgiving and praise and then serve Him with gladness throughout the day.

Monday

Read through the Bible: Mark 6
Family Worship: Mark 6:30–44

Who is "the good shepherd" (John 10:11)? What did Jesus feel for the crowds? Why? How did the Good Shepherd provide for their spiritual hunger? Their physical hunger? Did the disciples understand who Jesus was? **Mark 6:52.** Why not? How has Jesus been the Good Shepherd to our family? How can you follow His example of compassion for others? Let's pray for hearts filled with compassion for others.

Tuesday

Read through the Bible: Mark 7
Family Worship: Mark 7:1–13

Is it a good idea to wash your hands before eating? Is it a sin not to? What tells us whether something is sinful? Which were the Pharisees more focused on: God's Word or their traditions? How could honoring the Pharisees' tradition dishonor parents—and God? What's the difference between family rules and God's rules? Do we have any family rules or traditions that could dishonor God? Let's pray that God would show us those areas and help us honor Him by simple obedience to His Word.

Wednesday

Read through the Bible: Mark 8
Family Worship: Mark 8:22–25

Who is "the light of the world" (John 8:12)? What did Jesus do for the blind man? How well did he see the first time Jesus touched him? What happened when He touched his eyes again? How is the blind man's physical sight a picture of the spiritual sight of the disciples? *Mark 8:17–18*. How might it picture ours? *1 Cor. 13:12*. How can we improve our spiritual sight? *Ps. 119:18; Heb. 5:14*. Let's ask Jesus to open our spiritual eyes that we might see Him more clearly.

Thursday

Read through the Bible: Mark 9
Family Worship: Mark 9:42–48

Who is holy and hates sin? What does Jesus command us to do with things that cause us to sin? Does He really want us to cut off our hands or gouge out our eyes? *Mark 7:18–23*. What do these hyperboles teach us about the seriousness of sin? About the need to radically deal with temptations to sin? Reflect: What is something that tempts you to sin? How can you cut it out of your life? Let's pray for the grace to radically remove anything that causes us to sin.

Friday

Read through the Bible: Mark 10
Family Worship: Mark 10:35–45

Who—though equal with God—"emptied himself, by taking the form of a servant" (Phil. 2:7)? What did James and John request? How did the other disciples respond? Why? Who will be greatest in the kingdom of God? How did Jesus model greatness? What are some things you can do to model greatness in our family? Let's pray that God would help us realize true greatness by serving one another.

Saturday

Read through the Bible: Mark 11
Family Worship: Mark 11:15–19

Who is the true Temple? *John 2:21*. Who is the temple of the Holy Spirit? *1 Cor. 3:16; 6:19*. What did Jesus find in His temple? *Jer. 7:11*. What should have been happening there? *Isa. 56:7*. What would it have been like to worship there? What did Jesus do about it? Why are we going to church tomorrow? What are some things or attitudes that could distract us? How can we prepare for true worship? Let's ask Jesus to cleanse us and prepare us for worship.

Year 2 — Week 49

Sunday

Read through the Bible: Psalm 101
Family Worship: Psalm 101:1–8

What was David determined to do? What was he determined to remove from his heart, home, and kingdom? Did he live up to this standard? Have you? Whom is this psalm ultimately about? *Heb. 7:26; Matt. 13:41–43.* What do you need to remove from your life to "walk with integrity"? What do you need to add? *Gal. 5:22–23.* Let's pray for the grace to "walk with integrity of heart."

Monday

Read through the Bible: Mark 12
Family Worship: Mark 12:18–27

What did the Sadducees falsely teach? How did they try to prove that there was no resurrection? How did Jesus correct them? Did they really know the Bible? Did they really know God? Who is "the resurrection and the life" (John 11:25)? Liberals today deny the bodily resurrection of Christ—what would you say to them? Let's praise God for His Word, His power, and the truth of the resurrection.

Tuesday

Read through the Bible: Mark 13
Family Worship: Mark 13:1–13

Who "shall come again, with glory, to judge both the living and the dead" (Nicene Creed)? What did Jesus say would happen first? How would it be like "birth pains"? Which of these things have happened? What hasn't? Whom did He say would be saved? How can we guard against false Christs? A fragmented family? False faith? Let's pray for the grace to endure in the faith as a family.

Wednesday

Read through the Bible: Mark 14
Family Worship: Mark 14:26–31, 66–72

What did Jesus say was going to happen? *Zech. 13:7.* Who is "the good shepherd" (John 10:11)? How did Peter respond? What did he do? What does Peter's denial teach us about the danger of spiritual pride? *Prov. 16:18.* The danger of being in the wrong place? *2 Sam. 11.* The danger of peer pressure? How can we guard against denying Christ? Let's pray for the humility to know our weakness and for the strength of grace to stand for Christ no matter what.

Thursday

Read through the Bible: Mark 15
Family Worship: Mark 15:6–15, 21

Who is "the King of the Jews?" Did Pilate find any guilt in Jesus? Why, then, did he order Him to be crucified? When someone tempts you to do something wrong by saying, "Everybody's doing it," what should you do? What did Simon of Cyrene do? How do his actions picture discipleship? **Mark 8:34.** How can you be like Simon instead of Pilate? Let's pray for the faith to be cross carriers rather than crowd pleasers.

Friday

Read through the Bible: Mark 16
Family Worship: Mark 16:1–7

What did the women find when they went to the tomb? Why didn't they find Jesus? Who is "the resurrection and the life" (John 11:25)? What did the angel tell the women to do? Why do you think he singled out Peter? How do you think Peter felt when he heard—and later saw—Jesus? *Luke 24:34; 1 Cor. 15:5.* How did it change his life? How has it changed yours? Whom do we need to "go, tell"? Let's praise God for the resurrection, and let's "go, tell" with lips and lives.

Saturday

Read through the Bible: Jeremiah 1
Family Worship: Jeremiah 1:4–9

When did God know Jeremiah? When did He plan his life? When did God know us and plan our lives? *Ps. 139:16.* What is a prophet? Whose words were in Jeremiah's mouth? Whose words are these in the Bible? Did Jeremiah want to be a prophet? Why not? Can young people like you speak God's Word? Can you live God's Word? Let's praise God for giving us His precious words and pray for the grace to faithfully live and speak them whether young or old.

Year 2 — Week 50

Sunday

Read through the Bible: Psalm 102
Family Worship: Psalm 102:1–2, 23–27

Whom did the psalmist turn to during his trial? Which person of the Trinity do these verses refer to? **Heb. 1:10–12.** Which of Christ's attributes did the psalmist highlight? How can focusing on the timelessness and immutability of Christ the Creator help us have the proper perspective on our trials? *2 Cor. 4:17-18.* Let's pray for eyes to see our trials—and all of life—through the lens of Christ's glorious attributes.

Monday

Read through the Bible: Jeremiah 2
Family Worship: Jeremiah 2:11–13

Would you rather drink water from a pure, bubbling fountain or a broken pail? What shocking thing did Israel do? Who is the fountain of living water? *John 4:10.* What are some of the false sources of living water people seek to satisfy their souls? How can we guard our hearts from going after that stagnant water? Let's pray for hearts thirsty only for the fountain of living water.

Tuesday

Read through the Bible: Jeremiah 3
Family Worship: Jeremiah 2:1–2; 3:20

How had Israel's relationship with God been like a new bride with her husband? How was she now like a treacherous wife? Who is the church's Bridegroom? *Eph. 5:25.* What kind of things can cool our devotion for Christ? *2 Cor. 11:3-4, Matt. 6:24.* What can we do to stay passionately devoted to God? *Rev. 2:4-5; 2 Tim. 1:6.* Let's pray that God would rekindle our passion for Him and cause the flame of devotion to grow and mature in faithfulness.

Wednesday

Read through the Bible: Jeremiah 4
Family Worship: Jeremiah 4:22

What were God's people "wise" in? Were they really wise? Who is true Wisdom? *1 Cor. 1:30.* What are we supposed to be wise in? **Rom. 16:19.** Is knowing what is good and evil enough? How can you "be wise as to what is good"? How can you be "innocent as to what is evil"? Let's pray for the grace to be wise as to what is good and innocent as to what is evil.

Thursday

Read through the Bible: Jeremiah 5
Family Worship: Jeremiah 5:30–31

What were the prophets doing? The priests? What did God think of this? What did the people think? Why did they love false teaching? **Jer. 5:3, 23**; *John 3:19; 2 Tim. 4:3*. Whose "eyes look for truth?" What are some examples of false teaching that people love today? How can we guard ourselves from these? Let's pray for hearts to love the truth—even if it hurts.

Friday

Read through the Bible: Jeremiah 6
Family Worship: Jeremiah 6:16

What kind of "paths" did the Lord say to look for? What are "the ancient paths"? What will we find on the ancient paths of God's Word? How did Judah respond to the ancient paths? **Jer. 6:10, 19.** How is this similar to attitudes today? What would you say to someone touting a modern teaching, saying the Bible was old-fashioned? How can we cultivate a love for the ancient paths in our home? Let's pray for hearts to cherish the ancient paths of God's Word.

Saturday

Read through the Bible: Jeremiah 7
Family Worship: Jeremiah 7:1–15

What "deceptive words" were the people trusting in? How were God's words different? Whose words are truth? *John 17:17*. Some say you can live any way you want but if you "believe in Jesus" you'll be saved. What kind of words are these? Will God be pleased if we go to church but are selfish or defiant? *Mark 11:17*. How can we prepare for worship tomorrow? Let's trust the true words of God and repent of any hypocrisy in our lives.

Year 2 — Week 51

Sunday

Read through the Bible: Psalm 103
Family Worship: Psalm 103:1–13

What "benefits" does the psalmist bless God for? If the Lord dealt with us according to our sins, what would happen? How far does He remove our transgressions from us? How great is His steadfast love? Who is our Father in heaven? How is God like a father? *Dad: Are you a good role model?* How should we respond to God for all these benefits? Let's bless the Lord with all that is within us!

Monday

Read through the Bible: Jeremiah 8
Family Worship: Jeremiah 8:5–6, 8–9, 11, 22

If you were deathly ill and only a bitter medicine could save you, would you rather take it or a sugar pill? Why? What deadly wound did Judah have? What biblical medicine did they reject? *1 John 1:9.* What sugar pill did they take instead? Who is the Great Physician? *Matt. 9:12.* What balm does He have for our sin-sick souls? *1 John 1:7.* Have you taken His prescription of repentance? Let's confess our sin and pray for the healing balm of Christ's precious blood.

Tuesday

Read through the Bible: Jeremiah 9
Family Worship: Jeremiah 9:2–6, 23–24

Do you know the president? What is the difference between knowing him and knowing about him? Whom did Judah "refuse to know"? What is the difference between knowing God and knowing about Him? How can church members know about God but not really know Him? *Matt. 7:21-23.* How can our lives reflect the true knowledge of God? Let's pray for hearts to delight in knowing and reflecting God.

Wednesday

Read through the Bible: Jeremiah 10
Family Worship: Jeremiah 10:6–16

Who is "the living and true God" (1 Thess. 1:9)? How is the living God different from idols? How is the true God different from false ideas of "God" today?

What do all people owe the "King of the nations?" *Rev. 15:4; BCF 21:1*. How can you show proper reverence for God in worship? In your thoughts? In your actions? Let's pray for hearts filled with a reverent, loving fear of God.

Thursday

Read through the Bible: Jeremiah 11–12
Family Worship: Jeremiah 12:14–17

Who are the Lord's "evil neighbors"? What did He promise them? How is this being fulfilled today? *Compare Jer. 11:16 and Rom. 11:13–24*. As former evil neighbors now grafted into Israel, what do we need to do? How can we "diligently learn the ways of [God's] people"? Where do we find them? *Deut. 6:6-7*. Let's praise God for including us in His people and pray He would help us "diligently learn" His ways.

Friday

Read through the Bible: Jeremiah 13
Family Worship: Jeremiah 13:23

Can a man change the color of his skin? Can a leopard change his spots? Can sinful man make himself good? How, then, can we be saved? **Mark 10:26-27.** For whom are all things possible? How can we do good? *John 15:5; BCF 16:3, 6*. Let's confess our utter spiritual helplessness and pray for the grace to do good in Christ.

Saturday

Read through the Bible: Jeremiah 14–15:9
Family Worship: Jeremiah 14:11–16

What did the Lord say He was going to do to Judah? What did the false prophets say? Whose "word is truth" (John 17:17)? What did the Lord think of their prophecies? How would you respond if someone said to you, "It doesn't matter what you believe, as long as you are sincere you will be saved"? *John 3:36; 14:6*. How can we know whether something said about God is true? *Acts 17:11*. Let's pray for the discernment to be good "Bereans."

Year 2 — Week 52

Sunday

Read through the Bible: Psalm 104
Family Worship: Psalm 104:24–35

Who created and preserves all things and creatures? **Neh. 9:6**; *Col. 1:16–17*. How does creation glorify God? *Ps. 19:1*. How does God's providence over creation bring Him glory? *BCF 5:1*. How did the psalmist respond to the wonder of creation? How do unbelievers? *Rom. 1:18–23*. How should we? How can we glorify God in our stewardship of creation? Let's glorify and enjoy God for and in His creation. *Hymn: "All Creatures of Our God and King."*

Monday

Read through the Bible: Jeremiah 15:10–ch 16
Family Worship: Jeremiah 15:16

Name a food that you delight to eat. What was Jeremiah's favorite spiritual "food"? What does "eating" God's words picture? How healthy is your spiritual diet? *1 Peter 2:2–3; Heb. 5:12–14*. How can we make sure God's words are going inside us and not just outside? *Deut. 6:6–9; Pss. 1:2; 119:11, 34*. Let's pray for hearts to delight in reading, studying, memorizing, and especially, living God's words.

Tuesday

Read through the Bible: Jeremiah 17
Family Worship: Jeremiah 17:9–10

What is the heart like apart from grace? *Ezek. 36:26*. "Who can understand it?" *Rom. 8:27; 1 Cor. 4:5*. Some people say, "Just trust your heart to lead you." What is wrong with doing this? Instead of trusting our hearts to lead us, what should we do? **Ps. 139:23–24**. Let's pray as David did: "Search [us], O God, and know [our] heart[s] . . ."

Wednesday

Read through the Bible: Jeremiah 18
Family Worship: Jeremiah 18:1–12

When a potter is making something out of clay, what does he do if it's ruined? Who is the Potter? How is God like the potter and Israel like the clay? *Rom. 9:20–24*. What was God "shaping" against Judah? How should they have responded? How did they? How should we respond to this warning? Let's repent of our sin and pray that the sovereign Potter would shape us into "vessels of mercy" (Rom. 9:23).

Thursday

Read through the Bible: Jeremiah 19–20
Family Worship: Jeremiah 19:1–2, 10–15

What did the Lord tell Jeremiah to do with the flask? How did this picture what He was going to do to Judah? How did the hardened flask picture the people's hearts? What did they refuse to hear? How can we keep our hearts from being hardened? *Heb. 3:12-13*. Let's pray for hearts that remain pliable in the Potter's hands—teachable and quick to repent.

Friday

Read through the Bible: Jeremiah 21–22
Family Worship: Jeremiah 22:24–30

What curse did God pronounce on Jeconiah? Since he was the last surviving king of Judah, how could God fulfill His promise to raise up for David a forever king? **Jer. 23:5-6; 33:17**. Who is the forever King? *Jesus, the virgin-born, greater Son of David, inherited the legal right to the throne (but not the curse) through His "adoptive" father Joseph (Matt. 1:11-16; Luke 1:31-33)*. How should we respond to King Jesus, who delivered David's line from this curse and Adam's line from the curse of sin (by becoming a curse for us)? Let's worship Him!

Saturday

Read through the Bible: Jeremiah 23
Family Worship: Jeremiah 23:16–18, 21–29

What were the false prophets doing? Could they hide what they were doing from God? Why not? Who fills heaven and earth? What were they supposed to do? How can we ensure we are teaching the right things about God? *Acts 17:11*. What is like fire and a hammer? What power does the faithful teaching of the Word have? *Isa. 55:11; Heb. 4:12*. How can we make sure God's Word has its full impact in our family? *Deut. 6:6-9*. Let's pray for the wisdom to stand in God's council and faithfully teach and live His Word.

"And these words that I command you today shall be **on your heart**."
– Deuteronomy 6:6

Year 3   Week 1

Sunday

Read through the Bible: Psalm 105
Family Worship: Psalm 105:1–6

What does the psalmist exhort us to do? Who does "wondrous works"? What are some of the wondrous works of God we've learned about in the last two years of family worship? What are some wondrous works the Lord has done for our family? For you? How should we respond to the Lord for all His wondrous works? Let's "give thanks to the LORD" and "sing praises to him."

Monday

Read through the Bible: Jeremiah 24
Family Worship: Jeremiah 24:1–10

What did Jeremiah see? How were the exiles like good figs? How were those left behind like bad figs? What made the difference? *Compare Jer. 24:7 and 17:9.* Who is able to give us new hearts? How did the exile cleanse, or purge, Israel? *John 15:1–6.* How is the church like the good figs? *1 Peter 1:1.* How should we live as elect exiles? *1 Peter 1:17–18; 2:11.* Let's pray for hearts of elect exiles with the fruit of our lives to match.

Tuesday

Read through the Bible: Jeremiah 25
Family Worship: Jeremiah 25:15–16

What "cup" did the Lord tell Jeremiah to give the nations? Was it a literal cup? What did it symbolize? What cup will the wicked have to drink? **Rev. 14:9–10.** Who drank the cup of God's wrath for believers? **Mark 14:36.** How does this background of the cup of wrath help us better understand Jesus's struggle in the garden? How should knowing more fully what Jesus did for you impact your life? Let's ask God to "dissolve [our] heart[s] in thankfulness, and melt [our] eyes in tears." *Hymn: "Alas! And Did My Savior Bleed?"*

Wednesday

Read through the Bible: Jeremiah 26
Family Worship: Jeremiah 26:1–15

What did the Lord command Jeremiah to speak? How did the people respond? Did the people's response mean that Jeremiah's ministry was a failure? Was

Jeremiah responsible for results or for obedience? *Isa. 6:9-13*. What are we responsible for? What if others ridicule us or try to stop us from obeying God? Let's pray for the faith and courage of Jeremiah to obey God no matter the results or consequences.

Thursday

Read through the Bible: Jeremiah 27
Family Worship: Jeremiah 27:1–7, 12

Who is sovereign over all He created? What did God tell Jeremiah to put on his neck? What is a yoke used for? What did it symbolize here? What yoke does Christ command us to put on? **Matt. 11:28–30.** What does it symbolize? How can you take up Christ's yoke of discipleship? *1 John 5:3*. How can you serve Him by serving others today? Let's pray for hearts to joyfully take Christ's yoke and serve Him in love.

Friday

Read through the Bible: Jeremiah 28
Family Worship: Jeremiah 28:1–17

What did Hananiah say would happen? How was his prophecy different from Jeremiah's? *Jer. 25:11; 27:9*. Which one came true? Who is the only one who can tell us infallibly what will happen in the future? How can we test people's predictions or so-called prophecies of what is going to happen in the future? *Acts 17:11; Deut. 18:21-22; 13:1-3*. Let's pray for the discretion to not be misled by any "Hananiahs."

Saturday

Read through the Bible: Jeremiah 29
Family Worship: Jeremiah 29:1, 4–7, 10–14

What did the Lord tell the exiles in Babylon to do? What did He promise them? How are we like those exiles? *1 Peter 1:1, 17; Heb. 11:13; Phil. 3:20*. Who promised to return, rescue us from exile, and bring us to our heavenly home? *John 14:2-3*. How can we work for the welfare of our place of exile? *Col. 3:17-24; 2 Tim. 2:1-2*. Let's begin by praying for our president and "all who are in high positions" (1 Tim. 2:2).

Year 3   Week 2

Sunday

Read through the Bible: Psalm 106
Family Worship: Psalm 106:47

Who promised to rescue His people from exile? *Jer. 29:10–14.* What did the psalmist ask God to do? Why? How did God answer him? *Ezra 1.* How is the church now being gathered from the nations? *Matt. 28:19.* How will we be finally gathered? *Matt. 24:31.* How can we cooperate with God's work of gathering His people? Let's begin by praying the psalmist's prayer for ourselves and the elect in every nation.

Monday

Read through the Bible: Jeremiah 30
Family Worship: Jeremiah 30:1–3

What did the Lord tell Jeremiah to do? Where is this book now? Whose words are these in the Bible? What promise did the Lord give him? Did God keep His promise? *Ezra 1.* Will God keep all His promises? *2 Cor. 1:20; Heb. 6:17–18.* In light of the sure promises of God's Word, how should we live? Let's begin by praising God for the firm foundation of His Word. *Hymn: "How Firm a Foundation." (Note all the promises this hymn recounts).*

Tuesday

Read through the Bible: Jeremiah 31
Family Worship: Jeremiah 31:31–34

What did the Lord promise to make with Israel and Judah? Whom will all in the new covenant know? What was God's law written on in the old covenant? What would it be written on in the new? How has this been fulfilled? *Heb. 8:8–12; Luke 22:20.* How should the law written on your heart affect your life? *Rom. 2:14–15; Ezek. 36:26–27, 31.* Let's pray for the grace to joyfully obey the family rules that our Father has written on our hearts.

Wednesday

Read through the Bible: Jeremiah 32
Family Worship: Jeremiah 32:36–41

Who rejoices to do us good? What did the Lord promise to do for His people? What would He put in their hearts? Why? How long would it last? Why do we need God to put His fear in our hearts? *Jer. 17:9.* How should the fear of God in your heart affect your life? *Ezek. 36:26–27, 31.* Let's pray that God would indeed put His fear in our hearts and lives.

Thursday

Read through the Bible: Jeremiah 33
Family Worship: Jeremiah 33:1–3

What did the Lord promise Jeremiah? How does God tell us these "great and hidden things" we would not otherwise know? What are some of the great and hidden things God has shown us recently in family worship? What would our lives be like had God not revealed these things to us? How should we respond to God's gracious offer? Let's call to God and ask for hearts eager to learn and experience the great and hidden things He has revealed in His Word.

Friday

Read through the Bible: Jeremiah 34–35
Family Worship: Jeremiah 35:1–19

Who commands us to obey His Word? Why didn't the Rechabites drink the wine Jeremiah offered? How were they role models for Judah? For us? How did God reward their obedience? How were they an example of God's promise in the fifth commandment? *Eph. 6:1–3.* How do children learn how to obey God? How can you be more like a Rechabite? Let's pray for obedient hearts like the Rechabites.

Saturday

Read through the Bible: Jeremiah 36
Family Worship: Jeremiah 36:1–3, 20–32

What did the Lord tell Jeremiah to do? Why? Where are these words written today? How did the king respond to the reading of God's Word? How was this different from his father Josiah's response? *2 Kings 22:11.* How do you respond when God uses His Word to expose sin in your life? How should we? *James 1:22–25; Isa. 66:2.* Let's pray for hearts that tremble at and are quick to obey God's Word.

Year 3   Week 3

Sunday

Read through the Bible: Psalm 107
Family Worship: Psalm 107:1–3, 21–22

In the Old Testament, how did the Lord gather His people "from the lands"? *Ps. 106:47; Ezra 1.* How is He doing so today? *Matt. 28:19.* What does it mean to redeem something? *"To buy back; to free from captivity by payment of ransom."*[4] Who redeemed us by His blood? *Eph. 1:7.* How is our redemption a release from captivity? *John 8:34–36; Col. 1:13–14.* How does the psalmist urge us to respond to God for our redemption? Let's "give thanks to the LORD."

Monday

Read through the Bible: Jeremiah 37
Family Worship: Jeremiah 37:1–2, 15–17

Who spoke through Jeremiah? How did the people respond to God's Word? Did Jeremiah give up because no one listened? Did he give up after being beaten and imprisoned? How do people respond to God's Word today? What should we do if others ridicule us or even oppose us for obeying God's Word? Let's pray for persevering hearts like Jeremiah to obey God no matter how others respond.

Tuesday

Read through the Bible: Jeremiah 38
Family Worship: Jeremiah 38:6–13; 39:15–18

What did the officials of Judah do to Jeremiah? What did a foreigner do about it? In whom did he put his trust? How was he an example of working faith? Of sovereign grace? *Acts 8:26–39.* How did God reward him? Is there anyone we know that is suffering injustice? What can we do to help? How can your faith work at home? Let's pray for the grace and working faith to help those in need.

Wednesday

Read through the Bible: Jeremiah 39
Family Worship: Jeremiah 38:14–23; 39:1–9

Who spoke through Jeremiah? How did King Zedekiah respond to God's Word? What was the cost of disobedience for him? For his family? For the

---

4   Merriam-Webster Online, s.v. "redeem," accessed October 8, 2019, https://www.merriam-webster.com.

nation? What is the ultimate cost of disobedience? *John 3:36.* What has God been teaching you in His Word? How have you responded? Let's pray for hearts to obey—no matter how hard.

Thursday

Read through the Bible: Jeremiah 40–41
Family Worship: Jeremiah 40:1–6

Before the exile, what cost had Jeremiah paid for obedience? *Jer. 37:15; 38:6.* How was he rewarded? Which was costlier: Jeremiah's obedience or Zedekiah's disobedience? Who told us to "count the cost" (Luke 14:28)? What is the cost of following Christ? **Luke 14:33.** What is the reward for giving up all to follow Christ? *Phil. 3:7–11; 2 Tim. 4:7–8.* Which will you choose: the cost of obedience or disobedience? Let's "count the cost" and pray for hearts to choose obedience.

Friday

Read through the Bible: Jeremiah 42–43
Family Worship: Jeremiah 42:1–17; 43:1–7

Who spoke through Jeremiah? What did the people ask Jeremiah to do? What did they vow to do? Did they do as they vowed? How do you typically respond when you are told to do something you already want to do? What if it is something you don't want to do? Which is the test of true obedience? Let's pray for hearts to obey—even if it's something we don't want to do.

Saturday

Read through the Bible: Jeremiah 44
Family Worship: Jeremiah 44:1–19

Who judged Judah? Why? How did God warn the people who fled to Egypt? How did they respond? Did they learn anything from the consequences of their sin? What happens to people who willfully defy God's Word? *Heb. 10:26–27.* What are the consequences for defying your parents? Do you humble yourself and learn from the consequences or harden yourself further? Let's pray for the grace to quickly humble ourselves, repent, and learn our lesson.

Year 3　　　　　　　　　　　　　　　　　　　　　　Week 4

Sunday

Read through the Bible: Psalm 108
Family Worship: Psalm 108:1–6, 12–13

What did David praise God for? Whose "steadfast love is great above the heavens"? What did David ask God to do? Why did he ask God and not somebody else? What do we need God to do in our family? What "foes" do we need Him to "tread down"? Is there anybody else who can do these things? Let's pray that God would be exalted and glorified by doing what only He can do in our family.

Monday

Read through the Bible: Jeremiah 45–47
Family Worship: Jeremiah 36:4; 45:1–5

Whose words did Baruch write? What was bothering him? What made his ministry difficult and discouraging? What did the Lord say to him? Does God promise that life will be easy? Will the ministry He gives us always be exciting and fruitful? Will you be fulfilled by seeking great things for yourself? *Mark 10:43; Phil. 4:11–13.* What should we do instead? *1 Cor. 10:31.* Let's pray for hearts content with the life God has given us.

Tuesday

Read through the Bible: Jeremiah 48
Family Worship: Jeremiah 48:29–30, 42

Why would God judge Moab? *Isa. 16:6.* What are the different synonyms for *pride* in the verses we read? How is a child defying his parents rooted in pride? How is being insolent (extremely rude) to a sibling a fruit of pride? In contrast, who is "gentle and lowly in heart" (Matt. 11:29)? How can you be more like Christ and less like Moab? Let's repent for the pride in our lives and pray for humble hearts.

Wednesday

Read through the Bible: Jeremiah 49
Family Worship: Jeremiah 49:34–39

What would God do to Elam? Who faced God's "fierce anger" on behalf of His people? *Mark 15:34.* After judging them, what did He promise to do? How was this fulfilled on the day of Pentecost? **Acts 2:8–9.** In what sense are all children of Adam under judgment? *Rom. 6:23.* What provision has God made to restore our fortunes? *Acts 2:37–39.* What do we need to do to receive this promise? Let's repent, receive, and rejoice.

Thursday

Read through the Bible: Jeremiah 50
Family Worship: Jeremiah 50:1–5

What would the Lord do to Babylon? How would His people respond? How was this initially fulfilled? *Ezra 1; Ps. 126.* How will it be finally fulfilled in spiritual Babylon? *Rev. 18:2, 21.* Who is leading us to heavenly Zion? *Heb. 2:22.* God has promised to deliver His people from the judgment on worldly Babylon—how should we respond? Let's "seek the LORD [our] God" with tears of repentance and joy as we follow Him to heavenly Zion.

Friday

Read through the Bible: Jeremiah 51
Family Worship: Jeremiah 51:6, 11–12, 24, 45

Who was going to judge Babylon? How would God judge her? Why? Why should we never avenge ourselves on those who wrong us? *Rom. 12:19.* What were God's people to do? What is God going to do to spiritual Babylon? *Rev. 18:2, 4–6.* How should God's people respond? What "Babylonian" attitudes and actions do you need to flee from? *2 Tim. 2:22.* Let's pray for the grace to flee from the sins of Babylon.

Saturday

Read through the Bible: Jeremiah 52
Family Worship: Jeremiah 52:12–14, 17–19

What happened to the temple? Why did this happen? **2 Chron. 7:19–22.** Who always does what He says in His Word? *Jer. 1:12.* Did the people pay attention to the warnings God gave through Solomon and all the prophets to Jeremiah? *Jer. 44:4–5.* What are some warnings God has given us? *Heb. 2:1–3.* How have you responded? How should we? *2 Peter 1:19.* Let's pray for hearts that pay attention to the warnings in God's Word.

Year 3 — Week 5

Sunday

Read through the Bible: Psalm 109
Family Worship: Psalm 109:1–5

Have you ever had a friend betray you or tell lies behind your back? How did it feel? Were you tempted to lash back? How did David respond when it happened to him? Which greater Son of David was betrayed by a friend? *Ps. 109:8; Acts 1:20.* Reflect: Have you used any "words of hate" or deceit lately? How should we respond when others speak evil of us? Let's pray for the grace to "give [ourselves] to prayer."

Monday

Read through the Bible: Lamentations 1
Family Worship: Lamentations 1:16–18

Why was Jerusalem sent into captivity? Who was "in the right" for doing this? Who is always in the right? When confronted with a mistake you made, do you typically make excuses, blame someone, or admit fault? When the Holy Spirit convicts us of sin, how should we respond? *Prov. 28:13; 1 John 1:9.* Let's pray for hearts that honestly and humbly confess when we are in the wrong.

Tuesday

Read through the Bible: Lamentations 2
Family Worship: Lamentations 2:13–14

What did the false prophets "see" for Jerusalem? What did they fail to do? If an X-ray exposed a problem in your body, would you want the doctors to tell you? Would you want them to do surgery if necessary? Whose word is like an X-ray? How is it like a scalpel? *Heb. 4:12–13.* How can we be healed of our sin sickness? Let's pray that the Great Physician would use His Word to expose and heal us of our sin.

Wednesday

Read through the Bible: Lamentations 3
Family Worship: Lamentations 3:19–24, 46–48

How did Jeremiah respond to the destruction of Jerusalem? During his mourning, what did he remember? Whose "mercies . . . are new every morning"? What did focusing on God do for his faith? When we go through difficult times, what do we need to remember? What do we need to do? Let's praise God that His mercies are new every morning and pray for hearts that "hope in him."

Thursday

Read through the Bible: Lamentations 4–5
Family Worship: Lamentations 5:1–3, 15–22

What happened to Judah's "joy" and "dancing?" Why? Who said, "Blessed are those who mourn, for they shall be comforted" (Matt. 5:4)? What did Jeremiah remember about God? What did he ask God to do? *Ps. 85:4-7*. When someone says to you flippantly, "I'm sorry," how does it make you feel? When you repent, are you more like that person or Jeremiah? Let's ask God to restore us to Himself—giving us hearts that mourn over sin.

Friday

Read through the Bible: Ezekiel 1
Family Worship: Ezekiel 1:1, 26–28

Whom did Ezekiel see? *Rev. 4:2-3*. Based on what he saw, what is God like? *1 Tim. 6:16; 1 John 1:5*. How did he respond? *Rev. 1:17*. How do you think this vision encouraged the exiles? How would you respond if Jesus appeared in our home in all His glory? How might it change your view of yourself? Your problems? Your priorities? Let's pray for eyes to see a glimpse of God's glory in His Word and view all of life in its light. *Hymn: "Holy, Holy, Holy!"*

Saturday

Read through the Bible: Ezekiel 2–3
Family Worship: Ezekiel 2:1–2; 3:10–11

What was Ezekiel to receive in his heart? What else did the Lord tell him to do with His words? What was he to do if God's people refused to hear? **Ezek. 2:7.** Was he responsible for obedience or results? Who is responsible for the effect of His word? **Isa. 55:11.** What are we to do with God's words in our family? *Deut. 6:6-7*. What are we responsible for: obedience or results? Let's pray for hearts that trust and obey. *Hymn: "Trust and Obey."*

Year 3   Week 6

Sunday

Read through the Bible: Psalm 110
Family Worship: Psalm 110:1–3

Whom is David talking about? **Matt. 22:41–46.** How can Jesus be both David's Lord and his Son? What is pictured by Christ's enemies being made a "footstool"? When will our Lord conquer all His enemies? **1 Cor. 15:24–26.** What "do you think about the Christ?" Let's pray for hearts that "offer [ourselves] freely" as loyal subjects of our divine King.

Monday

Read through the Bible: Ezekiel 4–5
Family Worship: Ezekiel 5:1–6, 11–13

Why was God angry with Jerusalem? How would His anger be satisfied? How (upon whom) was the Lord's holy anger satisfied for our sins? **Rom. 3:23–25a; Mark 15:34; BCF 8:5.32.** *Note: "Propitiation" is satisfaction of God's just wrath.* What would happen if, instead, the Lord treated us with strict justice? Christ received God's fury that you might be forgiven—how will you respond to Him? Let's praise Him: "Hallelujah! What a Savior!" *From the hymn: "Man of Sorrows."*

Tuesday

Read through the Bible: Ezekiel 6
Family Worship: Ezekiel 6:1–10*

*AC v. 9. How was Israel like an unfaithful wife? How was the Lord like a broken-hearted husband? What would happen to most of Israel? How would the surviving remnant respond? Who is the church's heavenly Husband? *Eph. 5:25.* How can we keep our hearts and eyes faithful to Christ? *Deut. 6:4–9.* Let's pray that God would "like a fetter, bind [our] wandering heart[s] to Thee." *From the hymn: "Come Thou Fount of Every Blessing."*

Wednesday

Read through the Bible: Ezekiel 7
Family Worship: Ezekiel 7:1–4, 19

What was going to happen to Israel? Why? Could the people's silver and gold deliver them? Why not? What can money do for us when we die? *Luke 12:20.* What can it do for us on judgment day? Whom should we trust to deliver us?

How can we keep our affections focused on God rather than the gifts He gives? *1 Tim. 6:17.* Let's pray for hearts that value and trust in the riches of a relationship with God.

Thursday

Read through the Bible: Ezekiel 8–9
Family Worship: Ezekiel 9:3–4

When you write your name on something, what does it signify? What did God tell the angel with the writing case to do? What did this mark signify? What was different about those marked? Who marks us with His name? *Rev. 3:12; 9:4; 22:4.* How should those marked as belonging to God live? *Rom. 6:3-4.* Let's pray for lives that clearly show God's stamp of ownership.

Friday

Read through the Bible: Ezekiel 10
Family Worship: Ezekiel 10:4, 18–19; 11:22–23

What happened to the glory of God? Why did it leave the temple? *2 Chron. 7:1, 19-22.* Do you think the people of Jerusalem noticed? Who is the true Temple and radiance of God's glory? *John 1:14; 2:21; Heb. 1:3.* How did people respond to the arrival of the glory of Christ? *John 1:10-11.* How can we experience the glory of God? *John 1:12-13; 1 Cor. 3:16; 2 Peter 1:16-21.* Let's pray for hearts passionate for the presence of God's glory through His Spirit and His Word.

Saturday

Read through the Bible: Ezekiel 11
Family Worship: Ezekiel 11:14–20

What did God promise to do for His people? What does your physical heart do for you? *Listen to one another's heartbeats.* What would happen if your heart was made of stone? Spiritually speaking, what is a stony heart like? *Eph. 2:1-3.* A heart of flesh? All are born with spiritually stony hearts—who can help us? *Eph. 2:4-5.* What does your "spiritual" heart sound like? Let's pray that God would indeed give us hearts of flesh that beat passionately for Him.

Year 3 — Week 7

Sunday

Read through the Bible: Psalm 111
Family Worship: Psalm 111:10

If someone knows a lot about the Bible but doesn't do what it says, is he wise? Why not? What is the beginning of wisdom? Who is Wisdom personified? *1 Cor. 1:30.* How can you tell when someone truly understands the fear of the Lord? *Ps. 119:100.* How can we more fully practice the fear of God in our family? Let's pray for the grace to practice the fear of the Lord—and so give Him enduring praise.

Monday

Read through the Bible: Ezekiel 12
Family Worship: Ezekiel 12:21–28

What had the people been saying about God's word? Was it true? What did God promise? God told the people through Ezekiel and Jeremiah that Judah would go into exile—what happened? Is there any chance that God will fail to perform any of His promises? *Isa. 55:11.* Who is watching over His word to perform it? *Jer. 1:12.* Since God will perform His word, what should we do? Let's pray for the grace to trust and obey. *Hymn: "Trust and Obey."*

Tuesday

Read through the Bible: Ezekiel 13
Family Worship: Ezekiel 13:1–6

What does a wall do for a city under attack? What is required if there is a breach in the wall? What did the false prophets fail to do? **Ezek. 22:30.** How do these actions picture the ministry of the Word and prayer? *1 Cor. 3:10–11; Ps. 106:23.* Who always stands in the breach for us? *Heb. 7:25.* How can we build up the wall of our family? *Deut. 6:6–7.* How can we stand in the breach? Let's do so now and pray for the grace to build up the wall of our family by the Word.

Wednesday

Read through the Bible: Ezekiel 14–15
Family Worship: Ezekiel 14:1–8

What did the elders of Israel take into their hearts? Who should have been dwelling in their hearts? *Eph. 3:17.* Was God fooled by their outward show of seeking Him? What did He tell them to do? John Calvin wrote, "Man's nature . . . is a perpetual factory of idols."[5] Reflect: What is being produced in the factory of your heart? *Mark 7:21-22 (AC).* Let's pray for hearts filled with Christ and free of idols. F*athers: Pray Eph. 3:14-19 for your family.*

Thursday

Read through the Bible: Ezekiel 16
Family Worship: Ezekiel 16:59–63

How had Israel broken covenant with God? What did the Lord promise? How would His people respond? Reflect: When you sin, are you typically ashamed, or do you proudly try to justify yourself? Who atoned for our sin? Do we have anything to be proud of in salvation? *Eph. 2:8-9.* Why not? *Eph. 2:1-5.* How have you responded to God for His amazing grace? Let's praise Him. *Hymn: "Amazing Grace."*

Friday

Read through the Bible: Ezekiel 17
Family Worship: Ezekiel 17:22–23

The "cedar" represents David's dynasty—who is the "sprig" that will become a "noble cedar"? **Matt. 13:31-32.** How is the "mustard seed" like this sprig? How is God's kingdom like a mustard seed? How do both parables illustrate this truth: "Don't despise humble beginnings"? What has God begun in you? *Phil. 1:6.* In our family? In His church? What will it grow into? Let's pray that God would indeed cause His kingdom to grow in the world—and in us.

Saturday

Read through the Bible: Ezekiel 18
Family Worship: Ezekiel 18:20, 23, 25–32

Who is always just? Does God eternally punish one person for the sins of another? Does God like to punish people? *2 Peter 3:9.* What does He command people to do so they will not be condemned for their sin? *Acts 17:30-31.* Will you be condemned for my sin? Will you be saved because of my faith? What do you need to do? Let's pray for hearts to cast our sins away and that run to our merciful God in repentance.

---

5 John Calvin, *Institutes of the Christian Religion*, ed. John T. McNeill, trans. Ford Lewis Battles (Philadelphia: Westminster, 1977), 1.11.8.

Year 3   Week 8

Sunday

Read through the Bible: Psalm 112
Family Worship: Psalm 112:1–2

What does a God-fearing man delight in? *Pss. 1:2; 119:24, 35, 47, 77, 92, 174.* How will his family be blessed? What else does a godly man delight in? **Ps. 111:2.** How does he show his delight in God's works? What do you delight in? How can you show your delight in God's Word today? *2 Tim. 2:15 (KJV).* In His works? Let's pray for hearts to delight in and study God's Word and His works.

Monday

Read through the Bible: Ezekiel 19
Family Worship: Ezekiel 19:1–9

How do these lions picture the kings of Judah? How do they show the need for a greater Lion King? Who is that greater "Lion of the tribe of Judah"? **Rev. 5:5.** How is King Jesus greater? *Gen. 49:9–10.* What do you need King Jesus to conquer for you? In you? *BCF 8:10.46.* Let's praise God for the true Lion King and pray He would indeed conquer all His enemies—including the sin in our hearts.

Tuesday

Read through the Bible: Ezekiel 20:1–44
Family Worship: Ezekiel 20:33–38, 43–44

Who is the "King of kings" (Rev. 19:16)? As King, what did God promise to do for His people? What did He promise to purge from Israel? Would He give them what they deserved? How would the remnant respond? Why is self-loathing an appropriate response to grace? *Job 42:5–6; Rom. 2:4.* Has God treated us as our sins deserve? How should we respond? Let's pray for eyes to see our sin in the light of grace—and repent with self-loathing. *Hymn: "Amazing Grace."*

Wednesday

Read through the Bible: Ezekiel 20:45-ch 21
Family Worship: Ezekiel 21:25–27

What was the last king of Judah like? What did God tell him to take off? To whom would He give the crown of Israel? *John 1:49; Rev. 19:12.* What kind of crown did He have to wear first? *Matt. 27:29.* How was the low exalted and the exalted brought low? *Phil. 2:5-11.* How can we exalt our risen King? Let's worship Him. *Hymn: "Crown Him with Many Crowns."*

Thursday

Read through the Bible: Ezekiel 22
Family Worship: Ezekiel 22:1–2, 7

What are some of the "abominations" Jerusalem was guilty of? *2 Tim. 3:1-5.* What are some ways that children treat their parents with contempt? Can a child dishonor his parents and honor God? **Deut. 27:16**; *21:18-21; Rom. 1:28-32.* How should children treat their parents? **Deut. 5:16.** Who always honors His Father? *John 8:29.* What are some specific ways you can honor your father and mother? Let's pray for hearts to honor our heavenly Father by honoring our parents.

Friday

Read through the Bible: Ezekiel 23 (AC)
Family Worship: Ezekiel 22:26; 44:23

What did the priests fail to do? **Lev. 10:10.** What effect did this have? What does it mean for something to be holy? **2 Tim. 2:20-21.** Who is perfectly holy? *Heb. 7:26.* As God's holy people, how should we be distinguishable from the world? *2 Tim. 2:22.* How can we be more "useful to the master"? What are some "dishonorable" things you need to cleanse yourself from? Let's pray that the Master would make us honorable vessels—set apart and useful for Him.

Saturday

Read through the Bible: Ezekiel 24
Family Worship: Ezekiel 24:15–24

What did God take away from Ezekiel? What was He going to take away from Judah? How was Ezekiel a sign? What indestructible Temple is now the delight of God's eyes? *John 2:21.* What everlasting bride is the delight of Jesus's eyes? *Isa. 62:4; Eph. 5:25; Rev. 21:9.* What is the delight of your eyes? *Pss. 37:4; 112:1.* Let's pray for eyes that delight in God, even as He delights in us.

Year 3 — Week 9

Sunday

Read through the Bible: Psalm 113

Family Worship: Psalm 113:1–9

Who is "high above all nations"? In what ways is God high above us? Does this mean that God is impersonal—uninvolved in people's lives? What kind of things does God do for His people? What has He done for our family? How should we respond? Let's "praise the name of the LORD!"

Monday

Read through the Bible: Ezekiel 25–26

Family Worship: Ezekiel 25:1–7

How did the Ammonites respond when God judged Jerusalem? How would the Lord respond to them? Should we rejoice over an enemy's punishment? **Prov. 24:17–18.** Why not? *2 Cor. 5:10.* Should you rejoice over a sibling's punishment? What should you do instead? Who told us to love and pray for our enemies? *Matt. 5:44.* Let's pray for humble hearts that fear God and love our enemies.

Tuesday

Read through the Bible: Ezekiel 27

Family Worship: Ezekiel 27:1–9, 25–36

How was the city of Tyre like the *Titanic*? How important was money when the *Titanic* was sinking? Beauty? Worldly treasures? How is the world like Tyre or the *Titanic*? *Rev. 18:11–19.* How important will worldly treasures be when the world sinks in judgment? What kind of treasure should we store up? Who told us to store up treasures in heaven? **Matt. 6:19–21.** How can we do that? *1 Tim. 6:17–19.* Let's pray for hearts fixed on those treasures that will never sink.

Wednesday

Read through the Bible: Ezekiel 28

Family Worship: Ezekiel 28:11–19

Who is this? What was Satan like when God first created him? Why did his heart become proud? Is Satan truly beautiful? *2 Cor. 11:14; Rev. 12:9.* How is the beauty of Christ different? *Isa. 53:2; Ps. 27:4.* What kind of beauty is precious to God? *1 Peter 3:4; Prov. 31:30.* How are you tempted to be like Satan? Whom should you be like instead? What is one way you can be more like Christ? Let's repent of the ugliness of pride and pray for the beauty of Christlike character.

Thursday

Read through the Bible: Ezekiel 29
Family Worship: Ezekiel 29:6–9a, 16

What would happen if you tried to lean on a staff made of a flimsy reed? How was Egypt like this to Israel? Whom should Israel have leaned on? What are some "staffs of reed" people try to lean on today? *Prov. 3:5.* Are you leaning on any of these? How can we instead lean on Christ the Rock? Let's pray for the grace to lean on Christ the Rock.

Friday

Read through the Bible: Ezekiel 30
Family Worship: Ezekiel 30:6, 10–13

Who is sovereign over the nations? What kind of kingdom was Egypt in its heyday? What kind of kingdom is it today? **Ezek. 29:15.** What happened? Why? How could America be like Egypt? What can we do to help our nation? *1 Tim. 2:1-2; Matt. 5:13-16.* Let's pray for our nation and for the grace to be salt and light to help preserve it. *Hymn: "To Thee Our God We Fly."*

Saturday

Read through the Bible: Ezekiel 31
Family Worship: Ezekiel 31:1–12, 18

Who "opposes the proud, but gives grace to the humble" (1 Peter 5:5)? What was Assyria like? What happened to it? Why? How would Egypt be like this also? What will happen if we exalt ourselves? *Matt. 23:12.* What should we do instead? *1 Peter 5:5-6.* What is the difference between humbling yourself and being humbled? Name one thing you can do to humble yourself today. Let's pray for the grace to humble ourselves so we don't need to be humbled.

Year 3   Week 10

Sunday

Read through the Bible: Psalm 114
Family Worship: Psalm 114:1–8

What awesome miracles did God do when redeeming His people from Egypt? What does the earth do at His presence? Why? At whose death and resurrection did the earth tremble? *Matt. 27:50-51; 28:1-2*. What should our attitude be in His presence? *Jer. 5:22*. How can you reflect this attitude in family worship? Church? Let's pray for hearts that "tremble . . . at the presence of the Lord."

Monday

Read through the Bible: Ezekiel 32
Family Worship: Ezekiel 32:1–4

What did Pharaoh think of himself as? What did God say he was? Who is the true Lion? *Rev. 5:5*. What will He do to the dragon? *Rev. 12:9; 20:10*. Which is more important: what we think of ourselves or what God says about us? How should we think of ourselves? **Rom. 12:3.** Let's pray for the grace to think of ourselves (and all of life) from God's perspective.

Tuesday

Read through the Bible: Ezekiel 33
Family Worship: Ezekiel 33:1–9

What does a watchman do for a city? What happens if the watchman fails to do his duty? What happens if the people ignore the watchman's warnings? How was Ezekiel like a watchman? Who is our watchman? **Heb. 13:17.** Who appointed pastors and teachers to be watchmen over the church? *Eph. 4:11-12*. What have the watchmen been warning us about? Have you been listening? Let's pray for hearts that heed the warnings from God through our watchmen.

Wednesday

Read through the Bible: Ezekiel 34
Family Worship: Ezekiel 34:11–16

What did the Lord promise to be for His people? Who is the Good Shepherd? *John 10:11*. How is Jesus like a shepherd? How are we like sheep? *Isa. 53:6*. Do sinners seek God, or does God seek sinners? *Gen. 3:8-9; Luke 19:10*. Parents:

How did Jesus seek you? Children: How is Jesus seeking you? How are you responding? *Isa. 55:6*. Let's pray for hearts to seek the One who sought us first.

Thursday

Read through the Bible: Ezekiel 35–36:15
Family Worship: Ezekiel 36:8–11

Who is for us? *Rom. 8:31*. What did the Lord promise to do for Israel? How was this partially fulfilled in ethnic Israel? How is this being fulfilled spiritually in the new Israel? *Acts 6:7*. How will this be ultimately fulfilled in the new heaven and earth? *Rev. 7:9*. How can our family be part of the fulfillment? *Acts 2:39; Matt. 28:19-20*. Let's pray that God would indeed multiply His people throughout the earth and in multiple generations of our family.

Friday

Read through the Bible: Ezekiel 36:16–38
Family Worship: Ezekiel 36:22–32

What did God promise to do for His people? Why would He do so? *Matt. 6:9*. How would they respond? How does a stony heart view sin? Self? God? *Rom. 1:18-23*. How does a new heart view sin? Self? God? *Ps. 51*. Reflect: Which is your heart more like? Who alone can give us new hearts? *John 3:3-8*. Let's pray for new hearts which loath our sin and love our Savior.

Saturday

Read through the Bible: Ezekiel 37
Family Worship: Ezekiel 37:1–14

What did Ezekiel see in the valley? What did he speak to the dry bones? What happened when he spoke God's word to them? What were they missing? What happened next? How does this vision depict the return from exile? The new birth? *Ezek. 36:26-28; John 3:3-8; 5:25*. The resurrection of life? *John 5:28-29*. How would this vision have encouraged the exiles? How can it encourage us? *1 Thess. 4:13-18; 1 Cor. 15:50-58*. Let's pray for the breath of life to live with the end in sight.

Year 3   Week 11

Sunday

Read through the Bible: Psalm 115
Family Worship: Psalm 115:1–3

What does the Lord do? *Ps. 135:6.* Can anyone stop Him from doing what he pleases? *Dan. 4:35.* Why not? *Isa. 46:9–10.* Who, then, should get the glory for everything? What are some things we can give God glory for? Let's give glory to the name of our God.

Monday

Read through the Bible: Ezekiel 38
Family Worship: Ezekiel 38:1–4, 7–9, 16–23

Who will attack God's people in the latter days? **Rev. 20:7-10.** How will God show His greatness and holiness? *Ezek. 39:21; Isa. 5:16.* How would it feel to be surrounded by evil? Do you ever feel like this? Who will completely destroy all evil? *1 Cor. 15:24-26.* How can the certainty of God's final defeat of evil strengthen our faith at such times? Let's praise God for His certain triumph over evil and pray He would remind us of this when we are surrounded by evil today.

Tuesday

Read through the Bible: Ezekiel 39
Family Worship: Ezekiel 39:7–8

What will the Lord do with His holy name? What will He no longer allow at the judgment? *Ex. 20:7.* How can believers profane God's holy name through their actions? *Ezek. 20:39; Rom. 2:21-24.* How can we instead honor His holy name? *1 Peter 4:14-16; Ps. 115:1.* Who taught us to pray, "Hallowed be thy name" (Matt. 6:9)? Let's pray for the grace to hallow God's name with our lips and our lives.

Wednesday

Read through the Bible: Ezekiel 40
Family Worship: Ezekiel 40:1–4; 43:6–7a*; 48:35

*AC 43:7b. What did Ezekiel see? **Rev. 21:1-4.** Who will dwell with us there? How would a vision of the new Jerusalem have encouraged the exiles? How would it have encouraged John in exile on Patmos? How can it encourage us in

our trials? Let's pray for spiritual eyes to see what Ezekiel and John saw and for hearts to live with the end in sight.

Thursday

Read through the Bible: Ezekiel 41–42
Family Worship: Ezekiel 42:15–20; Revelation 21:15–17

In both visions, what was the angel doing? What did the measurements reveal about the perfection and beauty of the new Jerusalem? How do we "measure up" to God's perfect standards? **Ezek. 43:10**; *Rom. 3:23*. How can we get ready to be a part of the perfect city? *Eph. 5:25–27; Heb. 12:22–23; 2 Cor. 7:1*. Who promised to make us ready? *Phil. 1:6; 1 Thess. 5:23-24*. Let's confess our imperfection and pray that God would indeed prepare us for the perfect city with His perfect Word.

Friday

Read through the Bible: Ezekiel 43–44
Family Worship: Ezekiel 43:1–5; Revelation 21:22–23

What did Ezekiel see? How was what John saw similar? Different? What is the purpose of a temple? Why will there be no need of a temple building in the new Jerusalem? Who is our Temple, our way to God? *John 1:14; 14:6*. How did Ezekiel respond to this vision of the glory of God? How should we? Let's worship our living Temple with reverence and awe.

Saturday

Read through the Bible: Ezekiel 45–46
Family Worship: Ezekiel 45:17

What was the prince's duty? Who is the true Prince? How did He fulfill this duty? **Heb. 9:11–12**. Will there ever be a need to offer any more sacrifices? Why not? *Heb. 10:14*. How should we respond to our perfect Prince, who offered Himself as the once for all sacrifice? Let's "offer up a sacrifice of praise to God, that is, the fruit of lips that acknowledge his name" (Heb. 13:15).

Year 3   Week 12

Sunday

Read through the Bible: Psalm 116
Family Worship: Psalm 116:1–9, 12–19

Who is the giver of every good and perfect gift? *James 1:17.* When someone gives you a gift, how do you respond? How did the psalmist respond when the Lord gave him the gift of life? What are some of the gifts or benefits the Lord has given us? *1 Cor. 4:7.* Can we repay God? *Rom. 11:35.* What "shall [we] render to the LORD for all His benefits to [us]?" Let's "offer to [God] the sacrifice of thanksgiving," then show our thanks by enjoying the gifts and the Giver.

Monday

Read through the Bible: Ezekiel 47–48
Family Worship: Ezekiel 47:1, 12; Revelation 22:1–2

What did Ezekiel see? How is it similar to John's vision? How are both like the garden of Eden? *Gen. 2:9-10.* Who alone can give the water of life? *John 4:10.* Who can drink from the water of life? **Rev. 21:6; 22:17;** *Isa. 55:1.* How does thirst picture faith? How do these visions picture complete salvation? What are you thirsty for? Let's pray for hearts thirsty for Christ and the water of life He freely gives.

Tuesday

Read through the Bible: Daniel 1
Family Worship: Daniel 1:1–16

Who always obeys His Father? *John 8:29.* What was Daniel like when he was taken away from his family to Babylon? What do you act like when you're away from home? Many people grow up in Christian families but then fall away from God when they leave home—how can you prepare to be like Daniel instead? Let's pray for hearts that resolve to obey God—even when away from home in spiritual Babylon.

Wednesday

Read through the Bible: Daniel 2
Family Worship: Daniel 2:1–5, 24–49

What did Nebuchadnezzar see in his dream? Whose kingdom is like a rock that will smash the kingdoms of this world? *Rev. 11:15.* In what sense has Christ's kingdom already come? *Matt. 13*. How did the dream affect Nebuchadnezzar? How might it have encouraged the exiles? How can it encourage us? *Rev. 11:16–18*. Let's worship the King of Kings and pray: "Your kingdom come . . ." (Matt. 6:10).

Thursday

Read through the Bible: Daniel 3
Family Worship: Daniel 3:1–30

What did Nebuchadnezzar command the people to do? Who didn't obey him? Why? Whom alone are we to worship? *Ex. 20:4–5*. How did they respond to the king's threats? *Acts 5:29*. How did God deliver them? How are these three men an example for believers facing persecution today? Facing peer pressure? Let's pray that God would enable us and our brothers around the world to stand in faith whether facing persecution or peer pressure.

Friday

Read through the Bible: Daniel 4
Family Worship: Daniel 4:28–37

Who is in control of everything? Who can stop God from doing His will? What happened to Nebuchadnezzar? Why? What did he learn? Note how many times he uses personal pronouns in verse 30—do you ever sound like that? When we accomplish something good, who should get the glory for it? Why? *1 Cor. 4:7; John 3:27*. Let's praise God for His absolute sovereignty and pray for hearts that respond by giving credit where credit is due. *Hymn: "To God be the Glory."*

Saturday

Read through the Bible: Daniel 5
Family Worship: Daniel 5:1–9, 17–31

Who raises up and puts down kings and kingdoms? In whose hand is our breath? *Job 12:10; Acts 17:25*. How did Belshazzar dishonor God? Did he learn anything from what God did to Nebuchadnezzar? How did God humble Belshazzar? How should we treat things that belong to others? That belong to God? How can we honor God's name? Word? Church? Let's pray, "Hallowed be your name" (Matt. 6:9), and then do so—with all God's things.

Year 3   Week 13

Sunday

Read through the Bible: Psalm 117
Family Worship: Psalm 117:1–2

Who does the psalmist say should praise the Lord? Who came to save people from every nation? *Rev. 5:9.* Why? **John 3:16, Rom. 15:8–11.** How can we join God on mission so that all peoples praise Him? *Matt. 28:18–20.* How should we respond to God for His mercy to Gentiles like us? Let's praise and glorify God for His mercy and steadfast love!

Monday

Read through the Bible: Daniel 6
Family Worship: Daniel 6:1–23

What was Daniel like as a civil servant? As a servant of God? Why did he get in trouble? *2 Tim. 3:12.* In being unjustly condemned, who was Daniel like? *1 Peter 2:22.* What should we do if the state told us we couldn't teach you the Bible? *Acts 5:29.* How can you be more like Daniel? Let's pray for the integrity and faithfulness of Daniel, whether in prosperity or persecution.

Tuesday

Read through the Bible: Daniel 7
Family Worship: Daniel 7:13–14

Who is the "son of man"? Who is "the Ancient of Days"? What did God the Father give His Son? In what sense has this occurred already? **Matt. 28:18.** In what sense is this not yet? *Matt. 16:27; 24:30; 26:64.* What needs to happen first? *Matt. 24:14;* **28:19–20.** How can we join King Jesus on mission to expand His kingdom? Let's pray that God would empower us to make disciples in our home who are passionate to make disciples of all nations.

Wednesday

Read through the Bible: Daniel 8
Family Worship: Daniel 8:9–12, 23–25

What will this "little horn" be like? *2 Thess. 2:3–12.* What will he do to the truth? What will he try to replace it with? How would you respond to someone who said, "There is no absolute truth"? *Note: This is itself an absolute truth claim!* What is truth? **John 17:17.** Who is truth? *John 14:6.* How can you be prepared to counter the deceit prospering in our culture? Let's ask the One who is Truth to sanctify us in the truth.

Thursday

Read through the Bible: Daniel 9
Family Worship: Daniel 9:1–3, 9–13, 17–19

What is truth? *John 17:17.* What did Daniel learn when studying the Bible? *Jer. 25:11–12.* Note: *The first year of Darius was Daniel's sixty-seventh year in exile (605–538 BC).* How did he respond? How was his response to God's Word different from Israel's? How can we gain insight by the truth? *Ps. 119:97–104.* What has God been teaching you from His Word? How should we respond? Let's thank God for what He's taught us in His Word—and pray for the grace to obey it.

Friday

Read through the Bible: Daniel 10
Family Worship: Daniel 10:1–14

What is truth? *John 17:17.* Is everything in God's Word easy to understand? What was Daniel's heart set on doing? *Ezra 7:10.* How long did he mourn and wait before God gave him understanding of the vision? What means did God use to help him? What means does God normally use to help us? *Deut. 6:6–7; Eph. 4:11–16.* Reflect: How much effort have you been putting into understanding God's Word? Let's pray for hearts set on understanding God's Word.

Saturday

Read through the Bible: Daniel 11
Family Worship: Daniel 11:36, 32; 2 Thess. 2:1–12

Who will come in glory to destroy all evil? Who must appear before Jesus returns? What will he be like? How will he be destroyed? How will he deceive people? Why will people believe in him? How will God increase their condemnation? Why? What is the difference between acknowledging and loving the truth? How can we keep from being deceived? Let's pray for hearts that love the truth and so be saved.

Year 3   Week 14

Sunday

Read through the Bible: Psalm 118
Family Worship: Psalm 118:22–24, 28–29

What would happen if we built a house on a foundation that wasn't level or square? What is the purpose of a cornerstone? Who is the cornerstone of God's kingdom? **Matt. 21:42-43.** How did the nation of Israel treat the Cornerstone? What were the consequences? How can we build our lives on the Cornerstone? *Matt. 7:24.* Let's begin by joining the psalmist in praising God for Christ, our marvelous Cornerstone.

Monday

Read through the Bible: Daniel 12
Family Worship: Daniel 12:1–3

How is death like sleep? *John 11:11-13; compare BCF 31:1; Rev. 6:9-11.* Who is "the resurrection and the life" (John 11:25)? What will happen to those who sleep in death when Jesus returns? *1 Thess. 4:13-16; John 5:28-29.* Who will rise to everlasting life? *John 3:16.* Everlasting contempt? *John 3:18, 36. Note: We are justified by faith but judged by works—what we do shows what we believe.* Until then, what do the wise do? How can we turn many to righteousness? Let's pray for eyes to live with the end in sight and hearts passionate to help others do so as well.

Tuesday

Read through the Bible: Hosea 1
Family Worship: Hosea 1:6–10

What did God tell Hosea to name his daughter? Why? His son? Why? What did God promise Israel after this? **Hos. 2:23.** How did God expand this promise in the New Testament? **Rom. 9:23-26.** Who died to make us God's people? *Eph. 2:12-13.* How should we respond to the One who, in mercy, has called us "my people"? Let's declare, "You are my God," and worship Him!

Wednesday

Read through the Bible: Hosea 2
Family Worship: Hosea 2:16–20

How is marriage a type of the relationship God has with His people? **Eph. 5:22-33.** Who is the church's heavenly Husband? How are wives to respond to their husbands? How is the church to respond to her heavenly Husband? Did Israel respond this way? How can we do better? Let's pray for "a sincere and pure devotion to Christ" (2 Cor. 11:3).

Thursday

Read through the Bible: Hosea 3–4
Family Worship: Hosea 3:1–2

What did Hosea do for his wife? How are Hosea's actions toward his wife similar to what Christ has done for the church? **Eph. 5:25–30**; *Acts 20:28, 1 Cor. 6:20; 7:23*. Who is the church's heavenly Husband? How are husbands to be like Christ? *Dad: What kind of example are you?* How can you love sacrificially? Let's praise God for His self-sacrificing love and pray He would help us love one another as He loves us.

Friday

Read through the Bible: Hosea 5–6
Family Worship: Hosea 6:1–6

What was Israel's love for God like? Which did they focus on more: relationship with God or religious duties? How were the Pharisees also like this? **Matt. 9:9–13.** How was Jesus different? Who desires "mercy, and not sacrifice"? How can people be modern Pharisees? How can we keep our focus on relationship rather than mere religion? Let's pray for hearts that "press on to know the LORD."

Saturday

Read through the Bible: Hosea 7–8
Family Worship: Hosea 8:7a; Galatians 6:7–10

If we were to sow tomato seeds, what should we expect to reap? What does it mean to sow to the flesh? To the Spirit? *Gal. 5:16–25 (AC vv. 19–21).* What do you reap from each? Does this mean we earn eternal life by doing good? *Good works are the fruit—not the root—of salvation. Eph. 2:8–10; BCF 16:2.* Who gives us the power to do good works? *John 15:5; BCF 16:3.* What did Israel sow and reap? **Hos. 7:13–14.** How can you sow to the Spirit? Let's pray for hearts empowered to live and walk by the Spirit.

Year 3 — Week 15

Sunday

Read through the Bible: Psalm 119:1–24
Family Worship: Psalm 119:9–16

How "can a young man keep his way pure?" What did the psalmist do with God's word? What specifically did he do with his heart? Lips? Eyes? What did he delight in? How was his approach to God's word both a discipline and a delight? What do you need to do to be more like him? Let's pray that God would enable our discipline to be a delight as we memorize, meditate on, and obey His Word.

Monday

Read through the Bible: Hosea 9–10
Family Worship: Hosea 10:12

What would happen if we sowed seed on hard-packed dirt? What would we need to do to make it grow? Whose word is like seed? *Luke 8:11*. What happens when the seed of God's Word is sown to hard hearts? *Luke 8:5–6, 12–13*. What did Israel need to do to prepare for God's seed and rain? How can we practice these things in our family? Let's pray for hearts plowed up by grace—ready to receive and produce the fruit of righteousness.

Tuesday

Read through the Bible: Hosea 11–12
Family Worship: Hosea 11:1

What kind of relationship did Israel have with God? How was Israel like a son? How was God like a father? Who is the ultimate Son and true Israelite? **Matt. 2:13–15.** How was Christ a better Son? *Luke 2:51–52; John 8:29.* How is God a Father to us? How can you be more like Christ and less like Israel? Let's ask our Father to give us the hearts of true sons.

Wednesday

Read through the Bible: Hosea 13–14
Family Worship: Hosea 13:14

How would the Lord judge Israel for its idolatry? What do we deserve for our sin? *Rom. 6:23.* Who overcame the plague and sting of death for His people? **1 Cor. 15:50–57.** How did Jesus destroy the power of death? *Heb. 2:14–15;*

1 Cor. 15:3–4. How should we respond to the One "who gives us the victory" over sin and death? Let's give thanks to God for turning the judgment of death into victory!

Thursday

Read through the Bible: Joel 1
Family Worship: Joel 1:1–3

Whose word came to Joel? What did Joel tell the people to do with God's word? Whom were their children to tell? Whom were their grandchildren to tell? What would happen if you didn't tell your children? What can we do so that successive generations of our family hear God's Word? *Deut. 6:6-7*. Let's pray that God would enable each generation of our family to faithfully teach His Word to the next.

Friday

Read through the Bible: Joel 2
Family Worship: Joel 2:28–29

What did Joel prophesy would happen? On whom would God pour out His Spirit? Who always fulfills His word? How was this prophecy fulfilled? **Acts 2:1-18.** What were the special signs of the Spirit's filling at Pentecost? What are the normal signs of the Spirit's filling today? *Eph. 5:18-21; Gal. 5:22-23*. How might our home be different if the Lord poured out His Spirit on us? Let's pray for the outpouring of the Spirit and the evidence of His power in our lives.

Saturday

Read through the Bible: Joel 3
Family Worship: Joel 3:12–16

Why is the Lord going to gather the nations? In "the valley of decision," who is doing the deciding? *Matt. 25:32*. What will the Lord be for His people there? On that day, it will be too late for people to decide—what decision do we need to make now? *Deut. 30:19-20; Josh. 24:15*. What is your decision? Let's pray for hearts united in this decision: "As for me and my house, we will serve the Lord" (Josh. 24:15).

Year 3 — Week 16

Sunday

Read through the Bible: Psalm 119:25–48
Family Worship: Psalm 119:33–37

Whose word has eternal worth? In comparison, what are some "worthless things" we are tempted to focus on? What effect can this have on our devotion for Christ and delight in His Word? What are you going to focus on today? Let's ask the Lord to turn our eyes away from worthless things and, instead, incline our hearts to His precious Word.

Monday

Read through the Bible: Amos 1–2:5
Family Worship: Amos 2:4–5

What is truth? *John 17:17.* What did Judah do with God's word? What did they follow instead? Apart from grace, what do all people do with the truth about God? **Rom. 1:18, 25.** What are some lies about God people prefer to the truth? What are the consequences for "exchang[ing] the truth about God for a lie"? How can we protect ourselves from believing lies about God? *Ps. 119:97.* Let's pray for hearts that love the truth.

Tuesday

Read through the Bible: Amos 2:6–ch. 3
Family Worship: Amos 3:1–2

What is the difference between knowing about someone and truly knowing him? Who had known Israel? In what sense did God know Israel distinctly from all other nations? *Deut. 7:6.* Today, who does God know in this way? **1 Cor. 8:3; Gal. 4:9.** How should being known by God change our lives? *1 Peter 2:9-25.* Let's praise God for knowing us and pray for the grace to live as those who know Him.

Wednesday

Read through the Bible: Amos 4–5
Family Worship: Amos 5:21–24

Who alone can tell us how to worship God? *John 4:24; BCF 22:1.* What did God think of Israel's worship? Why? *2 Tim. 3:1-5.* Instead of empty religion, what does He desire? What is the difference between being religious and practicing true religion? **James 1:26–27.** What are some practical ways you can practice true religion? Let's pray for the grace to practice true religion.

Thursday

Read through the Bible: Amos 6–7
Family Worship: Amos 7:7–9

Make a plumb line and ask: What is a plumb line used for? What would happen if we tried to build a wall without making sure it was straight? What plumb line does God use to measure His people? *Isa. 28:17; Eph. 4:13.* How did Israel measure up? If the Lord measured you with His plumb line, what would He find? *Rom. 3:23.* What, then, do we need? Let's confess our crookedness and pray for the grace to build our lives by the plumb line of Christ and His Word.

Friday

Read through the Bible: Amos 8–9
Family Worship: Amos 9:11–12; Acts 15:13–18

What did God promise to rebuild? What is "the tent of David"? *Isa. 16:5.* Who now reigns on David's throne? *Luke 1:31–33.* What connection did James see between this prophecy and what God was doing in the church? How should we respond to the One who is calling Gentiles like us to be a people for His name? Let's "seek the Lord," worship Him, and pray, "Your kingdom come . . ." (Matt. 6:10).

Saturday

Read through the Bible: Obadiah 1
Family Worship: Obadiah 1:10–15

How were the people of Edom related to Israel? *Gen. 25:30.* What did Edom do when his brother nation was being taken into captivity? What would God do to Edom for this? Who "will repay each person according to what he has done" (Matt. 16:27)? How do you typically respond when your sibling is being punished? How should you? Let's pray for humble hearts to never gloat over another's punishment.

Year 3   Week 17

Sunday

Read through the Bible: Psalm 119:49–72
Family Worship: Psalm 119:57–60

Some people say, "I'll obey God when I'm older—for now I'm going to have my fun." What's wrong with this attitude? How was the psalmist's attitude different? What did he hasten to obey? Why do you think he hastened to obey God's word? Which attitude is more like yours? How can we hasten to obey God's Word? *Eph. 6:1–4.* Let's pray for hearts that "hasten and do not delay" to obey God's Word.

Monday

Read through the Bible: Jonah 1–2
Family Worship: Jonah 1:1–2:1, 10

Who is omnipotent and omnipresent? What did God tell Jonah to do? How did he respond? *Gen. 3:8; compare Ps. 119:60.* Why couldn't he really run away from God? *Ps. 139:7–12.* How did God show His sovereignty over creation? His mercy to Jonah? What are some ways that people still try to run away from God? Instead of running *from* Him, how can we run *to* Him? Let's pray for hearts that repent and run to God.

Tuesday

Read through the Bible: Jonah 3–4
Family Worship: Jonah 3:1–10

Who is "gracious . . . and merciful, slow to anger and abounding in steadfast love" (Jonah 4:2)? When given another chance, what did Jonah do? How did the people of Nineveh respond? How was this different from Israel's response to Jesus's preaching? **Matt. 12:38–41.** How is Nineveh an example for us? How can they be an encouragement for missions? Let's pray for hearts quick to repent and passionate for the repentance of the nations.

Wednesday

Read through the Bible: Micah 1–2
Family Worship: Micah 1:1, 2:6, 11

Whose word did Micah preach? How did the people respond to Micah's preaching? How was this different from the Ninevites? What kind of preachers did they want? **2 Tim. 4:1–5.** What do people's "itching ears" want to hear today? What should we do when the teaching of God's Word is unpopular? *Deut. 6:6–7.* Let's pray for ears that love to hear the sound teaching of God's Word.

Thursday

Read through the Bible: Micah 3–4
Family Worship: Micah 4:1–4

What will the nations do with their swords? What does this picture? A statue at the United Nations depicts a man doing this; will man bring about universal peace? **Joel 3:9–10;** *Matt. 24:7.* Who will? Since there won't be perfect peace until Christ returns, should we work for peace today? **Matt. 5:9.** How can you be a peacemaker? *Rom. 12:18; 1 Tim. 2:1–2.* How can the just use of the sword bring peace? *Rom. 13:4; Neh. 4:13–18.* Let's pray for the grace to be peacemakers.

Friday

Read through the Bible: Micah 5
Family Worship: Micah 5:2

Who is this ruler? Where was He born? **Matt. 2:1–6.** This describes Christ's human origin, but in His divine nature does He really have an origin? *John 1:1–3.* How does the incarnation display both the humility and greatness of Christ? *Phil. 2:5–11.* How should we respond to this amazing prophecy of our amazing Savior? *Matt. 2:10–11.* Let's pray for hearts filled with joy and wonder as we worship the One who is both God and man.

Saturday

Read through the Bible: Micah 6–7
Family Worship: Micah 7:18–19

What does God delight in? Is there anything we can do to earn His love? **Mic. 6:6–7.** Who gave His firstborn for our transgressions? *John 3:16.* What does the Lord require of His covenant people? **Mic. 6:8.** How can we practice justice in our home? Mercy and kindness? Walking humbly with God? Let's pray for the grace to magnify the greatness of Christ's love by reflecting it in our home.

Year 3 — Week 18

Sunday

Read through the Bible: Psalm 119:73–96
Family Worship: Psalm 119:89

What would it be like to measure with a changing ruler? What is the only measure of truth? *John 17:17*. What are some changing rulers that people use to measure truth? Can God's word ever change? How long will God's word endure? How can these truths about God's truth embolden us when facing the enemies of truth? *Optional: Discuss Martin Luther's stand at the Diet of Worms.* Let's praise our eternal and unchanging God for His eternal and unchanging word.

Monday

Read through the Bible: Nahum 1–3
Family Worship: Nahum 1:1, 14; 3:1

Who "is slow to anger and . . . will by no means clear the guilty" (Nah. 1:3)? What did Nineveh do when Jonah preached? Nahum lived about one hundred years later—what was Nineveh like then? What did the Lord do for that earlier generation? **Nah. 1:7**. What would He do to the later generation? **Nah. 1:8**. How can we keep this from happening to future generations of our family? Let's pray for the grace of continual repentance and revival throughout the generations of our family.

Tuesday

Read through the Bible: Habakkuk 1–2
Family Worship: Habakkuk 1:1–11

Who ordained all things for His glory? What did Habakkuk ask God? How did God respond? *Read next cycle:* **Hab. 1:12–13; 2:2–4**. What was his second question? How did God respond? Which is more important: understanding why God does something or trusting Him? How did God tell him (and us) to live? **Heb. 10:36–39**. Have you ever felt like Habakkuk? How can we live by faith during those times? Let's pray for the grace to live by faith and not by sight.

Wednesday

Read through the Bible: Habakkuk 3
Family Worship: Habakkuk 3:17–19

Review yesterday's lesson. What did Habakkuk resolve to do amid the coming troubles? How does this demonstrate what it means to live by faith? By whose strength would he be able to do this? How do you typically respond to trials? How can you be more like Habakkuk? *1 Thess. 5:16; James 1:2-4.* Let's pray for hearts that rejoice in the Lord always—even amid trials.

Thursday

Read through the Bible: Zephaniah 1–2
Family Worship: Zephaniah 1:1, 17–18

A bumper sticker says, "He who dies with the most toys wins." What is wrong with this statement? Which is worth more: riches or righteousness? Why? **Zeph. 2:3; Prov. 11:4.** Who is righteousness? *1 Cor. 1:30.* How can you put more priority on seeking righteousness? Let's pray for hearts that "seek first the kingdom of God and his righteousness" (Matt. 6:33).

Friday

Read through the Bible: Zephaniah 3
Family Worship: Zephaniah 3:14–17

What is something so special it makes you want to sing and shout for joy? What reason was Israel to rejoice? Who is the King of Israel in our midst? *John 1:49.* What is so special to our King that He would sing and shout for joy? *Luke 15:7, 20-24.* Think about God Himself rejoicing and singing over us—how does that make you want to respond to Him? Let's "sing aloud, . . . shout, . . . rejoice and exult" in our King.

Saturday

Read through the Bible: Haggai 1–2
Family Worship: Haggai 1:1–8

Prepare a bag with holes and coins inside. Whose word came to Haggai? Which were the people putting more priority on: their houses or God's? What was the result? What would happen if we kept our money in a "bag with holes"? *Demonstrate.* How does this show what was happening? What is God's house today? *1 Cor. 3:16-17.* How can we give greater priority to God's house—people? *2 Cor. 9:6-8; 1 Peter 4:10-11.* What may happen if we don't? Let's pray for hearts that cheerfully give our time, talent, and treasure to God.

Year 3   Week 19

Sunday

Read through the Bible: Psalm 119:97–120
Family Worship: Psalm 119:97–104

What did the psalmist love? Hate? What did love for God's Word motivate him to do? What does it mean to meditate on God's Word? What did meditation on God's Word give him? What did obeying God's Word give him? How can you gain more understanding than your teachers? How can we grow in our love for God's Word? Let's pray for hearts that love, meditate on, and obey God's Word all day long.

Monday

Read through the Bible: Zechariah 1–2
Family Worship: Zechariah 1:1–6

Whose word stands forever? *Ps. 119:89*. What had the Lord told earlier generations? How did they respond? What happened to them? What was He now telling this generation? What did He promise? *Zech. 1:16; 2:5, 11*. How did they respond? What is God telling us to do? *2 Peter 1:19; Acts 17:30*. How will you respond? Let's pay attention and return to the Lord now through repentance.

Tuesday

Read through the Bible: Zechariah 3–4
Family Worship: Zechariah 4:6–9

What did God promise Zerubbabel? By whose power would he complete it? Who is his greater Son? *Matt. 1:12*. What temple is He building? *Matt. 16:18; Eph. 2:19–22*. How do we work with Him to build His church? *Matt. 28:19–20*. By whose power are disciples made? *Titus 3:5*. How can we build a godly family? *Deut. 6:6–7*. By whose power? *Gal. 5:22–23*. Let's ask God to work mightily by His Spirit in our family and church.

Wednesday

Read through the Bible: Zechariah 5–6
Family Worship: Zechariah 6:9–15

Who was Joshua? What did a high priest normally do? How would this priest, "the Branch," be different? Who does this picture? How is Jesus both king and priest? *BCF 8:9–10*. What is our King-Priest building? Who shall come and help Him? *Eph. 2:11–22*. How can we help Him? *1 Cor. 3:9–17*. Let's praise our King-Priest for calling us who were "far off," and pray He would make us His fellow builders.

Thursday

Read through the Bible: Zechariah 7–8
Family Worship: Zechariah 8:16–17

What does God want us to do? What does He not want us to do? What does God hate? **Prov. 6:16–19; 12:22.** Why do you think He hates lies? Who is truth? *John 14:6.* Who is the father of lies? *John 8:44.* When we lie, who are we like? What about when we exaggerate or shade the truth? How can you be more Christlike with your words? *Eph. 4:15, 25, 29.* Let's pray for hearts that hate lies and love truth.

Friday

Read through the Bible: Zechariah 9–10
Family Worship: Zechariah 9:9–10

What would Israel's returning king be like? How far will His rule extend? Who is this? **Matt. 21:1–9.** How was this "triumphal entry" different from what you would expect from a conquering king? *Rev. 19:11–16.* In what sense is Jesus now conquering the nations? *Matt. 28:18–20.* How did the people receive their king? How can we honor Christ as king? Let's begin by worshiping our risen King.

Saturday

Read through the Bible: Zechariah 11–13:1
Family Worship: Zechariah 12:10; 13:1

What did God promise to pour out on His people? What would be the effect? Who is the One they pierced? **John 19:33–37.** Why would they mourn? *Acts 2:36–39.* What "fountain" did God open for them? *1 John 1:7; Rev. 7:14.* What will happen to those who laugh at sin now? **Luke 6:25; Rev. 1:7.** How do you respond when you realize you've sinned? How should we? *Matt. 5:4.* Let's pray that God would pour out His Spirit on us, that we would mourn over our sin and be cleansed. *Hymn: "There Is a Fountain Filled with Blood."*

Year 3 — Week 20

Sunday

Read through the Bible: Psalm 119:121–144
Family Worship: Psalm 119:130

Prepare a note folded up several times. What do you need to do to read this note? How is God's Word like a folded-up note when we don't understand it? How do we "unfold" God's "notes" to us? Who can help us unfold God's words? *John 16:13; Eph. 4:11–12; Deut. 6:7.* What results from unfolding God's words? Let's ask the "Spirit of truth" (John 16:13) to help us unfold, understand, and obey the words He inspired.

Monday

Read through the Bible: Zechariah 13:2–14:21
Family Worship: Zechariah 13:7*

*Read through "scattered." Who is the Shepherd who was struck? **Matt. 26:31–32.** In what sense was He struck? Why did God strike the Good Shepherd? *Isa. 53:4–6; John 10:14–15.* What happened to the sheep at first? Why? How does the truth that the Good Shepherd was struck for your sin make you want to respond to Him? Let's run to Him with hearts stricken over our sin and overflowing with thankfulness.

Tuesday

Read through the Bible: Malachi 1–2:16
Family Worship: Malachi 2:13–16

Why didn't God accept the men's offerings? *1 Peter 3:7.* How is marriage a covenant? What is God seeking in covenant marriage? Who or what should marriage picture? *Eph. 5:22–33; Ruth 2:12; 3:9.* What happens to these purposes when the marriage covenant is broken? Is it ever right to break the marriage covenant? *Rom. 7:2; Matt. 19:3–9 (AC); 1 Cor. 7:10–16.* How can you prepare for faithful, covenant marriage? Let's pray for the grace to be Christlike in all our relationships.

Wednesday

Read through the Bible: Malachi 2:17–4:6
Family Worship: Malachi 3:1; 4:5–6

Whom did the Lord promise to send? What would he do? Whose way would he prepare? How was this fulfilled? **Luke 1:13–17; Matt. 11:7–10, 13–14.** How did John the Baptist prepare people for Jesus? How did he prepare families? What are some things that can turn the hearts of children away from their parents? What can turn the hearts of parents away from their children? How can we guard against these things? Let's pray for hearts turned toward home.

Thursday

Read through the Bible: Luke 1:1–38
Family Worship: Luke 1:26–38

Who appeared to Mary? What did he tell her? How was Mary different from any other mother? *Isa. 7:14.* Who was her Son? How was Jesus different from any other son? *John 1:14.* From any other king? *2 Sam. 7:16.* How did Mary respond to this shocking, life-changing word from God? How do you respond when God speaks to you through His Word? Let's pray for servants' hearts to reply as Mary did.

Friday

Read through the Bible: Luke 1:39–80
Family Worship: Luke 1:39–55

Who was in Elizabeth's womb? Who was in Mary's womb? How did John respond when Jesus came near? How was this possible? *Luke 1:15; Matt. 21:16.* How did Elizabeth respond? How did Mary respond? What does Mary's response tell us about her love for God's Word? *1 Sam. 2:1–10.* How should we respond to the amazing truth that God became a baby? Let's magnify the Lord and rejoice in God our Savior. *Hymn: "Joy to the World."*

Saturday

Read through the Bible: Luke 2
Family Worship: Luke 2:1–20

Where would you expect a great king to be born? Who is the "King of kings" (Rev. 19:16)? Where was Jesus born? *2 Cor. 8:9; Isa. 6:1–5.* How could our hearts sometimes be like that crowded inn? How did the angels respond to the Creator becoming a creature? How did the shepherds respond to the angels? To their announcement? To the Christ child? God has now chosen us to receive this birth announcement—how should we respond? Let's glorify and praise God!

Year 3   Week 21

Sunday

Read through the Bible: Psalm 119:145–176
Family Worship: Psalm 119:160–168

What is the supreme standard of what is true and false? *John 17:17*. Are there any errors anywhere in God's Word? What was the psalmist's attitude toward God's inerrant Word? What actions flowed from this attitude? What do your actions say about your attitude toward God's Word? Let's pray for hearts that stand in awe of God's infallible Word.

Monday

Read through the Bible: Luke 3
Family Worship: Luke 3:1–14

Whose way was John the Baptist preparing? What did John demand from the people before he would baptize them? What is repentance? *BCF 15:3*. What is the difference between repentance and religiosity? *Luke 18:9–14*. What are the fruits of repentance? What would John the Baptist say if we asked him, "What shall we do"? Let's pray for the grace to "bear fruits in keeping with repentance."

Tuesday

Read through the Bible: Luke 4
Family Worship: Luke 4:16–30

Who always fulfills His word? How did Jesus fulfill the Scripture in Isaiah? *Isa. 61:1–2*. How did the people of Nazareth show their spiritual blindness regarding Christ? **Mark 6:1–3.** Regarding themselves? How were they like the Israelites of Elijah and Elisha's time? Why did they get so angry? How can spiritual pride blind us to our sin? Reflect: How do you typically respond when your sin is revealed? How should we? *Ezek. 36:31*. Let's ask Jesus to open our eyes to our sin and lead us to repentance.

Wednesday

Read through the Bible: Luke 5
Family Worship: Luke 5:27–32

Who needs a physician? How is sin like a deadly sickness? *Jer. 17:9*. Who do the spiritually sick need? What is the Great Physician's prescription for sin? How were the Pharisees like a person with cancer who doesn't know it? How was

Levi (Matthew) different? Who are you more like? Let's confess our sin-sickness and apply the cure, repentance.

Thursday

Read through the Bible: Luke 6
Family Worship: Luke 6:40

What will a student or disciple become like? Who is the Teacher? How can we be more like Him? *Luke 6:35–36.* Who are some other teachers in your life? Are they people you want to be like? In what ways? Parents: What is one way you don't want your children to be like you? Let's pray for the grace to be more like our Teacher and Lord.

Friday

Read through the Bible: Luke 7
Family Worship: Luke 7:11–17

Who is "the resurrection and the life" (John 11:25)? How did the Lord show compassion for this hurting family? How are sinners like this dead son? *Eph. 2:1–3.* How does his resurrection picture salvation? *Eph. 2:4–9.* How do we need the Lord to show compassion for our family? Let's ask God to visit our family by His Spirit and "revive us again, that [we] may rejoice in [Him]" (Ps. 85:6).

Saturday

Read through the Bible: Luke 8
Family Worship: Luke 8:4–15

What does the seed represent? *James 1:21; 1 Peter 1:23.* What kind of heart is pictured by the path? Rocky soil? Thorn-infested soil? Good soil? How can we keep the Word sown in our home from being snatched away by the devil? Choked by thorns and weeds? What can we do to grow deep roots? *Col. 2:6–7; Eph. 3:17.* Let's pray for hearts of good soil that will "bear fruit with patience."

Year 3 — Week 22

Sunday

Read through the Bible: Psalm 120
Family Worship: Psalm 120:1–7

Who is "the truth" (John 14:6)? What kind of people did the psalmist live around? What did he do about it? What are the consequences of deceit? How is our world like his? How can our home sometimes be like this? How can we instead make our home a refuge from the deceit and strife of the world? *Eph. 4:25; Rom. 12:18.* Let's ask the Lord to deliver us from the deceit and strife of the world—and in our hearts.

Monday

Read through the Bible: Luke 9
Family Worship: Luke 9:23–26

Whom must we follow? What does it cost to follow Jesus? It's free to join the military, but you must surrender everything—how is discipleship like this? What is the cost of not following Jesus? What are some ways we can practice self-denying discipleship in our home? Let's pray for the grace to deny ourselves, take up our cross, and follow Jesus.

Tuesday

Read through the Bible: Luke 10
Family Worship: Luke 10:25–37

Who said, "You shall love your neighbor as yourself" (Lev. 19:18)? In Jesus's parable, which person loved his neighbor as himself? How can you tell? How was the lawyer who questioned Jesus like the priest and the Levite? What did this story reveal about his need for grace? *Rom. 3:20; Eph. 2:8–10.* How can we sometimes be like him? How can we instead be good Samaritans? Who is your neighbor? Let's pray for hearts that show mercy to anyone who needs our help.

Wednesday

Read through the Bible: Luke 11
Family Worship: Luke 11:14–22

Who is sovereign over demons and the devil? How was Jesus able to cast out demons? What did some people accuse Him of? How would this be an example of a civil war in Satan's kingdom? What happens to a divided kingdom? A divided household? How could a Christian household be divided today? How can we keep ours from being a divided household? Let's pray for the grace to make ours an undivided household where God's kingdom reigns.

Thursday

Read through the Bible: Luke 12
Family Worship: Luke 12:13–21, 34

What were the two brothers arguing over? In Jesus's parable, what did the rich man say to himself? Why did Jesus say he was a fool? Where was his heart? Where were the hearts of the divided brothers? How can you tell? What causes arguing in our home? What does this say about where our treasure is? Where (who) should our treasure be? Let's ask God to give us hearts that find their treasure in Him.

Friday

Read through the Bible: Luke 13
Family Worship: Luke 13:22–30

Do all roads lead to heaven? Who is the "narrow door" to salvation? *John 10:9; 14:6.* In what sense is it narrow? How does striving to enter picture true faith? *Heb. 4:11.* What reward awaits those who do? What will happen to those who try another way? What if they knew about Jesus? Went to church? Grew up in a Christian home? How can we "strive to enter through the narrow door"? **1 Tim. 6:12.** Let's pray for the grace to "fight the good fight of the faith."

Saturday

Read through the Bible: Luke 14
Family Worship: Luke 14:7–11

Should you take the best seat when invited to a special event? Why not? What happens to everyone who exalts himself? What happens to the one who humbles himself? How did Jesus demonstrate the truth of His own teaching? Who humbled Himself from heaven's glory to death on a cross? *Phil. 2:5-11.* What are some ways you can humble yourself and let others have the first or best in our family? What would our home be like if we all practiced this? Let's pray for the grace to humble ourselves.

Year 3 — Week 23

Sunday

Read through the Bible: Psalm 121
Family Worship: Psalm 121:1–8

Where does our help come from? Why is the Lord able to help us? What could happen if a guard at an important military post fell asleep? Does God ever sleep? What is the Lord for us? How long will He help us? What are some of the ways He has been your helper/shade/keeper? Let's lift up our eyes to the Lord and praise Him for His constant watch and care over us.

Monday

Read through the Bible: Luke 15
Family Worship: Luke 15:11–24

What did the younger son ask for? What did he do with it? What happened when the money ran out? What did he realize when in the pig slop? How do his actions picture repentance? Who does the father represent? How is he like God? Does a child have to leave home to realize he's in the pig slop of sin? What stage of the prodigal's life can you most relate to now? Let's repent of the pig slop of sin in our hearts and run to the loving arms of the Father.

Tuesday

Read through the Bible: Luke 16
Family Worship: Luke 16:19–31

What was the rich man like? How was Lazarus different? What happened to each when he died? Can anyone have a second chance at heaven? Some say that if a person came back from the dead, it would convince them to believe—is this true? *Matt. 28:11–15.* What does God use to bring us to repentance? *Rom. 10:17.* How can thinking about eternity change our lives today? Let's pray that God would use His Word to help us think and live with the end in sight.

Wednesday

Read through the Bible: Luke 17
Family Worship: Luke 17:7–10

What is a servant's duty? What do all creatures owe the Creator? Does God owe us anything as a reward? *BCF 7:1.* Who did all that God commanded? *John 8:29.* Have you? *BCF 16:4–5.* After we've done something that God has commanded, should we be proud? Why not? *BCF 16:6*. How should we respond instead? Let's confess that we are unworthy servants—in need of grace even to do our duty.

Thursday

Read through the Bible: Luke 18
Family Worship: Luke 18:9–14

Who "opposes the proud, but gives grace to the humble" (James 4:6)? For whom did Jesus tell this parable? How did the Pharisee view himself? Others? How was the tax collector different? Which one was self-righteous? Which one was declared righteous (justified) by God? Why? *Rom. 4:5; BCF 11:1*. Reflect: Do you think of yourself as better than others? How can we be more like this tax collector? Let's ask God to be merciful to us—unworthy sinners.

Friday

Read through the Bible: Luke 19
Family Worship: Luke 19:1–10

Who "came to seek and to save the lost"? What was Zacchaeus seeking? How did he go about it? What was Jesus seeking? What evidence is there that Jesus had indeed saved Zacchaeus? *Lev. 6:1–5; Luke 18:18–27*. What evidence is there that salvation has come to our house? *Eph. 4:1–3*. Whom do we need Jesus to seek and save? Let's pray that the Son of Man would indeed seek and save the lost.

Saturday

Read through the Bible: Luke 20
Family Worship: Luke 20:19–26

What were the chief priests and scribes trying to do? What would have happened had Jesus answered yes or no? Should we pay taxes to "Caesar"? *Rom. 13:1–7*. Who ordained civil government? What are we to render to Caesar? To God? *Rom. 12:1*. Should the state tell us how to worship? *Acts 5:29*. Should the church run the state? How can we honor God as American citizens? *Jer. 29:7*. Let's pray for the wisdom to honor God as citizens of heaven and earth.

Year 3   Week 24

Sunday

Read through the Bible: Psalm 122
Family Worship: Psalm 122:1–9

How did David respond when called to worship at the house of the Lord? Why? *Ps. 27:4*. What kind of tabernacle did he worship in? Who is our greater tabernacle? *John 1:14*. How is the Jerusalem we ascend to greater? *Heb. 12:22–24; Gal. 4:26*. When we are called to worship, how much greater should be our joy? Let's pray for hearts that are glad and say, "Let us go to the house of the LORD!"

Monday

Read through the Bible: Luke 21
Family Worship: Luke 21:25–28, 34–36

Who is "the Son of Man"? What will it be like just before Jesus returns? What should we do to get ready? What would it be like to swim with heavy clothes weighing you down? What type of things can weigh our hearts down and keep us from being ready? How can we keep our hearts free from these things? Let's pray for the "strength to escape all these things . . . and to stand before the Son of Man."

Tuesday

Read through the Bible: Luke 22
Family Worship: Luke 22:39–46

What did the Lord tell His disciples to pray? What did He pray for Himself? Why was He in "agony"? *2 Cor. 5:21*. Who was "crushed for our iniquities" (Isa. 53:5)? What was the Father's will for Him? *Isa. 53:10*. How did the Father answer Him? Does God always keep us from trials and temptation? *1 Cor. 10:13*. How can Jesus's example help us endure trials and temptation? *Heb. 12:2–3*. Let's pray that we "may not enter into temptation," but—if it's the Father's will—that He would strengthen us to endure like Jesus.

Wednesday

Read through the Bible: Luke 23
Family Worship: Luke 23:32–43

Who is "the King of the Jews"? How did the King respond to those who crucified Him? *Matt. 5:44*. How do you typically respond to those who mistreat you? How did the two criminals differ in their view of Christ? Of self? How is the repentant criminal an example of great faith? What did Jesus promise him? How does our view of Christ affect our view of self? Let's pray for the grace to see Christ and ourselves through the eyes of the repentant criminal.

Thursday

Read through the Bible: Luke 24
Family Worship: Luke 24:13–35

Who began to walk with Cleopas and his friend? Why didn't they recognize Him at first? How was their physical sight like their spiritual sight? What caused their spiritual eyes to open? What made their hearts burn? How did they change? How do we "see" Jesus today? How should we change as a result? Let's pray for eyes to see Christ in the Scriptures and hearts to burn with devotion for Him.

Friday

Read through the Bible: Acts 1
Family Worship: Acts 1:1–11

What kind of kingdom did the disciples ask about? What type of power did they expect to receive? *Matt. 19:28.* What kind of power did Jesus promise them? What effect would the power of the Holy Spirit have on them? What effect should the Holy Spirit's power have in our lives? How can our family be a witness for Christ? Whose power do we need? Let's pray for the Spirit's power to be His witnesses.

Saturday

Read through the Bible: Acts 2
Family Worship: Acts 2:32–41

Who is "both Lord and Christ"? How did the power of the Holy Spirit change Peter? Why were the men "cut to the heart"? *John 16:8.* What did Peter tell them to do? What did he promise them? Who can receive the gift of the Holy Spirit? Have you ever been "cut to the heart" by the conviction of sin? How should we respond when we are? Let's ask for the gift of the Holy Spirit to convict, convert, and consecrate us.

Year 3 — Week 25

Sunday

Read through the Bible: Psalm 123
Family Worship: Psalm 123:1–4

For what does a servant look to the hand of his master? Who is our Master? For what do we need to look to our Master's hand? *Acts 17:25; Matt. 6:11–13.* What did the psalmist need from the Master? What specifically do you need from the Master today? Let's ask the Master for these things—and for eyes which look to Him for everything.

Monday

Read through the Bible: Acts 3
Family Worship: Acts 3:1–16

What did Peter do for the lame man? By whose power was he able to heal him? Who was the crowd going to credit for this miracle? Whom did Peter credit? How did he use this as an opportunity to be a witness? What good works can we do "by our own power or piety"? *John 15:5; BCF 16:3.* Reflect: Who typically gets the credit for the good you do? How can giving God the glory help us be witnesses for Christ? Let's pray for hearts that give credit where credit is due.

Tuesday

Read through the Bible: Acts 4
Family Worship: Acts 4:1–13

By what power and name was the blind man healed? By what one and only powerful name must we be saved? By what power were Peter and John turned from ordinary men to powerful preachers? What did the rulers recognize about them? How can others recognize that we have been with Jesus? *John 13:35.* Let's pray for lives so transformed by the Spirit's power that people recognize we have been with Jesus.

Wednesday

Read through the Bible: Acts 5
Family Worship: Acts 4:32–5:11

What did Ananias and Sapphira give the church? Did they give all the money from the sale? Did they have to? Why do you think they lied about it? What were the consequences? Why was this lie especially heinous? To whom did they lie? Have you ever not told the whole truth to make yourself look good? What should we do instead? Let's pray for the integrity to always tell the whole truth.

Thursday

Read through the Bible: Acts 6
Family Worship: Acts 6:1–7

What was the problem? What was the solution? Why didn't the apostles personally oversee the food distribution? What was the result of this wise division of labor? What "continued to increase"? Who manages the temporal affairs of our church so that our pastor can focus on prayer and the Word? *1 Tim. 3:8–13.* What can each of you do to wisely divide the duties of our home? Let's pray for servants' hearts that look for ways to help.

Friday

Read through the Bible: Acts 7
Family Worship: Acts 6:8–7:1, 51–60

Summarize Stephen's sermon. What made the people so angry with Stephen? How were they like the Israelites of old? How did they "resist the Holy Spirit"? How do you typically respond when your sin is exposed? Whom did Stephen see in heaven? How was Stephen like Jesus? How can we be more like Stephen in boldness? In humility? Let's pray for hearts sensitive to the Spirit and empowered by Him for boldness and humility.

Saturday

Read through the Bible: Acts 8
Family Worship: Acts 8:26–40

What was the Ethiopian man reading? Why didn't he understand it? How did God help him understand? How did it change him? Do you understand everything in the Bible? Whom has God given to help the church understand it? *John 14:26; Eph. 4:11–16.* Whom has God given to help children understand His Word? *Deut. 6:7.* How should understanding the Word change our lives? Let's pray that God would transform our lives through the teaching of His Word.

Year 3   Week 26

Sunday

Read through the Bible: Psalm 124
Family Worship: Psalm 124:1–8

What problem had David faced? How are angry foes like a "flood" and "raging waters"? What would have happened to David had the Lord not been on his side to help him? What kind of life storms have we been through? Who was our Help during these? What could have happened if the Lord had not been on our side? Let's thank the Lord for being our ark of safety in the floods of life.

Monday

Read through the Bible: Acts 9
Family Worship: Acts 9:1–22

Why was Saul going to Damascus? Who changed his plans? Why did the Lord choose him? How was Saul's physical sight a picture of his spiritual sight? How did Saul change? Will every believer experience a dramatic conversion like Saul? How might the conversion of a child in a Christian home be different? What aspects should be the same? How has the Lord changed your life? Let's pray for the fruit of life-changing conversion through the light of the Word.

Tuesday

Read through the Bible: Acts 10
Family Worship: Acts 10:1–8, 34–48

Who appeared to Cornelius? Why? Why did Peter need to come? **Acts 11:13-14.** What happened when he started preaching the word? How was this like Pentecost? What do people need to hear to be saved? *Rom. 10:17.* How can we get the Word to the unreached peoples of the world? *Rom. 10:13-15.* Let's pray that God would raise up missionaries and Bible translators to share the Word with those who haven't heard.

Wednesday

Read through the Bible: Acts 11
Family Worship: Acts 11:19–26

What were the disciples first called in Antioch? Who are Christians named after? What did Barnabas "see" when he came there? What did he do? What was he like? How was he a "son of encouragement" (Acts 4:36) to the church?

To Saul? How can we be more like him? Let's pray that God's grace would be evident in our home as we encourage one another.

Thursday

Read through the Bible: Acts 12
Family Worship: Acts 12:1–17

What did Herod do to James? To Peter? What did the church do for Peter? How did God answer their prayers? Did they recognize the answer right away? Why not? Why do you think God rescued Peter but not James? Whose wisdom is infinite and unsearchable? *Rom. 11:33.* How was God glorified in both men? *Rev. 12:11.* What can we do for Christians who are being persecuted? Let's pray that God would be glorified in rescuing our persecuted brothers.

Friday

Read through the Bible: Acts 13
Family Worship: Acts 13:40–52

Who is "a light for the Gentiles"? *Isa. 49:6.* How did the Jews respond to the light? *John 1:11.* How did the Gentiles? How many believed? How does this passage show the sovereignty of God in salvation? The responsibility of man? How have you responded to the light of Christ in His Word? Let's rejoice and glorify God for the gift of salvation and pray He would fill us with joy and the Holy Spirit.

Saturday

Read through the Bible: Acts 14
Family Worship: Acts 14:8–18

What miracle did Paul do? Who gave him the power to do this? Why did God give His apostles this power? **Acts 14:3.** How did the people respond? How did Paul and Barnabas stop them? How had God shown them His grace? What kind of people are "idolized" in our culture? In the church? How can we properly honor people without idolizing them? Let's praise God for His grace in all its forms and pray for hearts free from the vanity of "celebrity worship."

Year 3 — Week 27

Sunday

Read through the Bible: Psalm 125
Family Worship: Psalm 125:1–2

Who is the Rock of our salvation? *Ps. 18:2; 1 Cor. 10:4.* What does a big mountain remind you of? How are those who trust in the Lord like Mount Zion? How is the Lord like the mountains that surround Mount Zion? How do storms affect a mountain? How can this mountain imagery secure our faith in the storms of life? *BCF 17:1.2.* Let's pray for the grace of persevering faith "which cannot be moved, but abides forever."

Monday

Read through the Bible: Acts 15
Family Worship: Acts 15:1–11

What did the Pharisees say was necessary to be saved? What did Peter say? Who was right? *Eph. 2:8–9.* Was the law a way of salvation or a way of life for God's people? *BCF 11:6; 19:6.* Since we are not saved by the law, can we live any way we want? Who said, "If you love me, you will keep my commandments" (John 14:15)? How can we show our appreciation for free grace? Let's receive it and rejoice!

Tuesday

Read through the Bible: Acts 16
Family Worship: Acts 16:16–34

What would you do if you were beaten and thrown in prison? What did Paul and Silas do? *James 1:2.* How might the story have been different had they whined and complained? What did the jailer do? What must we do to be saved? In whom must we believe? How did the jailer's family respond? Let's pray for the grace of an entire household that believes in the Lord Jesus—and worships Him amid trials.

Wednesday

Read through the Bible: Acts 17
Family Worship: Acts 17:10–12

How did the Berean Jews receive the word? What did they do after Paul and Silas preached? Why? What is the standard we use to verify all truth claims?

John 17:17; Ps. 119:160; BCF 1:10. How can we be good "Bereans"? Let's pray for the wisdom to verify all truth claims against the supreme standard of Scripture.

Thursday

Read through the Bible: Acts 18
Family Worship: Acts 18:24–28

What was Apollos like? How did Priscilla and Aquila help him? What was the result? What did he show "by the Scriptures"? Who is the Christ? What can happen if the Word of God is not taught accurately? How can you prepare to accurately teach the Word to your future family? *2 Tim. 2:15; 3:14–17.* Let's pray that God would use the teaching in our home to make you "competent in the Scriptures."

Friday

Read through the Bible: Acts 19
Family Worship: Acts 19:18–20

What did some of the new believers do? Why? How seriously does God view involvement in magic arts? *Deut. 18:9–14.* What was the cost of their obedience? Was it worth it? *Ps. 119:72.* What "increase[d] and prevail[ed] mightily"? What forms of magic and occult practices do we need to beware of? Do we have any books, movies, or video games that would be better off burned? Let's pray for wisdom in identifying and purging our home of any sources of evil.

Saturday

Read through the Bible: Acts 20
Family Worship: Acts 20:17–21, 26–27

What did Paul teach the Ephesian elders? Where do we find "the whole counsel of God"? *Ps. 119:160.* Why is it important to teach the whole counsel of God? *Acts 20:29–32; Ezek. 3:17–21.* Who is responsible to teach children the whole counsel of God? *Deut. 6:6–7.* How can we make sure we are? (*This is the purpose of On Your Heart!*) Let's pray for hearts passionate to teach—and to learn—"the whole counsel of God."

Year 3 — Week 28

Sunday

Read through the Bible: Psalm 126
Family Worship: Psalm 126:1–6

Who restored the fortunes of the exiles? How did He do so? *Ezra 1*. How did they respond? Why was there both laughter and tears? *Ezra 3:10–13*. What are some great things the Lord has done for us? What are some great things yet to come? *Rev. 21:1–4*. How should we live during this "already/not yet" time? *1 Peter 2:9; 1 Cor. 15:58*. Let's praise God for the great things He has done and for the great things yet to come.

Monday

Read through the Bible: Acts 21
Family Worship: Acts 20:22–24; 21:8–14; 23:11

Whose will was it for Paul to go to Jerusalem? What did the Holy Spirit say would happen to him there? Why didn't that dissuade him from going? What is the cost of obedience for our missionaries? The persecuted church? For us? Reflect: Is there any area of your life where you are failing to obey out of fear of the cost? What is the cost of disobedience? Let's pray for the tenacious faith to obey God no matter the cost.

Tuesday

Read through the Bible: Acts 22
Family Worship: Acts 22:1–10

What did Paul formerly do to the church? According to our Lord, whom was Paul ultimately persecuting? In what sense was Paul persecuting Jesus? *Col. 1:18*. What parts of the body of Christ are being persecuted today? What can we do to help them? *Heb. 13:3; see the Voice of the Martyrs website at www.persecution.com*. Let's begin by asking Jesus to encourage, strengthen, and deliver His persecuted people.

Wednesday

Read through the Bible: Acts 23
Family Worship: Acts 23:12–24

What did the Jews plot against Paul? Who exposed the plot? Who, by His providence, caused Paul's nephew to overhear the plot? What did he do? What did he risk by doing this? What should you do if a group of so-called friends is planning to do something wrong? What if they are adults? Would it be easy? What may it cost? Let's pray for the strength to stand for what's right no matter what others around us are doing.

Thursday

Read through the Bible: Acts 24
Family Worship: Acts 24:24–27

What and whom did Paul speak to Felix about? How did he respond? Why was he alarmed? How should we respond to the message of righteousness and the coming judgment? Why did he keep talking with Paul? Why didn't Paul give him a bribe and sugarcoat his message to gain release? Is it ever right to "soften" the gospel to make it less offensive to people? *Gal. 5:11.* Let's pray for the boldness and integrity to live and proclaim the truth without compromise.

Friday

Read through the Bible: Acts 25
Family Worship: Acts 25:1–12

What were the Jews planning to do to Paul? Was he guilty of breaking the law? How did he wisely use his rights as a Roman citizen? What rights do we have as American citizens? What responsibilities? Who said, "Render to Caesar the things that are Caesar's, and to God the things that are God's" (Mark 12:17)? How can we be good Christians and good citizens? *Rom. 13:1–7; Phil. 3:20; 1 Tim. 2:1–2.* Let's pray for the wisdom to be good citizens of heaven and earth.

Saturday

Read through the Bible: Acts 26
Family Worship: Acts 26:12–20

Who sent Paul to the Gentiles? Why? How did Paul respond? What did he declare wherever he went? What are "deeds in keeping with repentance"? What should they look like in our family? In your life? Let's praise God for opening our eyes and pray for the grace to perform deeds in keeping with repentance.

Year 3   Week 29

Sunday

Read through the Bible: Psalm 127
Family Worship: Psalm 127:3–5

How does the Lord view children? Who said, "Let the little children come to me" (Matt. 19:14)? How are children a heritage, a gift, a reward? *1 Chron. 13:14; 26:4–5.* If you were a warrior, how many arrows would you want? How are children like arrows for a family? *Parents: Hug each child and explain one way God has blessed you through him or her.* How can you continue to bless our family when you grow up? *3 John 4; Gen. 24:60; 1 Tim. 5:4.* Let's praise God for each child-gift.

Monday

Read through the Bible: Acts 27
Family Worship: Acts 27:9–26, 39–44

Whom did the Centurion listen to at the beginning of the voyage? To whom should he have listened? *Acts 27:31–32.* Should we listen to the worldly wisdom of the so-called experts or the heavenly wisdom of God? Where do we find God's wisdom? *Prov. 2:1–8.* Was the majority right in Paul's case? Is the majority always right today? Let's pray that God would show us any area where we are listening to worldly wisdom instead of His Word.

Tuesday

Read through the Bible: Acts 28
Family Worship: Acts 28:23–31

What did Paul do wherever he was? How was his imprisonment a blessing? *This is when he wrote Ephesians, Colossians, Philippians, and Philemon.* Who spoke through Isaiah? Who is speaking to us now through Luke and Paul? Since these are God's words, what authority do they have? Does this change if some disbelieve? Though not preachers, how can we boldly testify like Paul? *Deut. 6:6–7; 1 Peter 3:15.* Let's pray for hearts to boldly testify of Christ wherever we are.

Wednesday

Read through the Bible: Romans 1
Family Worship: Romans 1:16–17

What is the gospel? Where do we find it? *Rom. 1:1–2.* What does it reveal? How do we receive it? *Rom. 3:21-22*. What does it create in the elect? *Rom. 10:17; 1 Peter 1:23-25*. Does the gospel need to be added to or modified to reach people today? How did Paul show he was "not ashamed of the gospel"? How can we? Let's pray for hearts transformed by—and unashamed of—the gospel.

Thursday

Read through the Bible: Romans 2
Family Worship: Romans 1:18, 28–2:4

What are sinners like apart from grace? What do sinners deserve? What about those who consider themselves moral but judge others? Have you ever done any of these things? What has God provided for sinners like us? In whom has God shown us His kindness? *Eph. 2:1-7*. What should God's kindness lead us to? Let's pray that God's kindness would indeed lead us to repentance . . . right now.

Friday

Read through the Bible: Romans 3
Family Worship: Romans 3:9–20

Who is "the Judge of all the earth" (Gen. 18:25)? Imagine all mankind accused of sin before God in the heavenly courtroom. The prosecution (the law) presents verses 10–18 as evidence. What is the verdict: guilty or not guilty? Can we be justified (declared "not guilty") by the law? What, then, is the purpose of the law? How can we be justified? **Rom. 3:21-26.** Let's confess our guilt and praise God for the gift of justification by grace.

Saturday

Read through the Bible: Romans 4
Family Worship: Romans 4:1–8

What is *justification*? *BCF 11:1*. Was Abraham justified by faith or by works? How was David justified? How are we justified? *Rom. 4:22-25*. Was justification in the Old Testament different from the New Testament? *BCF 11:6*. Who "justifies the ungodly"? How can God do that and remain just? *Rom. 3:23-26; 2 Cor. 5:21*. Once justified, how should we live? *Rom. 5:1-2*. Let's praise our Lord for bearing the guilt and punishment we deserve so we might be declared not guilty—righteous.

Year 3   Week 30

Sunday

Read through the Bible: Psalm 128
Family Worship: Psalm 128:1–6

Whom are we to fear? How can you show that you fear the Lord? In general, how does God bless those who fear Him? How do the metaphors in verse 3 picture a blessed family? How has God blessed our family? How do you want God to bless your future family? Let's praise God for blessing our family and pray for hearts and future homes that fear God and walk in His ways.

Monday

Read through the Bible: Romans 5
Family Worship: Romans 5:1, 6–11

How did God show His love for us? Who died for sinners? Did Christ die for us because of something good in us? What were the people like that Jesus died for? What is reconciliation? In what sense has God made peace with former enemies? *Col. 1:21-22.* How should we respond to the One who redeemed us and reconciled us to God? Let's "rejoice in God through our Lord Jesus Christ."

Tuesday

Read through the Bible: Romans 6
Family Worship: Romans 6:14–23

Fill in the blanks: All people serve either ____ or ____. What do people become when they obey sin? How is living in sin like slavery? What are the wages of sin? What free gift does God offer sinners? How do we receive that gift? *Rom. 10:9-10.* After receiving it, should we "have fun" by living in sin? Why not? What (or whom) will you serve? *Josh. 24:15; Matt. 11:28-30.* Let's pray for hearts freed from sin and free to serve God.

Wednesday

Read through the Bible: Romans 7
Family Worship: Romans 7:14–25

Is it possible to be completely sinless in this life? *BCF 13:2.* Was Paul? What was he struggling with? How is the battle with remaining sin like a war? Have you ever felt like Paul? Who will "deliver [us] from this body of death" (remaining corruption)? How can we work together with God in this battle for sanctification? **Rom. 6:12–13; 8:13;** *BCF 13:3*. Let's pray for the grace to struggle obediently against remaining sin.

Thursday

Read through the Bible: Romans 8
Family Worship: Romans 8:31–39

Who is for us? If "God is for us," can anyone "be against us"? Can anyone "bring any charge against God's elect"? What if Satan says, "You've sinned—you don't deserve to go to heaven!"? Can anything or anyone "separate us from the love of Christ"? If bad things happen to us, does it mean that God has stopped loving us? *Rom. 8:28-29*. In what sense are we more than conquerors? *Rev. 12:11*. What "shall we say to these things?" Let's praise God for His never-ending love.

Friday

Read through the Bible: Romans 9
Family Worship: Romans 9:6–18

What do all sinners deserve? *Rom. 6:23*. Is God obligated to show mercy to any? Who "has mercy on whomever he wills"? Why was God merciful to Jacob but not to Esau? *Eph. 1:4-6*. Why did God soften Moses's heart but harden Pharaoh's? Are we any better than people like Esau and Pharaoh? How should we respond to God for showing sovereign mercy to undeserving sinners like us? Let's offer to Him humble, heartfelt praise and thanksgiving! *Hymn: "Amazing Grace."*

Saturday

Read through the Bible: Romans 10
Family Worship: Romans 10:5–13

How does a person attain "the righteousness . . . based on the law"? Have you obeyed all the commandments? Has anyone? How, then, can we be saved? Who is Lord? Can Christ be your Savior without being your Lord? How can we show by our lives that our confession of Christ as Lord is genuine? *Luke 6:46*. Let's pray for hearts to believe, mouths to confess, and lives to show that Jesus is Lord.

Year 3 — Week 31

Sunday

Read through the Bible: Psalm 129
Family Worship: Psalm 129:1–8

What problem did the psalmist (speaking for Israel) face? What does plowing on one's back picture? Whose back was "plowed" by scourging for our transgressions? *Isa. 53:5.* What does the cutting of cords picture? What does withering grass picture? *2 Thess. 1:5–10.* What spiritual enemies hate the church and "plow" on its back today? How can we help our persecuted brothers and sisters? Let's pray that God would strengthen their faith, free them, and judge their enemies.

Monday

Read through the Bible: Romans 11
Family Worship: Romans 11:13–24

Who is the Sovereign Savior? In the olive tree of God's people, who are the natural branches? Who are the wild olive branches? What happened to the natural branches? Why? Should the wild branches be proud of being grafted in? Why not? *Rom. 11:5–6.* How should they (we) respond instead? *Rom. 11:33–36.* Let's humbly and reverently worship our Sovereign Savior. *Hymn: "Amazing Grace."*

Tuesday

Read through the Bible: Romans 12
Family Worship: Romans 12:1–2

Who offered Himself as a full sacrifice for us? What are we to present ourselves as? How are "living sacrifices" similar to Old Testament animal sacrifices? How are they different? Reflect: Is there any part of your life that has crawled off the altar? What is the difference between being conformed and being transformed? How can we renew our minds? *Deut. 6:6–7; Eph. 4:11–16.* What should this result in? Let's worship God now by offering ourselves completely to Him—body and mind.

Wednesday

Read through the Bible: Romans 13
Family Worship: Romans 13:1–7

Who instituted civil government? How is civil government a servant of God? What power has God given civil government? *BCF 24:1.* What are the limits of the civil government's jurisdiction? *Mark 12:17; Acts 5:29*. What would happen if there were no civil government? How can we be good citizens of both heaven and earth? *Phil. 3:20; BCF 24:2–3*. Let's pray that God would enable our government to fulfill its role—and enable us to fulfill our role in it.

Thursday

Read through the Bible: Romans 14
Family Worship: Romans 14:10–12

To whom shall every knee bow? *Phil. 2:9–11*. Is it okay for other families to have different rules about things like hair, school, alcohol, and the like? Is it our place to judge or despise a Christian brother or sister? Why not? What will all people have to do on judgment day? Instead of judging others, whom should we judge? *2 Cor. 13:5*. Let's pray for the Spirit's help to judge ourselves and repent of any judgmentalism.

Friday

Read through the Bible: Romans 15
Family Worship: Romans 15:1–7

Whom should we seek to please? Why? Who is our ultimate example of how to treat others? What can you do to please someone else today? What is the ultimate authority for our lives? How do the Scriptures help us? *2 Tim. 3:16–17*. How can our family better live in harmony? What will this result in? Let's pray that God would grant us to live in such harmony that our family would give Him glory.

Saturday

Read through the Bible: Romans 16
Family Worship: Romans 16:17–19; Matthew 10:16

What should we watch out for? Why? How do false teachers deceive others? What is the difference between being naïve and being wise? What is the difference between knowing what is good and being wise? How can we equip ourselves "to be wise as to what is good and innocent as to what is evil"? Where do we find true doctrine? *1 Tim. 6:3; Titus 1:9*. Let's pray for the grace and discernment to be wise as to what is good and innocent as to what is evil.

Year 3 — Week 32

Sunday

Read through the Bible: Psalm 130
Family Worship: Psalm 130:1–8

If the Lord "should mark iniquities (i.e., keep a tally of our sins) who could stand?" Who bore the tally of our sins? *Isa. 53:5-6*. How did God display both His justice and mercy at the cross? *Rom. 3:23-26; 2 Cor. 5:21*. In light of God's justice, how did the psalmist respond to God's forgiveness? How should we? In loving reverence, let's praise God for not marking our sins against us.

Monday

Read through the Bible: 1 Corinthians 1
Family Worship: 1 Corinthians 1:18–25

Can we come to know God through human wisdom? Who is "the wisdom of God"? What means does God use to call people to Himself? What are different ways that people respond to "the word of the cross"? Why the difference? *1 Cor. 1:26-29; 2:14*. How have you responded to the word of the cross? Let's pray for hearts to reject the wisdom of the world (which is really foolishness) and receive the wisdom of God in His Word.

Tuesday

Read through the Bible: 1 Corinthians 2
Family Worship: 1 Corinthians 2:9–14

What has God revealed to us? *Ps. 139:17*. Where are the thoughts of God recorded? Who understands the thoughts of God? How can we understand His thoughts? Can a natural person (one without the Spirit) understand God's thoughts? Why not? What should we do with God's thoughts? Let's praise God for revealing His precious thoughts to us and pray for the Spirit's power to understand and obey them.

Wednesday

Read through the Bible: 1 Corinthians 3
Family Worship: 1 Corinthians 3:9–15

Who is the foundation of the church? What does fire do to gold, silver, and precious stones? What does it do to wood, hay, and straw? What type of works do each picture? What will happen to believers' works on the judgment day?

What works can you do that will survive the test of fire? *1 Peter 1:6-7; BCF 16*. Let's pray for the Spirit's power to do works that endure to the glory of God.

Thursday

Read through the Bible: 1 Corinthians 4
Family Worship: 1 Corinthians 4:14–17

What was Paul to the Corinthians? In what sense was he their "father"? *Acts 18:1-11*. What did he urge them to do? Whom did Paul imitate? **1 Cor. 11:1; Eph. 5:1**. Whom are you imitating? Who is your spiritual father? As your father, here are some ways I don't want you to imitate me: ____. As my beloved children, I urge you to imitate my ways in Christ, such as: ____. Let's pray for the grace to imitate Christ (and for me to be a better example of what that looks like).

Friday

Read through the Bible: 1 Corinthians 5
Family Worship: 1 Corinthians 5:6–8

Who is our Passover Lamb? How is Christ like a Passover lamb? *Ex. 12:3-13; John 1:29; 1 Peter 1:19*. What does a little leaven (yeast) do to a lump of dough? How is sin like that? How can we keep the leaven of sin from spreading in our lives? In our family? In our church? What should we replace the leaven with? Let's pray for the grace to remove the leaven of evil and replace it with sincerity and truth.

Saturday

Read through the Bible: 1 Corinthians 6
Family Worship: 1 Corinthians 6:19–20

What is the body of a believer? How should a temple of the Holy Spirit act? To whom do we belong? With what price were we "bought" (redeemed)? *1 Peter 1:18-19*. How, then, should we live? **1 Cor. 10:31**. What is "the chief end of man"? *"To glorify God and to enjoy Him forever" (Westminster Shorter Catechism)*. How can we glorify God and enjoy Him today? Let's pray for the grace to "do all to the glory of God."

Year 3   Week 33

Sunday

Read through the Bible: Psalm 131
Family Worship: Psalm 131:1–3

What is a weaned child like with his mother? How was the warrior David like a weaned child? *Matt. 18:1–4.* Does a weaned child need to understand everything his mother does or just be with her? How is this like our relationship with God? Who told us to "become like children" (Matt. 18:3)? In which of these aspects do you need to be more like a weaned child: humility, trust, or contentment? Let's pray for childlike hearts that are humble, trusting, and content.

Monday

Read through the Bible: 1 Corinthians 7
Family Worship: 1 Corinthians 7:39

Who instituted marriage? *Mark 10:6–9.* Should a believer ever marry an unbeliever? Why not? *2 Cor. 6:14.* What are some of the potential areas of conflict a believer may have with an unbelieving spouse? What are some unique joys believers can share in marriage? How can you prepare for a Christian marriage? Let's pray for our children and their future spouses that during their season of singleness they would "secure [their] undivided devotion to the Lord" (1 Cor. 7:35).

Tuesday

Read through the Bible: 1 Corinthians 8
Family Worship: 1 Corinthians 8:4–13

How many Gods are there? Is it wrong in and of itself to eat meat sacrificed to an idol? In what situation would it be wrong? Is it wrong to drink wine? *Ps. 104:15; John 2:1–11.* In what situation would it be wrong? **Rom. 14:21.** When we cause a weaker brother or sister to sin, whom have we ultimately sinned against? How can we show greater concern for our brothers and sisters than our rights? Let's pray for the discretion to enjoy our liberty in Christ without being a stumbling block.

Wednesday

Read through the Bible: 1 Corinthians 9
Family Worship: 1 Corinthians 9:24–27

How is the Christian life like a race? *Heb. 12:1–2*. What do athletes need to do to win the prize? What do we need to do to persevere in the Christian life? What is an area of your life that requires greater self-control? How can you exercise greater discipline in that area? Who gives us the power to have self-control? *Gal. 5:22–23*. Let's pray for the fruit of the Spirit of self-control.

Thursday

Read through the Bible: 1 Corinthians 10
Family Worship: 1 Corinthians 10:12–13

What happens to those who think they are above temptation? *Prov. 16:18*. What is different about the temptations we face from those in Bible times? Who always provides "the way of escape" from temptation? What way of escape did Jesus use when tempted? *Matt. 4:1–11*. How can we successfully face temptation? Let's pray for the grace to choose the way of escape of obedience when tempted.

Friday

Read through the Bible: 1 Corinthians 11
Family Worship: 1 Corinthians 11:23–32; 10:16–17

Who instituted the Lord's Supper? What does the Communion bread represent? The wine? Do these really become the body and blood of the Lord? Why do we celebrate the Lord's Supper? *BCF 30:1*. How is it like a special family meal? Who should partake of it? How should we prepare for it? Let's pray that God would reveal anything in us that could spoil communion with our risen Savior.

Saturday

Read through the Bible: 1 Corinthians 12
Family Worship: 1 Corinthians 12:12–27

How many parts does your body have? Do you need them all? What if your eye said to your hand, "I have no need of you"? Who arranged the parts of the body? How is the church like a body? What can we do to serve our church body? How is our family like a body? What can you do to help our family? Let's pray for the power of the Spirit to do our part in the body of Christ.

Year 3   Week 34

Sunday

Read through the Bible: Psalm 132
Family Worship: Psalm 132:11–18

What did the Lord promise David? Who is now on Zion's throne? *Luke 1:32-33.* Where is God's "dwelling place"? *John 1:14; Heb. 12:22; 1 Cor. 3:16; 6:19.* Who are His priests? *1 Peter 2:9.* His saints? *1 Cor. 1:2.* What has He done for His priests and saints? How should we respond? Let's "shout for joy" as we "proclaim the excellencies of him who called [us] out of darkness into his marvelous light" (1 Peter 2:9).

Monday

Read through the Bible: 1 Corinthians 13
Family Worship: 1 Corinthians 13:1–8a

What value is the greatest human achievement without love? What does love look like? Who perfectly demonstrated this kind of love? What are some things we can do to show this kind of love to one another? To those in our church? To our neighbors? Let's pray for the grace to love one another with Christlike love.

Tuesday

Read through the Bible: 1 Corinthians 14
Family Worship: 1 Corinthians 14:33a, 40

What would it be like driving a car with no order or rules? What would church be like if there were no order, but instead, everyone did what he felt was right? *1 Cor. 14:26.* Who created the universe with order and harmony? *Gen. 1.* How does order in church and society reflect God? How can our home better reflect the orderliness of God? Let's pray for the wisdom to do all things "decently and in order."

Wednesday

Read through the Bible: 1 Corinthians 15
Family Worship: 1 Corinthians 15:3–8, 35–49

What will our resurrection bodies be like? Who will we be more like? How will our new bodies be different from our current ones? How will the relationship between the two be like planting a seed? How should this glorious truth motivate us to live now? **1 Cor. 15:58.** Let's praise God for the resurrection and pray

He would enable us to be "steadfast, immovable, always abounding in the work of the Lord."

Thursday

Read through the Bible: 1 Corinthians 16
Family Worship: 1 Corinthians 16:13–14

What are some spiritual dangers we should be watchful for? What are we to stand firm in? *Jude 3*. Boys: Does acting like men mean we should be rough and unloving? Does being loving imply we are wimps? Who exemplifies perfect, manly love? How can you live out strong, Christlike love today? Let's pray for the strength to do everything in love.

Friday

Read through the Bible: 2 Corinthians 1
Family Worship: 2 Corinthians 1:3–11

Who is the "God of all comfort"? What does God do when we are afflicted? How has God comforted you in a time of affliction? How can affliction move us to rely more on God and less on ourselves? How can it enable us to help others who are afflicted? Is there someone you know who is afflicted? How can we help him or her? Let's pray that God would be the God of all comfort to him or her and use us as part of the means.

Saturday

Read through the Bible: 2 Corinthians 2
Family Worship: 2 Corinthians 2:14–16

What is a fragrance or aroma you find pleasant? What is an aroma that some find pleasant but others unpleasant? What or whom are believers the aroma of? What kind of fragrance is the aroma of Christ to a believer? To an unbeliever? Why the difference? What is the spiritual aroma of our home? Of your heart? How can we spread the fragrance of the knowledge of Christ? *Eph. 5:1–2*. Let's pray for the grace to be "the aroma of Christ."

Year 3 — Week 35

Sunday

Read through the Bible: Psalm 133
Family Worship: Psalm 133:1–3

What was it like in Israel when brothers would dwell in unity? What is it like in our home when brothers and sisters dwell in unity? What is it like when brothers and sisters fight? How can we promote greater unity in our family? Our church family? In whom does the church have unity? *John 17:22–23; Eph. 4:3.* Let's pray for "good and pleasant" unity in our family and the family of God.

Monday

Read through the Bible: 2 Corinthians 3
Family Worship: 2 Corinthians 3:17

Is freedom the ability to sin all you want? **Gal. 5:1, 13.** What is true freedom? **Rom. 8:2**; *BCF 9:4.* Who gives us true freedom? **John 8:36.** How can we experience true freedom? **John 8:31–32.** Let's ask the Holy Spirit to free us from our love of sin and empower us to know and abide in the truth.

Tuesday

Read through the Bible: 2 Corinthians 4
Family Worship: 2 Corinthians 4:3–6

What is a veil? In what sense is the gospel "veiled"? *2 Cor. 3:12–16.* Who has blinded the mind of unbelievers? Why? Who spoke light into the darkness of creation? Who speaks light into the darkness of human hearts? How can we keep the enemy from blinding us? *2 Peter 1:19; BCF 10:1.* Let's pray for hearts and minds unveiled by the Holy Spirit to see and pay attention to "the light of the gospel."

Wednesday

Read through the Bible: 2 Corinthians 5
Family Worship: 2 Corinthians 5:1–9

How are a tent and a building different? How does this picture the difference between our mortal bodies and our future resurrection bodies? What happens to believers who die before the resurrection? *Phil. 1:21, 23.* Whom do they go to be with? What did Paul long for? What was his aim? How can we aim to please the Lord today? *Col. 1:10; 3:20.* Let's praise God for the promise of an immortal body and pray for the grace to please Him now in our mortal bodies.

Thursday

Read through the Bible: 2 Corinthians 6:1–7:1
Family Worship: 2 Corinthians 6:14–7:1

What would happen if you tried to pull a plow with two animals of unequal strength? How does this picture an improper relationship between a believer and an unbeliever? How can we share Christ with unbelievers without becoming "unequally yoked" with them? What has God promised us? Who promises to dwell with us? How should these promises motivate us to live? Let's praise our Father for drawing us near as sons and daughters and pray He would show us anyone or anything that would hinder fellowship with Him.

Friday

Read through the Bible: 2 Corinthians 7:2–16
Family Worship: 2 Corinthians 7:8–11

What is "godly grief"? What does it produce? How is "worldly grief" different? What does it produce? What would godly grief look like when a child is disciplined? What would worldly grief look like? Reflect: Do you grieve merely for the consequences of sin or because you have offended our holy God? Who can grant us the godly grief that produces repentance? *2 Tim. 2:25.* Let's pray for the grace of godly grief which produces genuine repentance.

Saturday

Read through the Bible: 2 Corinthians 8
Family Worship: 2 Corinthians 8:9

Who was rich yet for our sake became poor? How was (is) Christ rich? *John 1:1-3; Col. 1:15-19; Heb. 1:2-3.* In what ways did He become poor? *Phil. 2:6-8.* How were we poor? *Eph. 2:1-3.* In what ways have we become rich through Him? *2 Cor. 5:21; Eph. 2:4-7.* How should we respond to His gracious generosity? Let's praise God for the amazing grace of our Lord Jesus Christ. *Hymn: "Amazing Grace."*

Year 3   Week 36

Sunday

Read through the Bible: Psalm 134
Family Worship: Psalm 134:1–2

What were those who stood by night in the temple told to do? What posture did they use? *1 Tim. 2:8.* Whom are we to bless? How often? **Ps. 34:1.** Reflect: What is in your mouth more often: praise or complaining? When should we rejoice, pray, and give thanks? **1 Thess. 5:16–18.** How can we foster an attitude of continual praise in our home? Let's pray for hearts, hands, and mouths to "bless the LORD at all times."

Monday

Read through the Bible: 2 Corinthians 9
Family Worship: 2 Corinthians 9:7

What kind of giver does God love? What is a "cheerful giver" like? What would be the opposite of a cheerful giver? Can we ever out-give God? **2 Cor. 9:15.** Who gave us an "inexpressible gift"? What is it? *2 Cor. 8:9; John 3:16; Eph. 2:8.* How can we practice cheerful giving at church? In our family? Let's pray for the grace to be a family of cheerful givers.

Tuesday

Read through the Bible: 2 Corinthians 10
Family Worship: 2 Corinthians 10:3–5

What kind of weapons do we fight with? *Eph. 6:10–18.* What do we destroy? What are we to take captive? Whom should our thoughts obey? How can we know if a thought is obedient to Christ? What kind of things should we think about? **Phil. 4:8.** Reflect: What are some thoughts you need to take captive? Let's pray for the grace to take every thought captive and love God with all our minds. *Matt. 22:37.*

Wednesday

Read through the Bible: 2 Corinthians 11
Family Worship: 2 Corinthians 11:3–4, 13–15

What does Satan disguise himself as? Why? Who are his servants? What do they disguise themselves as? What kind of "gospel" do they teach? What kind of "Jesus" do they proclaim? How can we recognize false teachers/teaching?

Ps. 119:97–104; Hos. 4:6. What is the supreme standard of truth? *Ps. 119:160; John 17:17.* Let's pray for hearts that so know and love the truth of God's Word that we will immediately recognize and reject false teaching.

Thursday

Read through the Bible: 2 Corinthians 12
Family Worship: 2 Corinthians 12:1–10

What amazing experience did Paul have fourteen years prior? Why did God then give him a "thorn" in the flesh? What do you think it was? What did Paul ask God to do? Why wouldn't He? Whose grace is sufficient for us? How is God's saving grace magnified in our weakness? *1 Cor. 1:26–29; Eph. 2:4–7.* How is God's grace magnified in our trials? *James 1:2–4.* Let's pray for eyes to see trials and weaknesses as opportunities to magnify God's grace.

Friday

Read through the Bible: 2 Corinthians 13
Family Worship: 2 Corinthians 13:5; Matt. 7:15–23

Who saves and sanctifies us? How could you test a tree to see whether it was an apple tree? How can we test ourselves to see whether we are in the faith? What kind of fruit should there be in our lives? *Gal. 5:22-23.* Is being outwardly religious sufficient fruit? "Examine yourselves"—what kind of fruit is evident in your life? Let's pray for the power of the Holy Spirit to produce a fruitful, obedient faith that will be tested genuine. *1 Peter 1:7.*

Saturday

Read through the Bible: Galatians 1
Family Worship: Galatians 1:6–9

What kind of "gospel" were some people teaching the Galatians? What was Paul's reaction? Mormons claim their founder received golden plates from an angel containing an addition to the gospel. What should we do if their "missionaries" come to our house to share this "different gospel"? *2 John 10.* Where do we find the true gospel? *Ps. 119:160; John 17:17.* Let's pray that God would enable us to passionately and respectfully "contend for the faith" (Jude 3).

Year 3 — Week 37

Sunday

Read through the Bible: Psalm 135
Family Worship: Psalm 135:1–7

Who "does all that he pleases" (Ps. 115:3)? What pleases the Lord? **1 Sam. 12:22.**[6] What would the world be like if God were not able to do all He pleased? How did the psalmist respond to God's pleasure in being God? How did Jesus? **Luke 10:21.** How should we? Let's praise God for doing all He pleases.

Monday

Read through the Bible: Galatians 2
Family Worship: Galatians 2:20

Who lived in Paul? In what sense was Paul "crucified with Christ"? *Rom. 6:4–6.* In what sense did he no longer live? *2 Cor. 5:17.* How did he live? What has Jesus done for us? How should we live? Reflect: What is one area of your life where you need to die to self and live by faith in Christ? Let's praise our Lord for giving Himself for us and pray for His help to give ourselves completely to Him by faith.

Tuesday

Read through the Bible: Galatians 3
Family Worship: Galatians 2:16, 21; 3:19, 24–26

Are we justified by works of the law or by faith in Christ? "Why then the law"—what is its purpose? *Rom. 3:20.* In Roman culture, a guardian was a slave responsible for the training and discipline of children. How is the law like a guardian? To whom does the law point? **Rom. 10:4.** How can the law help us become more like Christ? **Gal. 5:14; 6:2;** *BCF 19:5–6.* Let's pray that God would use the law to expose our sin and draw us to Christ.

Wednesday

Read through the Bible: Galatians 4
Family Worship: Galatians 4:1–7

Who is the Son of God? How are a slave and a son different? What did God's Son do so we could be adopted as sons? What does His Spirit do through adopted sons? *Abba* is a tender Aramaic term similar to a respectful *daddy*. How

---

[6] See also John Piper, *The Pleasures of God* (Colorado Springs: Multnomah, 2000).

is God like our "daddy"? What privileges do we have as His children? How should we live as adopted children of God? Let's praise our "Abba, Father" and ask Him to help us act like His sons and daughters and not like slaves.

Thursday

Read through the Bible: Galatians 5
Family Worship: Galatians 5:22–23

What fruit should be evident in a believer's life? Who perfectly lived the fruit of the Spirit? Of the fruit listed, which one is the biggest struggle for you? How can you better practice this quality in our family? Let's pray for the power of the Spirit to manifest the fruit of the Spirit—especially in the area we struggle with most.

Friday

Read through the Bible: Galatians 6
Family Worship: Galatians 6:1

Who gave the church the authority to discipline its members? *Matt. 18:15-20.* What should happen if a brother is caught in a sin? Who should do it? In what manner? What must the mature brother watch out for? What should you do if you catch a sibling doing something sinful? Let's pray for gentle and humble hearts whether correcting or being corrected.

Saturday

Read through the Bible: Ephesians 1
Family Worship: Ephesians 1:3–14

What has God blessed us with? In whom do we receive "every spiritual blessing"? Specifically, what spiritual blessings has God the Father given us? God the Son? God the Holy Spirit? Why has God done all these things? How can these blessings be a source of comfort for us? *Rom. 8:28-30.* A source of humility? *Rom. 9:16.* Praise? *Rom. 11:33-36.* Let's praise our triune God for the riches of His glorious grace. *Hymn: "Amazing Grace."*

Year 3 — Week 38

Sunday

Read through the Bible: Psalm 136
Family Worship: Psalm 136:1–9, 23–26

Who shows us steadfast love? How long does His steadfast love endure? How did God show His steadfast love to Israel? How has He shown His steadfast love to all people? *Acts 14:17; John 3:16.* How has He shown His steadfast love to us? How did the psalmist respond to God for His steadfast love? How should we? Let's "give thanks to the LORD, for He is good, for His steadfast love endures forever."

Monday

Read through the Bible: Ephesians 2
Family Worship: Ephesians 2:1–9

Preparation: Get a stuffed animal. If I pinch you, will you feel it? If I pinch this stuffed animal, will it feel it? Why not? Spiritually, how are sinners like this stuffed animal? To respond to God, what do sinners need? Who is able to make us alive? Do sinners made alive have anything to boast about? Why not? How should those made alive respond to God? Let's praise God for "the immeasurable riches of His grace." *Hymn: "Amazing Grace."*

Tuesday

Read through the Bible: Ephesians 3
Family Worship: Ephesians 3:20–21

What is the most amazing thing you can imagine? What is God able to do? What are some amazing things God has done for believers? *Eph. 1–2.* What are some amazing things He has done for you? What is something amazing you need God to do for you? *Eph. 3:14–19.* Is He able? Who should receive the glory for all this? Let's ask God "to do far more abundantly than all that we ask or think"—for His glory.

Wednesday

Read through the Bible: Ephesians 4
Family Worship: Ephesians 4:20–24

What are we to "put off"? What are we to "put on"? What is the "old self"? *Eph. 2:1–3.* What is the "new self"? *2 Cor. 5:17.* Who is the new self like?

Col. 3:9–10; Rom. 8:29. What type of behaviors belong to the old self? **Eph. 4:25–32.** How is the new self different? What is one thing you need to put off? What can you replace it with? Let's pray for the grace "to put off [the] old self . . . and to put on the new."

Thursday

Read through the Bible: Ephesians 5
Family Worship: Ephesians 5:18–21

Instead of being drunk, whom should believers be filled with? What do drunk people act like? How are Spirit-filled people different? *Gal. 5:22–23; Col. 3:16.* What would our home be like if we were all "filled with the Spirit"? Which of the characteristics in verses 5:19–21 need more emphasis in our home? Let's pray that God would fill us mightily with His Spirit.

Friday

Read through the Bible: Ephesians 6
Family Worship: Ephesians 6:1–4

How can children honor the Lord? What is an example of a child honoring his parents? What is an example of a child dishonoring his parents? What does God promise children who honor their parents? How can fathers honor the Lord? Have I provoked you to anger or frustration by my discipline? Who is the perfect example for fathers and children? How can we better honor the Lord as a family? Let's pray for the grace to honor the Lord by obedience.

Saturday

Read through the Bible: Philippians 1
Family Worship: Philippians 1:21–26

Complete this sentence: "To live is _____." What was Paul's attitude toward life? Toward death? How is dying "gain" for believers? *2 Cor. 5:8.* How is Paul's attitude different from the way most people think? *1 Cor. 15:32; 1 Thess. 4:13.* How can the promise of meeting Christ in death help us live boldly for Him in life? Let's pray for the grace to think biblically about life and death—and to live joyfully for Christ while we look forward to meeting Him.

Year 3 — Week 39

Sunday

Read through the Bible: Psalm 137
Family Worship: Psalm 137:1–6

Where was the psalmist? What was he doing? Why? What did the Babylonians want him to do? Why wouldn't he? Should we try to entertain Babylon with our worship? What did the psalmist long for? Why? Which "city" do we worship in? *Heb. 12:22.* Whose song do we sing there? How does your longing for the place of worship compare with the psalmist's? Let's pray for hearts passionate for worship.

Monday

Read through the Bible: Philippians 2
Family Worship: Philippians 2:3–11

Who is our perfect example for attitude and action? What "mind" (or attitude) are we to have? What attitude did Christ have during His earthly ministry? How does someone with the mind of Christ view others? How can you honor others as more important than yourself? What would our home be like if we all lived this way? *Rom. 12:10.* Let's pray for the grace to have the mind of Christ.

Tuesday

Read through the Bible: Philippians 3
Family Worship: Philippians 3:7–11

To Paul, what or who was the most valuable thing in life? How did he view all else compared to this? How can you tell what a person considers the most valuable? What does the world consider the most valuable? What are these compared to knowing Christ? What would others say you consider the most valuable thing in life? How can we treat knowing Christ as the most valuable? Let's pray for hearts passionate for "the surpassing worth of knowing Christ Jesus."

Wednesday

Read through the Bible: Philippians 4
Family Worship: Philippians 4:6–7

What are we not to do? What good does worrying do? What is the difference between worry, prudent concern, and carelessness? What are we to do instead of worrying? *Matt. 6:25-34.* What does God promise when we do? Who was our perfect role model in this? *Matt. 26:36–46.* What do you worry about? So now, "by prayer and supplication with thanksgiving [let's] let [our] requests be made known to God."

Thursday

Read through the Bible: Colossians 1
Family Worship: Colossians 1:15–20

Who is the image of the invisible God? Who is the creator of all things? Who holds all things together? In whom does all the fullness of God dwell? Who is preeminent in everything? How can we truly—not just nominally—honor Christ as preeminent (superior in rank and honor above all) in our home? Our lives? Let's praise God for His exalted Son and pray for hearts to honor Him as preeminent in everything.

Friday

Read through the Bible: Colossians 2
Family Worship: Colossians 2:8–10

In whom are "hidden all the treasures of wisdom and knowledge" (Col. 2:3)? What are we to beware of? What are some false philosophies and human traditions we need to beware of? How can we avoid being taken captive by false ways of thinking? **Col. 2:6-7.** How can you become "rooted and built up in him and established in the faith?" *Col. 3:16.* Let's pray that God would use His word to build us up in Christ.

Saturday

Read through the Bible: Colossians 3
Family Worship: Colossians 3:17, 23–24

In whose name should we do everything? If Jesus told you to do some school work or work around the house, how would you respond? What attitude would you have while working? How much effort would you put into it? How is this different from your typical attitude about work? Should it be different? How can you honor Christ in your work? Let's pray for the grace to "do everything in the name of the Lord Jesus, giving thanks to God the Father through him."

Year 3 — Week 40

Sunday

Read through the Bible: Psalm 138
Family Worship: Psalm 138:1–2

Who is the only "living and true God" (1 Thess. 1:9)? What has the Lord exalted above all things? If God treats His name and His word like this, how should we? How can we exalt God's name? How can we exalt His Word? *Deut. 6:6-7.* Is there anything in our home or hearts that we are exalting above God's name or His Word? Let's pray for hearts that exalt above all things God's name and His Word.

Monday

Read through the Bible: Colossians 4
Family Worship: Colossians 4:5–6

How are we to conduct ourselves toward those outside the church? How are we to speak with them? What does salt do to food? What is speech "seasoned with salt" like? *Eph. 4:29.* Reflect: What is most of your speech seasoned with? Whose ways and words are always perfect? *Ps. 18:30.* Let's pray for the grace to walk and talk wisely at all times—especially around unbelievers.

Tuesday

Read through the Bible: 1 Thessalonians 1
Family Worship: 1 Thessalonians 1:4–6

How did Paul know the Thessalonians had been chosen by God? How did they respond to the gospel? Who empowered them to respond this way? What does the "full conviction" of the Holy Spirit look like? *Ezek. 36:26-27, 31.* How have you responded to the gospel? Let's pray that the power, conviction, and joy of the Holy Spirit would accompany the teaching of the Word in our home.

Wednesday

Read through the Bible: 1 Thessalonians 2
Family Worship: 1 Thessalonians 2:7–8, 11–12

Who "calls [us] into his own kingdom and glory"? What is a nursing mother like with her children? How was Paul like this with the Thessalonians? What is a father like with his children? How was Paul like this? *Parents: How can you be more like Paul?* How is Paul exhorting us to walk? What aspect of your "walk" needs to change to be more "worthy of God"? Let's pray for the grace to walk in a manner worthy of God.

Thursday

Read through the Bible: 1 Thessalonians 3
Family Worship: 1 Thessalonians 3:1–5

What are believers destined for? How did God enable the Thessalonians to persevere through affliction? Whose coworkers are we to be? Who are God's coworkers that "establish and exhort you in your faith"? How can you be God's coworker in our home? Let's pray that God would enable us to be His coworkers—to mutually encourage one another always—especially in affliction.

Friday

Read through the Bible: 1 Thessalonians 4
Family Worship: 1 Thessalonians 4:13–18

How is death like sleep for a believer? *Dan. 12:2; John 11:11–13.* How should a Christian funeral be different from an unbeliever's funeral? Why? Who was the first to die and be resurrected? What will happen to those who have died in Christ when He returns? What will happen to living believers when He returns? How can we "encourage one another with these words"? Let's praise the Lord for the promise that we will meet Him in the air.

Saturday

Read through the Bible: 1 Thessalonians 5
Family Worship: 1 Thessalonians 5:1–11

Who "shall come again, with glory, to judge the living and the dead" (Nicene Creed)? What is "the day of the Lord"? *1 Thess. 4:15–17.* How will it be "like a thief in the night"? *Matt. 24:42–44.* How will it be different for believers and unbelievers? *2 Thess. 1:6–10.* How can we prepare for that day? How can we encourage and build one another up? Let's pray that God would help us to live as children of the light—encouraging one another as we live with the end in sight.

Year 3 — Week 41

Sunday

Read through the Bible: Psalm 139
Family Worship: Psalm 139:1–6, 13–17

Who forms babies in the womb? What do the metaphors "knitted" and "woven" imply about the Creator's care for us? Who plans out all our days? When did He do it? Is there anything God doesn't know? What was David's reaction to this revelation? How should we respond to our Creator for His intricate work in us? Let's praise God that we are fearfully and wonderfully made.

Monday

Read through the Bible: 2 Thessalonians 1
Family Worship: 2 Thessalonians 1:5–10

Who "shall come again, with glory, to judge the living and the dead" (Nicene Creed)? Is justice always served in this life? When will it be? What will happen to the persecuted when Christ returns? The persecutors? All unbelievers? How can the truth of God's glorious justice help our persecuted brothers to endure? How should it motivate us to live? Let's pray for justice for our persecuted brothers and for the grace to live with the end in sight.

Tuesday

Read through the Bible: 2 Thessalonians 2
Family Worship: 2 Thessalonians 2:13–15

What means does God work through to save His chosen ones? Who opens our hearts to believe? *Acts 16:14*. What does the Holy Spirit work through to call us to sanctification and belief in the truth? *BCF 10:1*. What are we to do with Paul's teaching? Where do we find "the traditions" taught by Paul? **1 Thess. 2:13**. Let's pray that the Holy Spirit would work through the teaching of God's Word in our home to save us, sanctify us, and enable us to "stand firm."

Wednesday

Read through the Bible: 2 Thessalonians 3
Family Worship: 2 Thessalonians 3:6–12

What kind of brothers should we keep away from? How hard did Paul work? What is Paul's command concerning those not willing to work? What should such people do instead of being idle? What work can you do to help our family?

Ultimately, who do we work for? *Col. 3:23*. Let's pray that God would help us be a family of hard workers.

Thursday

Read through the Bible: 1 Timothy 1
Family Worship: 1 Timothy 1:12–17

Who is "the King of ages"? What was Paul formerly? What happened to change him? Why did God save him? How did Paul respond to God for saving him? Can you relate to Paul? How has "the grace of our Lord overflowed for [you]"? How should we respond? Let's give "to the King of ages . . . honor and glory forever and ever. Amen." *Hymn: "Immortal, Invisible, God Only Wise."*

Friday

Read through the Bible: 1 Timothy 2
Family Worship: 1 Timothy 2:1–4

Who desires all types of people "from every tribe and language and people and nation" (Rev. 5:9) to be saved? Whom should we pray for? Why should we pray for the president and our political leaders? What are some specific things we can pray for them? *1 Kings 3:9*. Let's pray for the president and "all who are in high positions, that we may lead a peaceful and quiet life, godly and dignified in every way."

Saturday

Read through the Bible: 1 Timothy 3
Family Worship: 1 Timothy 3:8–13

Who "came not to be served, but to serve" (Mark 10:45)? The Greek word for *deacon* literally means "servant." How are deacons like servants? *Acts 6:1–6*. What are the requirements to be a deacon? Why is it important for deacons to manage "their own households well"? *1 Tim. 3:4–5*. Are these qualities just for deacons, or should they describe all Christians? Which of these areas do you need to work on to become a godlier servant? Let's pray for the grace to be godly servants.

Year 3   Week 42

Sunday

Read through the Bible: Psalm 140
Family Worship: Psalm 140:12–13

Who "will maintain the cause of the afflicted"? What will He do for the needy? Will this always happen in this life? *2 Thess. 1:6–10*. What does God promise for those He has made righteous? *John 14:2–3*. How, then, should we respond to God? Let's "give thanks to [His] name" and pray that the Lord would indeed draw us close to "dwell in [His] presence."

Monday

Read through the Bible: 1 Timothy 4
Family Worship: 1 Timothy 4:1–5

What does the Spirit say will happen? What are two good things created by God that false teachers try to forbid? Who created food? *Ps. 104:14–15*. How are we to receive the food that God has created? *1 Cor. 10:31*. How do you typically receive the food we serve? Let's praise God for the gifts of family and food and pray for hearts to glorify Him by enjoying with thanksgiving what He has created.

Tuesday

Read through the Bible: 1 Timothy 5
Family Worship: 1 Timothy 5:3–4, 8, 16

Who should take care of widows? Who commanded children to honor their parents? *Deut. 5:16*. What does God think of children who take care of their parents when they grow old? What does He think of those who do not provide for their family? What are some practical ways you can "show godliness" to our family? Let's pray for hearts to show godliness by how we care for one another.

Wednesday

Read through the Bible: 1 Timothy 6
Family Worship: 1 Timothy 6:6–10

What did we bring into this world? What can we take out of it? What should we be content with? How can you show contentment with what you have? What causes many people to fall into temptation? What is the root of all kinds of evils? Who said, "You cannot serve God and money"? **Matt. 6:24.** Reflect: Which master are you serving? Let's pray for hearts to love and serve God—not money.

Thursday

Read through the Bible: 2 Timothy 1
Family Worship: 2 Timothy 1:8–12

Who is the Sovereign Savior? Does God call people to salvation because of anything they do? Why, then, does He call them? When did God choose to give grace to His people? Can one called by God ever lose his or her salvation? Why not? *John 10:28-29.* Can you say with Paul, "I know whom I have believed"? How should we respond to the One who saves us and keeps us saved by His grace? Let's praise God for His amazing grace! *Hymn: "I Know Whom I Have Believed."*

Friday

Read through the Bible: 2 Timothy 2
Family Worship: 2 Timothy 2:3–4

What is a good soldier like? What are some hardships soldiers must endure? What are some hardships Christian soldiers must endure? What should soldiers avoid? Why? What kind of things could entangle Christian soldiers? What is a Christian soldier's mission? Who is our Commander? How can we please Him? Let's pray that God would make us good soldiers of Christ. *Hymn: "Onward Christian Soldiers."*

Saturday

Read through the Bible: 2 Timothy 3
Family Worship: 2 Timothy 3:14–17

What is able to make us "wise for salvation"? When did Timothy begin learning the Bible? From whom did he learn it? **2 Tim. 1:5.** Where does the Bible come from? *2 Peter 1:21.* Does the Bible always tell us what we want to hear? What is it profitable for? How can you ensure you're "equipped for every good work"? Let's pray that God would use His Word to teach, reprove, correct, and train us in righteousness.

Year 3   Week 43

Sunday

Read through the Bible: Psalm 141
Family Worship: Psalm 141:3–4

What did David ask the Lord to do with his mouth? His heart? Why? *Ps. 39:1; Prov. 4:23*. Where do sinful words and thoughts come from? *Mark 7:21*. What do our hearts naturally incline to? *Jer. 17:9*. Who never sinned with His words? *1 Peter 2:22*. Reflect: Have you made any unguarded statements lately that you need to make right? Let's pray that God would set guards of grace over our mouths and hearts.

Monday

Read through the Bible: 2 Timothy 4
Family Worship: 2 Timothy 4:6–8

Who is "the righteous judge"? How is the Christian life like a fight? *1 Tim. 6:12; Eph. 6:10–18*. How is it like a race? *1 Cor. 9:24–26; Heb. 12:1*. What did Paul's fight or race prove about his faith? *James 2:18*. What do you need to do to fight or race successfully? What reward was laid up for Paul? Who else receives this reward? Let's pray for the grace to fight and race faithfully until we can echo Paul's words.

Tuesday

Read through the Bible: Titus 1
Family Worship: Titus 1:5–9

What must an elder, overseer, bishop, or pastor be like? What must he not be like? What must he "hold firm to"? What must his children be like? Why? **1 Tim. 3:4–5**. Are these characteristics just for elders, or do they show how all believers should live? What is one area where you need help in becoming "above reproach"? Who is the perfect example of being above reproach? Let's pray for the grace to be above reproach.

Wednesday

Read through the Bible: Titus 2
Family Worship: Titus 2:1–10

Where do we find "sound doctrine"? What should older men be like? Younger men? Older women? Younger women? Slaves (workers)? How can this "adorn the doctrine of God our Savior"? What could be reviled if we disobey? How could disobedience cause God's Word to be reviled? What can you do to "adorn" the teaching of God's Word? Let's pray for the grace to honor God and His Word.

Thursday

Read through the Bible: Titus 3
Family Worship: Titus 3:3–7

When you're dirty from playing outside, what do you need? What do people filthy from sin need? What can sinners do to wash themselves? Who can wash away our sin? What do believers, who have been washed in regeneration but are defiled by sin, need? *Ps. 51:2; John 13:10; 1 John 1:9.* What do you need to be cleansed from? Let's pray for an outpouring of the washing, regenerating, and renewing Holy Spirit.

Friday

Read through the Bible: Philemon
Family Worship: Philemon 1:8–20

Who was Onesimus? What did he do? What happened to him when he met Paul? Who was Philemon? What did Paul ask him to do? What did Paul offer to pay? In redeeming and reconciling Onesimus, who was Paul like? *2 Cor. 5:18–21; Col. 1:21–22.* Are there any relationships in our family or church that require reconciliation? How can we help? Let's pray that God would help us be agents of reconciliation.

Saturday

Read through the Bible: Hebrews 1
Family Worship: Hebrews 1:1–4

How did God speak to His people in the Old Testament? In what new way did He speak in the New Testament? Who is the Son of God? What is He like? What has He done? What does He continually do? Whom is He superior to? In what ways? *Col. 1:15–20.* How should we respond to our glorious Creator-Redeemer? Let's praise the Son of God for His superiority in creation, revelation, and redemption.

Year 3 — Week 44

Sunday

Read through the Bible: Psalm 142
Family Worship: Psalm 142:1–7

What was happening to David? *1 Sam. 22:1.* To whom did he turn in his time of distress? What are some other things that people turn to in distress? What is a refuge? Who was David's refuge? What did David plan to do when God delivered him? Name a time when God has been your refuge. Let's give thanks to God for being our refuge in times of trouble.

Monday

Read through the Bible: Hebrews 2
Family Worship: Hebrews 2:1–4

To what must we "pay much closer attention"? *2 Peter 1:19.* Why? What happened to those who neglected God's word in the Old Testament? What will happen to those who reject the fuller revelation of the New Testament? How did God bear witness that the words of the apostles and prophets were His words? How can you pay closer attention to God's Word? Let's pray for hearts to pay much closer attention to God's Word.

Tuesday

Read through the Bible: Hebrews 3
Family Worship: Hebrews 3:1–6

Who is "the apostle and high priest of our confession"? What did Moses do? How was Jesus like Moses? How is He infinitely greater than Moses? *John 1:1–3; Heb. 1:1–3; compare 2 Cor. 3:7.* Who is His "house"? How can the superiority of Christ help us "hold fast our confidence" (faith) in Him? Let's worship our glorious High Priest and pray for His aid to hold fast our confidence firm to the end.

Wednesday

Read through the Bible: Hebrews 4
Family Worship: Hebrews 4:12–13

To whom must we give account? What is "sharper than any two-edged sword"? How is God's Word like a sword? What can it do that a regular sword can't? How is God's Word like a scalpel used to remove a cancerous tumor? Can anyone hide sin from God? What should we do when God's Word points out sin in our hearts? *Acts 2:37–38; 2 Kings 22:11.* Let's pray that God would use the sword of His Word to expose any sin in our hearts and lead us to repentance.

Thursday

Read through the Bible: Hebrews 5
Family Worship: Hebrews 5:11–14

Who drinks only milk? Why? Who eats solid food? What would happen if we drank only milk? Where do we find spiritual milk and meat? *1 Peter 2:2.* What is the "milk" of the Word? Who needs this kind of milk? What does solid food represent? Who is able to handle it? What can the spiritually mature discern? How can you ensure you will be fully trained and able to teach your family? Let's pray for healthy spiritual growth through the milk and meat of the Word.

Friday

Read through the Bible: Hebrews 6
Family Worship: Hebrews 6:11–12

Where do we find God's promises? What are some promises in God's Word? *Eph. 6:1–3; 2 Tim. 4:8.* How do we inherit them? Whom should we imitate? Name some saints whose faith we should imitate. What would a "sluggish" response to God's promises look like? What would an earnest response look like? Reflect: Which one better describes your response? Let's pray for earnest hearts to have the faith and patience that inherits God's precious promises.

Saturday

Read through the Bible: Hebrews 7
Family Worship: Hebrews 7:23–27

What does a priest do? *Heb. 5:1.* Who is our High Priest? How is Jesus a greater priest than Aaron and his successors? What can our eternal High Priest do for us that other priests could never do? What is He doing for us now? Is there someone we need to intercede for? How should we respond to our eternal High Priest? Let's draw near to God through Christ to praise Him and to pray for someone who needs His help.

Year 3   Week 45

Sunday

Read through the Bible: Psalm 143
Family Worship: Psalm 143:1–2

Why did David ask God not to enter into judgment with him? Who is righteous before God? **Rom. 3:10, 23.** How do people become righteous before God? Who took our sin and gave us His righteousness? **2 Cor. 5:21.** Do you, like David, recognize your helpless estate before a holy God? How, then, should we respond to Him? Let's praise God for entering into judgment with His Son so that we could be righteous before Him. *Hymn: "It Is Well with My Soul."*

Monday

Read through the Bible: Hebrews 8
Family Worship: Hebrews 8:6–12

Why is the new covenant better than the old? What are some of the specific promises that are better? Which is most precious to you? Upon whom does the fulfillment of this covenant depend? Are there any unbelievers in the new covenant? What does it mean to "know the Lord"? Do you know Him? What effect does knowing the Lord have on your life? Let's praise God for making us His people and pray for the grace to show, by our lives, that we are.

Tuesday

Read through the Bible: Hebrews 9
Family Worship: Hebrews 9:22–26

What is essential to the forgiveness of sins? Why? *Rom. 3:23–26; 6:23.* How is Christ's sacrifice better than those under the old covenant? Whose is the only blood that can wash away our sin? How can you be purified by that blood? *Rom. 3:28.* Let's make our only plea for pardon "nothing but the blood of Jesus." *Hymn: "Nothing but the Blood."*

Wednesday

Read through the Bible: Hebrews 10
Family Worship: Hebrews 10:19–25

Who is our great High Priest? How do we enter into the holy places? What are three things the writer of Hebrews encourages us to do as a result of Christ's priestly ministry? *Hint: Each begins with the phrase "Let us."* How can we "stir up one another to love and good works"? Let's pray for the grace to draw near to God, hold fast our confession, and encourage one another.

Thursday

Read through the Bible: Hebrews 11
Family Worship: Hebrews 11:1–7

What is faith? What is the only way to please God? What do we understand "by faith"? What did Abel do by faith? Who did Enoch walk with by faith? *Gen. 5:24.* What did Noah do by faith? What does true faith always produce? *James 2:17-18; BCF 11:2.* What can you do by faith? Let's pray that God would help us live out an obedient, living, reverent faith that pleases Him.

Friday

Read through the Bible: Hebrews 12
Family Worship: Hebrews 12:1–3

What kind of race are we in? What would happen to a runner who carried extra weight? How is sin like that? Reflect: Is there any dead weight of sin in your life you need to shed? Who is in the stands cheering us on, so to speak, by their example? Whom are we to focus on? How can Jesus's example encourage us? Let's pray that God would enable us to "run with endurance the race that is set before us."

Saturday

Read through the Bible: Hebrews 13
Family Worship: Hebrews 13:20–21

Who is the Great Shepherd? What did the Great Shepherd do for the sheep? *John 10:11.* What does He equip us to do? Where do we find God's will (that which pleases Him)? How does He equip us? *Eph. 4:11-12.* How can you please God today? Let's pray that the Great Shepherd would indeed equip and enable us to please Him—for His glory.

Year 3 — Week 46

Sunday

Read through the Bible: Psalm 144
Family Worship: Psalm 144:12–15

What did David pray for his sons? What is a full-grown plant like? How does this picture godly sons? *Ps. 1:3; John 15:1–8*. What does David pray for his daughters? What is a corner pillar in a palace like? How does this picture godly daughters? *Rev. 3:12*. Reflect: In which of these traits do you need to grow more? Who can give us the grace to grow in these ways? Let's pray that God would make our sons like fruitful plants and our daughters like beautiful pillars!

Monday

Read through the Bible: James 1
Family Worship: James 1:22–25

If you look in the mirror and see dirt on your face, what should you do? What mirror shows us what we look like spiritually? How is the Bible like a mirror? When the Bible shows us something about ourselves that needs to change, what should we do? If we don't obey, what are we like? What has God been showing you in the mirror of His Word? What have you done about it? Let's pray for the grace to "be doers of the word, and not hearers only."

Tuesday

Read through the Bible: James 2
Family Worship: James 2:14–19

Are good works the root or the fruit of salvation? *Eph. 2:8–10; ask the rhetorical questions in 2:14–16*. What is dead faith like? What is saving faith like? *Heb. 11; BCF 11:2; 14:2*. What kind of faith do demons have? What is the difference between saving faith and mental assent to the truth? How can you demonstrate living faith? What means does God use to create and strengthen faith in our hearts? *Rom. 10:17; BCF 14:1*. Let's pray for living faith shown by good works.

Wednesday

Read through the Bible: James 3
Family Worship: James 3:2–10

What is a bit? What is a rudder? How is the tongue like a bit or a rudder? What kinds of animals have been tamed by man? What "beast" has never been tamed? How are evil words like poison? What should our words be like? *Eph. 4:29.* Reflect: What have your words been like lately: gracious or poisonous? Who never sinned with His words? *1 Peter 2:22.* Let's pray for the grace to tame our tongues.

Thursday

Read through the Bible: James 4
Family Worship: James 4:1–3

What causes quarrels among people? What causes quarrels in our family? What was the most recent quarrel over in our family? What could have prevented it? How can you help prevent future quarrels? Instead of worldly passions, what or whom should we be passionate for? *Phil. 3:8-11.* Let's pray for hearts passionate for Christ and greater Christlikeness.

Friday

Read through the Bible: James 5
Family Worship: James 5:13–16

What should we do when we are suffering? Cheerful? Sick? Sick with sin? How powerful is the prayer of faith? Who is able to heal any sickness? What should we do if God doesn't appear to answer our prayers right away? *James 1:2-4, 12; 5:7-11.* Is there anything you need to confess to another in our family to make things right? Does anyone have any prayer requests? Let's "confess [our] sins to one another and pray for one another" and "sing praise" to God.

Saturday

Read through the Bible: 1 Peter 1
Family Worship: 1 Peter 1:22–25

What "remains forever"? How is God's Word different from a flower? Through what "seed" are we "born again"? *James 1:18; Rom. 10:17; BCF 14:1.* What does it mean to be born again? *Ezek. 36:26; Eph. 2:5; BCF 10:1.* How should those made alive by God's Word and Spirit live? How can you practice "sincere brotherly love" in our family? Let's pray for hearts transformed by God's Word and filled with "sincere brotherly love."

Year 3   Week 47

Sunday

Read through the Bible: Psalm 145
Family Worship: Psalm 145:1–7

Whose "greatness is unsearchable"? What shall one generation do for the next? How can we do this in our family? *Deut. 6:6–7*. How will you fulfill this for the next generation? What are some of God's "wondrous works"? How did David respond to God's greatness? How should we? Let's praise God for His "awesome deeds" and pray for the grace to faithfully commend them to the next generation.

Monday

Read through the Bible: 1 Peter 2
Family Worship: 1 Peter 2:2–3

What does a newborn infant long for? What does a newborn spiritual infant long for? Where do we find "pure spiritual milk"? What does milk do for babies? What does the pure spiritual milk of God's Word do for God's children? What do you enjoy eating? Why? How can we "taste and see that the LORD is good" (Ps. 34:8)? Let's pray for hearts that long for God and for the pure spiritual milk of His Word.

Tuesday

Read through the Bible: 1 Peter 3
Family Worship: 1 Peter 3:1–7

What kind of "adorning" should godly wives focus on? In whose sight is this "very precious"? Should a Christian wife submit to an unbelieving husband? Why? How should a husband live with his wife? What will happen if he doesn't? *Parents: How can you teach these truths by example? Children: How can you prepare for your future role as a wife or husband?* Let's pray for the grace to adorn ourselves with godly character.

Wednesday

Read through the Bible: 1 Peter 4
Family Worship: 1 Peter 4:12–19

What should believers not be surprised about? What kind of suffering should believers expect? *2 Tim. 3:12*. When persecuted, whose sufferings do we share?

What kind of suffering is inappropriate for Christians? How should we respond in suffering? How can you glorify God when being ridiculed for your beliefs? *1 Peter 2:23; 3:15-16*. Let's pray for the grace to glorify God in the name *Christian* no matter what.

Thursday

Read through the Bible: 1 Peter 5
Family Worship: 1 Peter 5:5–7

How should church members relate to the elders? *Heb. 13:17*. How should believers relate to one another? Who "opposes the proud but gives grace to the humble"? What should we do with our worries? What anxieties do you need to cast on the Lord? How is humility a corrective for both pride and worry? Let's confess our anxieties—and our pride—to the Lord and pray for the grace of humility.

Friday

Read through the Bible: 2 Peter 1
Family Worship: 2 Peter 1:3–11

What has God granted to us? Why? What are we to supplement our faith with? What other qualities are we to add? Of these, which one do you need to make the most effort to add? What will happen if these qualities are ours and increasing? How can we gain assurance that we are called and chosen by God? *BCF 18:2-3*. Who perfectly modeled these moral qualities? Let's pray for the grace to be more like Christ and so "make our calling and election sure."

Saturday

Read through the Bible: 2 Peter 2
Family Worship: 2 Peter 2:4–9

Who is both Judge and Savior? Whom did God judge? Whom did He rescue from judgment (save)? What will God do for the godly? The ungodly? How, then, should we live in the midst of this modern, ungodly world? *1 Thess. 1:9-10*. Let's pray for the grace to live holy lives as we wait for our Savior to rescue us from current trials and future judgment.

Year 3 — Week 48

Sunday

Read through the Bible: Psalm 146
Family Worship: Psalm 146:1–10

Whom should we *not* put our trust in? Why not? Whom should we put our trust in? Why? How is God greater than princes (rulers)? What does the Lord do that princes can't? In whom is your hope and trust today? How should people who trust in God live? Let's begin by praising our ever-faithful Lord and praying for hearts to daily trust in Him.

Monday

Read through the Bible: 2 Peter 3
Family Worship: 2 Peter 3:1–13

Who "shall come again, with glory, to judge the living and the dead" (Nicene Creed)? What do scoffers say about our Lord's return? What do they forget? Why hasn't the Lord returned yet? **John 6:37–39.** Whom is He being patient toward? **2 Tim. 2:10.** What will happen when He returns? What will the new heavens and earth be like? How can we prepare for that day? Let's pray that all our family would have grace to "reach repentance" and live "lives of holiness and godliness."

Tuesday

Read through the Bible: 1 John 1
Family Worship: 1 John 1:3, 5–7

What is it like to walk in a dark room? *Option: Demonstrate by shutting off the lights.* What do "light" and "darkness" picture? Who is light? *John 8:12.* What does it mean to walk in darkness? *John 3:19–21.* How can we instead "walk in the light"? *John 8:12.* What happens when we do? Let's pray for the grace to "walk in the light, as he is in the light" and enjoy fellowship with God.

Wednesday

Read through the Bible: 1 John 2
Family Worship: 1 John 2:15–17

Who created everything and saw "it was very good" (Gen. 1:31)? What happened to the world God created? What three things characterize the sinful corruption of the world? *Gen. 3:6.* Reflect: Which of these do you struggle with the most? What does it show when someone loves the world? What greater love or desires can we instead pursue? *Ps. 37:4.*[7] Let's pray for hearts filled with "the love of the Father" instead of the world.

Thursday

Read through the Bible: 1 John 3
Family Worship: 1 John 3:16–18

Who is the supreme example of love? *John 15:13.* How is Jesus's love an example for us? How can we "lay down our lives for the brothers"? *Phil. 2:3-4; ask the rhetorical question in 3:17.* How are we to love one another? What are some ways you can love others "in deed and in truth" this week? Let's pray for the grace us to love one another the way God loves us—in deed and in truth.

Friday

Read through the Bible: 1 John 4
Family Worship: 1 John 4:7–12, 20

Who is love? How did God show His love for us? How is God's love perfected in us? If we love one another, what assurance can we have? What does it show when a person does not love? What if he says he loves God but hates his brother? Do others know that we love God? How? Let's pray for the grace to show we are Christians by our love.

Saturday

Read through the Bible: 1 John 5
Family Worship: 1 John 5:14–15

How can we know that God will hear and answer our prayers? Where do we find God's revealed will? *Deut. 29:29; Isa. 55:11.* How did Jesus teach us to pray regarding God's will? **Matt. 6:10.** How did Jesus Himself pray for God's will? **Matt. 26:39.** How can we pray more like Jesus taught and showed us? Let's pray that God's will/word would be done in our family, as it is in heaven.

---

7 See also John Piper, *Desiring God* (Colorado Springs: Multnomah, 2011).

Year 3 — Week 49

Sunday

Read through the Bible: Psalm 147
Family Worship: Psalm 147:7–11

Who created the world and everything in it? What are some examples of how God cares for His creation? What does the Lord delight in? Note that fear and hope are parallel expressions—what is the connection between these? *Heb. 11:6.* Reflect: Which is stronger—your legs or your faith? How can we honor the Lord with both? *1 Cor. 6:20; 10:31.* Let's pray for hearts to fear and hope in God, then "sing to the LORD with thanksgiving."

Monday

Read through the Bible: 2 John, 3 John
Family Worship: 2 John 4; 3 John 3–4

What was John's greatest joy? Where do we find truth? *John 17:17.* Who is *the Truth*? *John 14:6.* What does "walking in the truth" picture? How can we walk (live) in the truth? **2 John 5–6.** What do you think my greatest joy is? Let's pray for the grace to walk in the truth as a family.

Tuesday

Read through the Bible: Jude
Family Worship: Jude 3

What did Jude want to write about? What did he have to write about instead? What is "the faith"? *Ps. 119:160; 1 Tim. 6:3.* Where do we find it? *2 Tim. 3:16–17.* Can it be added to or changed? *Deut. 4:2.* What are we to do with the faith? What does it mean to "contend" for something? How can we "contend for the faith"? *1 Peter 3:15–16.* Let's pray for the spiritual backbone to contend for the faith.

Wednesday

Read through the Bible: Revelation 1
Family Worship: Revelation 1:1–3

Whom does the book of Revelation reveal? Why did God give the Revelation? How did He give the Revelation? Whom does God promise to bless? How can we prepare to be blessed as we study the Revelation? *Ps. 119:18; James 1:22.* Let's pray for ears to hear our Savior's voice, eyes to behold His glory, and hearts to obey His words.

Thursday

Read through the Bible: Revelation 2
Family Worship: Revelation 2:1–5

Who "holds the seven stars in his right hand"? What was the problem with the Ephesian church? *Jer. 2:2.* Have you ever received a present you loved to play with at first, but after a while it wasn't very special anymore? How was this church's love like that? Reflect: How has your love for God changed since you first knew Him? Your love for others? What do we need to do if our love grows cold? Let's pray for hearts rekindled with a first-love, passionate devotion for Christ.

Friday

Read through the Bible: Revelation 3
Family Worship: Revelation 3:19–20

What does the Lord do for those He loves? Why? *Heb. 12:5-11.* What do we need to do when we sin? Who is knocking at the door of His church? *Luke 12:36.* How do we hear His voice? *Luke 24:32.* What does Jesus promise for those who hear and respond in faith? What has the Lord been saying to you? How shall we respond? Let's pray for ears to hear our Lord and hearts zealous to repent and fellowship with Him.

Saturday

Read through the Bible: Revelation 4
Family Worship: Revelation 4:1–11

Who is seated on the throne? What is God like? What do the four living creatures never cease to say? What does it mean to be holy? In light of God's holiness, what kind of people ought we to be? *1 Peter 1:15-16.* How do those in heaven respond to our thrice holy, almighty, sovereign Creator-King? How should we? Let's pray for hearts passionate to worship our King and to be more like Him in holiness. *Hymns: "Holy, Holy, Holy!" and "O Worship the King."*

Year 3 — Week 50

Sunday

Read through the Bible: Psalm 148
Family Worship: Psalm 148:1–14

Whose name alone is exalted? *Phil. 2:9-11*. What should everything and everyone in heaven and earth do? Why? How does the creation praise the Lord? *Ps. 19:1; Rom. 1:19-20*. How can we praise the Lord? How can we praise Him with our lives? *1 Cor. 10:31*. Let's "praise the LORD"! Hymn: "All Creatures of Our God and King."

Monday

Read through the Bible: Revelation 5
Family Worship: Revelation 5:9–14

Who is both Lion and Lamb? How is Jesus like a lion? How is He like a lamb? What is a ransom? Why do we need to be ransomed? *Rom. 6:23*. What was the ransom price? Whom did Jesus ransom? *John 10:15; Acts 20:28; Eph. 5:25*. What has Jesus made us? How does heaven—and all creation—respond to the Lion/Lamb of God? How will you respond? Let's worship Him!

Tuesday

Read through the Bible: Revelation 6
Family Worship: Revelation 6:9–11

Who is "the Judge of all the earth" (Gen. 18:25)? Who did John see under the altar? Why had they been slain? What did they ask the Lord? *Ps. 94:1-3*. What was the answer to their prayer? **Rev. 6:12-17.** How can this vision be a source of comfort to believers suffering injustice? To believers facing death? How can we be faithful witnesses like them? Let's pray for the grace to be bold witnesses no matter the cost.

Wednesday

Read through the Bible: Revelation 7
Family Worship: Revelation 7:9–12

How many people did John see in heaven? Where did they come from? *Rev. 5:9*. How can this vision encourage foreign missions? *Matt. 28:19; 2 Tim. 2:10*. To whom does the work of salvation belong? *Jonah 2:9*. How do the angels respond to God's great work of saving sinners? How should we? Let's praise

God for salvation and pray He would empower His church to make disciples from every nation.

Thursday

Read through the Bible: Revelation 8
Family Worship: Revelation 8:2–5; 5:8; Ps. 141:2

Who delights in the prayers of His people? *Prov. 15:8 (KJV).* What is incense like? *Ex 30:34–38.* How is prayer like a sweet aroma to God? Reflect: Do you treat your prayers as seriously as God does? Revelation 8:5 and following appears to be the answer to these prayers. If so, what prayers might these be? *Rev. 6:10; Ps. 94:1–3.* How can we make sure our prayers are pleasing to God? *1 John 5:14.* Let's pray: "Your kingdom come, your will be done, on earth as it is in heaven" (Matt. 6:10).

Friday

Read through the Bible: Revelation 9
Family Worship: Revelation 9:1–6, 20–21*

*AC v. 21. How do unbelievers respond to the judgments described in this chapter? What do they refuse to do? Why won't they repent and be saved? *John 3:19-21.* How does this show the irrational nature of sin? The incredible hardness of the human heart? *Jer. 17:9.* Reflect: How did you respond the last time you were disciplined—were you sorry for your sin or just for the consequences? Who can change our hearts? Let's pray for hearts softened by grace and quick to repent.

Saturday

Read through the Bible: Revelation 10
Family Worship: Revelation 10:8–11

What was John told to eat? What did it taste like? What did it do to his stomach? What was he told to do afterward? Whose words were on the scroll? **Ezra 2:8-3:4.** How is God's Word sweet as honey? *Jer. 15:16; Ps. 119:103.* In what sense is it bitter? How can we spiritually ingest God's Word? *Ezra 3:10.* What should we do afterward? *Rev. 1:3; 22:7.* Let's pray for hearts to hunger for, receive, and obey God's Word.

Year 3 — Week 51

Sunday

Read through the Bible: Psalm 149
Family Worship: Psalm 149:1–5

Who is our Maker and King? Who especially should worship God? Why should God's children worship Him? How should we worship Him? Where? When? What does God take pleasure in? *Ps. 147:11.* How can we take pleasure in God today? Let's pray for hearts to be glad in our Maker, and let's rejoice in our King, whether in the assembly or on our beds.

Monday

Read through the Bible: Revelation 11
Family Worship: Revelation 11:15–18

What happened when the seventh angel blew his trumpet? Who "shall reign forever and ever"? How did the twenty-four elders respond to the announcement of Christ's reign? In what sense has Christ's kingdom already come? *Matt. 13:31–33.* In what sense is it yet future? How can we prepare for the fullness of His kingdom? Let's worship and serve our King in godly fear, praying, "Your kingdom come . . ." (Matt. 6:10).

Tuesday

Read through the Bible: Revelation 12
Family Worship: Revelation 12:7–11

Who is the dragon? What are the different names given for Satan? What does he do to people? *Gen. 3:1; Job 1:9–11.* How do the people of God conquer Satan? How can we conquer him "by the blood of the Lamb"? *Eph. 1:7.* How can we conquer him "by the word of [our] testimony"? *Rom. 1:16; 2 Tim. 1:8.* By loving not our lives "even unto death"? *Rev. 2:10.* Whose strength do we need to conquer the dragon? Let's pray for the grace of the Lamb to conquer the dragon.

Wednesday

Read through the Bible: Revelation 13
Family Worship: Revelation 13:1–8

What is the beast like? What is it allowed to do? How is it that the beast conquers the saints, yet the saints conquer the dragon and the beast? *Rev. 12:11; 15:2; Phil. 1:21.* How does the world respond to the beast? How is the beast a counterfeit of Christ? How does the beast picture the persecuting power of the state? *Dan. 7*. How can we help our persecuted brothers and sisters? How might we be tempted to idolize the power of the state? Who is sovereign over the dragon and the beast? Let's pray for the grace of the Lamb to conquer the beast.

Thursday

Read through the Bible: Revelation 14
Family Worship: Revelation 14:12–13

How are the saints described? What is the connection between faith and keeping God's commandments? *James 2:18; BCF 16:2*. What are the saints called to do? Who "endured the cross" for us (Heb. 12:2)? Who is blessed? Why? In what sense do our deeds follow us to heaven? *2 Cor. 5:10; Matt. 25:21*. How, then, shall we live? *Gal. 6:9–10*. Let's pray for the grace to endure in the obedience of faith.

Friday

Read through the Bible: Revelation 15
Family Worship: Revelation 15:1–4

Who is the "King of the nations"? Who are those who have conquered the beast? *Rev. 12:11; 14:13*. What are they doing? What attributes of God do they praise in "the song of the Lamb"? How is the holiness of God exalted in the Revelation? Who will not fear God one day and glorify His name? *Phil. 2:9–11*. How can we show reverence for God and honor His name today? Let's begin by worshiping Him and praying: "Hallowed be thy name" (Matt. 6:9).

Saturday

Read through the Bible: Revelation 16
Family Worship: Revelation 16:1–11

What did the angels pour out? Who are the recipients of God's wrath? Why are they judged? *Rev. 6:10*. How is God's justice glorified in these judgments? How do unbelievers respond to the justice they deserve? What do we deserve for our sin? *Rom. 6:23*. Who received what we deserve? *Isa. 53:4–6*. How were God's justice and grace exalted at the cross? *Rom. 3:23–26*. How shall we respond to God for the grace we don't deserve? Let's worship Him! *Hymn: "Amazing Grace."*

Year 3 — Week 52

Sunday

Read through the Bible: Psalm 150
Family Worship: Psalm 150:1–6

Whom should we praise? Why? What are some of "his mighty deeds"? What are some attributes of "his excellent greatness"? What kind of musical instruments can we use to "praise the LORD"? Who should praise the Lord? When will "everything that has breath praise the LORD"? **Rev. 5:13–14**; *Phil. 2:11*. How can we praise the Lord today? Let's praise the Lord! *Hymn: "The Doxology."*

Monday

Read through the Bible: Revelation 17
Family Worship: Revelation 17:3,* 12–14, 17

*AC vv. 1–2, 4. What do the ten horns on the beast picture? What will they do? Who ultimately controls them? *Prov. 21:1*. What will the Lamb do to them? Who is the Lamb? Who is with the Lamb? Whose words are always fulfilled? How can the truth of God's sovereignty encourage us to be faithful in the fight against evil? Let's pray for the grace to be faithful followers of the King of Kings as He conquers all evil.

Tuesday

Read through the Bible: Revelation 18
Family Worship: Revelation 17:18–18:2,* 4–8

*AC vv. 3, 9. Revelation 17–18 depicts the world's power to allure us to sin as an immoral woman/city named *Babylon*. What does this "Babylon" think of herself? What does God think of her? Who will judge her? Why? What are His people to do? *2 Cor. 6:17*. Why? How can we "come out of her" when we live in spiritual Babylon? *John 17:14–15; Dan. 1:8*. Let's pray for the grace to be in the world but not of it.

Wednesday

Read through the Bible: Revelation 19
Family Worship: Revelation 19:11–21

Who is the rider on the white horse? What are the different names given for Him? What will Christ do to the anti-Christian forces of this world, pictured by the "beast" and the "false prophet"? To those who follow them? Who follows the King of Kings into His final battle? *Rev. 17:14.* How can we follow our King in the daily battle against evil? *1 John 5:4; BCF 13:2–3.* How can this vision of victory strengthen our faith? Let's praise our conquering King and pray He would help us live by overcoming faith with the end in sight.

Thursday

Read through the Bible: Revelation 20
Family Worship: Revelation 20:11–15

Who is seated on the throne? **2 Cor. 5:10.** Who is standing before the throne? What will everyone be judged by? Since we are saved by grace through faith, why will we be judged by works? *James 2:18.* What will happen to those whose names are not written in the Book of Life? How can we prepare for judgment day? *2 Cor. 5:11; Matt. 25:14–40.* Let's praise God for His glorious grace and glorious justice and pray He would help us live by working faith with the end in sight.

Friday

Read through the Bible: Revelation 21
Family Worship: Revelation 21:1–4

What did John see? Who is the bride of Christ? *Rev. 19:7–8.* Who will dwell with His bride? How does this bride/holy city contrast with the harlot/unholy city of "Babylon"? *Rev. 17–18.* What will Jesus do for His bride? What are some things we shed tears over today? What will happen to these in the new heaven and earth? How can God's promise comfort and encourage us today? Let's pray for the grace to live with the end in sight—even through tear-filled eyes.

Saturday

Read through the Bible: Revelation 22
Family Worship: Revelation 22:1–5

What will the new earth be like? What will be there? What will not be there? How is it similar to the garden of Eden? **Gen. 2:8–10.** How is it far better? Whose face will we see? How will our fellowship with God be different? How can we prepare for the new earth? Let's pray that God would grant us fellowship with Him now by His Spirit (*1 John 1:3*), as we look forward to that time when we "will see his face."

Appendix: Read through the Bible Chart

In the table below you will find a reading plan to take you through the entire Bible during the course of this devotional (3 years). Every Sunday you will read the psalm listed. Monday through Saturday, the books and chapter numbers to be read are arranged from left to right.

WK	SUN (Pss.)	MON	TUE	WED	THU	FRI	SAT
1	1	Gen. 1	2	3	4	5	6
2	2	7	8	9	10	11	12
3	3	13	14	15	16	17	18
4	4	19	20	21	22	23	24
5	5	25	26	27	28	29	30
6	6	31	32	33	34	35	36
7	7	37	38	39	40	41	42
8	8	43	44	45	46	47	48
9	9	49	50	John 1	2	3	4
10	10	5	6	7	8	9	10
11	11	11	12	13	14	15	16
12	12	17	18	19	20	21	Ex. 1
13	13	2	3	4	5	6	7
14	14	8	9	10	11–12:20	12:21–51	13
15	15	14	15	16	17	18	19
16	16	20	21	22	23	24	25
17	17	26	27	28	29	30	31
18	18	32	33	34	35	36	37
19	19	38	39	40	Lev. 1–2	3–4	5–6
20	20	7	8	9–10	11–12	13	14
21	21	15	16	17–18	19	20	21
22	22	22	23	24	25	26	27
23	23	Num. 1	2	3	4	5	6
24	24	7	8	9	10	11	12
25	25	13	14	15	16	17	18
26	26	19	20	21	22	23	24
27	27	25	26	27	28	29	30
28	28	31	32	33	34	35	36
29	29	Deut. 1	2	3:1–4:8	4:9–49	5	6
30	30	7	8	9	10	11	12
31	31	13	14	15	16	17	18
32	32	19	20	21	22	23	24
33	33	25	26	27	28	29	30
34	34	31	32	33	34	Josh. 1	2
35	35	3	4	5	6	7	8
36	36	9	10	11	12	13	14
37	37	15	16	17	18	19	20
38	38	21	22	23	24	Judg. 1	2
39	39	3	4	5	6	7	8
40	40	9	10	11	12	13	14
41	41	15	16	17	18	19	20
42	42	21	Ruth 1	2	3	4	1 Sam. 1
43	43	2	3	4	5	6	7
44	44	8	9	10	11	12	13
45	45	14	15	16	17	18	19
46	46	20	21	22	23	24	25
47	47	26	27	28	29	30	31
48	48	2 Sam. 1	2	3	4	5	6
49	49	7:1–17	7:18–29	8	9–10	11	12
50	51*	13	14	15	16	17	18
51	50*	19	20	21	22	23	24
52	52	1 Kings 1	2	3	4:1–28	4:29–5:18	6

Read through the Bible Year 2

WK	SUN (Pss.)	MON	TUE	WED	THU	FRI	SAT
53	53	7	8	9	10	11	12
54	54	13	14	15	16	17	18
55	55	19	20	21	22	2 Kings 1	2
56	56	3	4	5	6:1–23	6:24–7:20	8
57	57	9	10	11	12	13	14
58	58	15	16	17	18	19	20
59	59	21	22	23:1–30	23:31–24:20	25	Matt. 1
60	60	2	3	4	5	6	7
61	61	8	9	10	11	12	13
62	62	14	15	16	17	18	19
63	63	20	21	22	23	24	25
64	64	26	27	28	1 Chron. 1–5	6–10	11
65	65	12	13	14	15	16	17
66	66	18	19–20	21	22	23	24
67	67	25	26	27	28	29	2 Chron. 1
68	68	2	3–4	5–6:11	6:12–42	7	8
69	69	9	10	11	12	13	14
70	70	15	16	17	18	19	20
71	71	21	22	23	24	25	26
72	72	27–28	29	30	31	32	33
73	73	34	35	36	Ezra 1–2	3	4
74	74	5	6	7	8	9	10
75	75	Neh. 1	2	3	4	5	6
76	76	7	8	9	10	11	12
77	77	13	Est. 1	2	3–4	5–6	7–8
78	78	9–10	Song 1–2	3–4	5–6	7–8	Job 1
79	79	2	3	4–5	6–7	8–9	10–11
80	80	12	13	14	15	16–17	18–19
81	81	20	21	22	23–24	25–26	27–28
82	82	29–30	31	32	33	34	35–36:21
83	83	36:22–ch37	38	39–40:5	40:6–ch41	42	Prov. 1
84	84	2	3	4	5	6	7
85	85	8	9	10	11	12	13
86	86	14	15	16	17	18	19
87	87	20	21	22	23	24	25
88	88	26	27	28	29	30	31
89	89	Eccl. 1	2	3	4	5	6
90	90	7	8	9	10	11	12
91	91	Isa. 1	2	3–4	5	6	7
92	92	8	9	10	11	12–13	14
93	93	15–16	17–18	19	20–21	22	23
94	94	24	25	26	27	28	29
95	95	30	31–32	33	34–35	36	37
96	96	38–39	40	41	42	43	44
97	97	45	46–47	48	49	50–51	52–53
98	98	54–55	56–57	58–59	60–61	62–63	64–65
99	99	66	Mark 1	2	3	4	5
100	100	6	7	8	9	10	11
101	101	12	13	14	15	16	Jer. 1
102	102	2	3	4	5	6	7
103	103	8	9	10	11	12–13	14–15:9
104	104	15:10–ch16	17	18	19–20	21–22	23

Read through the Bible Year 3

WK	SUN (Pss.)	MON	TUE	WED	THU	FRI	SAT
105	105	24	25	26	27	28	29
106	106	30	31	32	33	34–35	36
107	107	37	38	39	40–41	42–43	44
108	108	45–47	48	49	50	51	52
109	109	**Lam.** 1	2	3	4–5	**Ezek.** 1	2–3
110	110	4–5	6	7	8–9	10	11
111	111	12	13	14–15	16	17	18
112	112	19	20:1–44	20:45–ch21	22	23	24
113	113	25–26	27	28	29	30	31
114	114	32	33	34	35–36:15	36:16–38	37
115	115	38	39	40	41–42	43–44	45–46
116	116	47–48	**Dan.** 1	2	3	4	5
117	117	6	7	8	9	10	11
118	118	12	**Hos.** 1	2	3–4	5–6	7–8
119	119:1–24	9–10	11–12	13–14	**Joel** 1	2	3
120	119:25–48	**Amos** 1–2:5	2:6–ch.3	4–5	6–7	8–9	**Obad.** 1
121	119:49–72	**Jonah** 1–2	3–4	**Mic.** 1–2	3–4	5	6–7
122	119:73–96	**Nah.** 1–3	**Hab.** 1–2	3	**Zeph.** 1–2	3	**Hag.** 1–2
123	119:97–104	**Zech.** 1–2	3–4	5–6	7–8	9–10	11–13:1
124	119:121–144	13:2–ch14	**Mal.** 1–2:16	2:17–ch4	**Luke** 1:1–38	1:39–80	2
125	119:145–176	3	4	5	6	7	8
126	120	9	10	11	12	13	14
127	121	15	16	17	18	19	20
128	122	21	22	23	24	**Acts** 1	2
129	123	3	4	5	6	7	8
130	124	9	10	11	12	13	14
131	125	15	16	17	18	19	20
132	126	21	22	23	24	25	26
133	127	27	28	**Rom.** 1	2	3	4
134	128	5	6	7	8	9	10
135	129	11	12	13	14	15	16
136	130	**1 Cor.** 1	2	3	4	5	6
137	131	7	8	9	10	11	12
138	132	13	14	15	16	**2 Cor.** 1	2
139	133	3	4	5	6:1–7:1	7:2–16	8
140	134	9	10	11	12	13	**Gal.** 1
141	135	2	3	4	5	6	**Eph.** 1
142	136	2	3	4	5	6	**Phil.** 1
143	137	2	3	4	**Col.** 1	2	3
144	138	4	**1 Thess.** 1	2	3	4	5
145	139	**2 Thess.** 1	2	3	**1 Tim.** 1	2	3
146	140	4	5	6	**2 Tim.** 1	2	3
147	141	4	**Titus** 1	2	3	**Philem.** 1	**Heb.** 1
148	142	2	3	4	5	6	7
149	143	8	9	10	11	12	13
150	144	**James** 1	2	3	4	5	**1 Peter** 1
151	145	2	3	4	5	**2 Peter** 1	2
152	146	3	**1 John** 1	2	3	4	5
153	147	**2 John–3 John**	**Jude** 1	**Rev.** 1	2	3	4
154	148	5	6	7	8	9	10
155	149	11	12	13	14	15	16
156	150	17	18	19	20	21	22

A. J. Genco's Testimony

My Life before Following Christ

I grew up in a loving home with a mother and father who taught me the value of integrity, education, and hard work. However, they did not emphasize spiritual matters. We stopped going to church when I was in grade school. The only time I ever read the Bible was once in a hotel room during a family vacation. After reading a paragraph, I made fun of it and put it away.

In my teen years I considered myself an agnostic. I believed there was a God but He wasn't personal or involved in human affairs. In high school I was promiscuous and drank a lot of alcohol. I continued this lifestyle through my first year of college. I did well in school but began to feel there had to be more to life. A girl from one of my classes brought me to a lecture given by Josh McDowell, who discussed historical proofs for the resurrection of Christ. Intellectually, I was convinced. Although this was an important first step, I fell short of genuine faith in Christ. I believed Jesus was the Son of God and that He rose from the dead, but this knowledge didn't change my life. After that semester I enlisted in the Air National Guard and left for basic training, where my life would change forever.

How I Became a Christian

In May of 1982, at age nineteen, I went to basic training in San Antonio, Texas. Five of the fifty men assigned to my flight were Christians; I immediately noticed they were different. They didn't act crudely like the rest of us, and they had a peace and inner strength I admired. When I talked with them, the conversation usually ended up centered on Jesus. In frustration one day, I asked them where they found out all this information about Jesus. They told me it was in the Bible. One of them gave me a New Testament, and I read it whenever I got a chance. I fell in love with Jesus. I saw a connection between His life and the actions of my friends.

That Sunday, I went to chapel with my Christian friends. They brought me to a smaller, evangelical service led by a civilian pastor. I could tell the people there were genuine—they really believed the Bible and acted on its truth. The pastor preached about sin, righteousness, and hell—and I couldn't wait to leave. But I continued reading my Bible and realized what the pastor had said was true. I knew I was going to hell. I went back to chapel the next Sunday. At the close of the service, the pastor asked if there was anyone who wasn't sure that if they died they would go to heaven. I felt like everybody was looking right at me. They weren't, of course, but the Holy Spirit was dealing with me. I raised my hand, went forward, and prayed with the pastor. I confessed that I was a sinner. I knew Jesus was the Son of God, and I asked Him to save me. I felt like someone took a huge weight off my shoulders. I knew I had eternal life as well as purpose and meaning in this life.

My Life Since Following Christ

I told others in my flight what Jesus did for me. I bought my own Bible and read it as fast as I could. I grew rapidly in my newfound faith. By the time I returned home from Texas, my life was noticeably different. I stopped drinking alcohol and sleeping around. I became very involved in church and Bible study. I began to care more about others, and I shared my faith. My parents didn't understand the changes in my life, which caused considerable friction while I stayed at home. Since then our relationship has healed, but they still have not responded to the gospel. Some of my college friends also noticed the changes in my life. One asked what happened to me, and I shared my testimony with him. He received Christ as his Savior about two weeks later. I quickly found out I still had problems in life. However, God gave me the peace and inner strength to overcome them as I had earlier admired in my Christian friends.

Has anything like this ever happened to you?

On Campus & Distance Options Available

GRACE BIBLE THEOLOGICAL SEMINARY

Interested in becoming a student or supporting our ministry?
Please visit gbtseminary.org

www.ingramcontent.com/pod-product-compliance
Lightning Source LLC
Chambersburg PA
CBHW062041080426
42734CB00012B/2529